GENE
HACKMAN

Also by Allan Hunter

WALTER MATTHAU
FAYE DUNAWAY

GENE
HACKMAN

Allan Hunter

St. Martin's Press
New York

Library of Congress Cataloging-in-Publication Data

Hunter, Allan.
     Gene Hackman.

     "A Thomas Dunne book."
     1. Hackman, Gene.   2. Motion picture actors and actresses—
United States—Biography.   I. Title.
PN2287.H16H8   1989   791.43′028′0924   [B]   88-30625
ISBN 0-312-02579-3

First published in Great Britain by W.H. Allen & Co.

First U.S. Edition

10 9 8 7 6 5 4 3 2 1

Acknowledgments

With a list of credits that includes *Bonnie and Clyde, The Poseidon Adventure, Young Frankenstein* and *Superman*, Gene Hackman has appeared in some of the most popular films ever made. He has been nominated on three occasions for the coveted Oscar and won in 1972 for his role as 'Popeye' Doyle in *The French Connection*. Despite these notable achievements he stubbornly remains a consistently under-valued actor. His own discomfort with the spotlight of stardom and his defensive brand of self-effacement have often succeeded in camouflaging his prodigious talents. I am therefore indebted to Joe O'Reilly of W. H. Allen who suggested writing a biography of Hackman and allowed me the opportunity to renew acquaintance with a body of screen work that is as diverse as it is distinguished.

Among those who responded with alacrity to my requests for assistance were: Anne Bancroft, Sir Michael Hordern, Jane Lapotaire, Gay Cox of Filmhouse in Edinburgh, Brian M. Burton of Rank Film Distributors in London, Lois Abrams of Orion Pictures in New York, Richard Winnie of Lorimar Telepictures in Los Angeles, Caroline Binnie and Trevor Pake.

An undertaking of this kind would now be unimaginable without the resources of the British Film Institute, the Kobal Collection and the National Film Archive. To the staff of these indispensable institutions I offer my continuing appreciation and gratitude.

Allan Hunter

Introduction

Writing in *New York*, the film critic David Denby once described Gene Hackman as 'the greatest seemingly ordinary actor in American movies.' Movie stars are expected to possess qualities far removed from those of everyday men and women. They are supposed to be handsome, fascinating, larger-than-life figures who justify the label of screen gods and goddesses. Yet, paradoxically, Hackman was an actor who became a movie star on the strength of his normality. 'I guess the audiences respond to the proletarian man they see in me,' he has suggested. 'The working guy who's doing vicariously what they would like to do. I think that's why, essentially, *The French Connection* worked.'

Audiences do identify with Hackman. He doesn't have a gimmick or a unique personality that charms them into repeatedly renewing their acquaintance with him. He is not some fantasy hero through whom they can escape their everyday woes. He is their own representative among the pantheon of cinema greats; an ambling, fallible, often nondescript human being who sweats and toils and could be our fellow worker down at the factory or the coach of the local sports team. Hackman has an integrity and a conviction of truth in his work that convinces his audience that he is what he pretends to be – the common man. He was once, fittingly, dubbed a 'Brando for the masses'.

To some extent his face has been his fortune. It has been tactlessly described as everything from a manhandled melon to a bowl of mashed potatoes. 'I hate watching myself on the screen,' he says. 'I don't even notice my acting: I just look at that pudding face and think, "Oh God, I look like my grandfather." ' When Hackman was growing up, his idea of a movie idol was a dashing swashbuckler like Errol Flynn or Tyrone Power, and he has found it difficult to reconcile an unflattering image of himself with other people's assertions that he is a star. He contends that he doesn't look like a star and doesn't feel like a star – he is an actor.

The concept of stardom is a problematic one for him, fraught with unresolved difficulties but also replete with certain advantages. After *The French Connection* the concept slowly corroded his higher principles and he jumped at every lucrative offer that came along, insecure and fearful that his good fortune couldn't last. Later, the reluctant star began to view his status as a bonus that could allow him to play a wide variety of challenging leading roles.

'It's true that I've had a greater versatility in the roles I've played because I've fallen somewhere between star and character actor,' Hackman says. 'I've never allowed myself to become totally typecast and I can do a number of things. I don't think that I'm actually a character actor as such; on the other hand, I don't like to think of myself as a star. I suppose, all right, if one had to analyze, then I really *am* a character actor, but I don't like to put a label on it.'

Stardom, its pitfalls and pleasures, has been the central issue in Hackman's career. Some observers claim that a good character actor was ruined by the receipt of an Oscar and promotion to leading-man roles. Hackman himself has been uncomfortable with star status, craving its benefits at some points and rueing its drawbacks at others. He can only regret the toll it has exacted in his private life.

However, the range and accomplishments of his career are staggering and virtually unrivalled in terms of consistency and versatility. A roll call of his most memorable performances would have to include his doomed gangster in *Bonnie and Clyde*, the emotionally thwarted son in *I Never Sang for My Father*, the feisty hobo in *Scarecrow*, the conscience-stricken surveillance expert in *The Conversation*, the baffled private eye in *Night Moves*, the blind hermit in *Young Frankenstein*, the beseiged gold baron in *Eureka*, the adulterous steelworker in *Twice in a Lifetime*, and most famous of all, the tough, obsessive narcotics cop 'Popeye' Doyle in *The French Connection*.

Contemporary American cinema would be the poorer without Gene Hackman's vital and prodigious presence. He may have been a reluctant star but he has proved an uncommonly fine actor.

Chapter One

Eugene Alden Hackman was born on 30 January 1930 in San Bernardino, California. His father, Eugene Ezra, was a veteran newspaperman, continuing a distinguished family tradition of service within the journalism profession. Gene's paternal grandfather had spent almost half a century as a reporter and, as a teenager, the future Oscar winner briefly considered the family trade as his vocation.

The Hackman family moved from California when Gene was still a youngster and his formative years were spent in the small mid-West town of Danville in Illinois. Situated deep in the cornbelt region, with a population of around 10,000, Danville was a quiet backwater where the highlight of the week was the Saturday night parade down Main Street.

Hackman never enjoyed a settled childhood; his schooling was completed at a variety of establishments, his family never seemed to own a home of their own and his father was a somewhat puritanical patriarch who separated from his mother when Hackman was thirteen. Hackman remained in Danville with his mother, but years later he recalled, 'We always had enough to eat, but we lived with my grandmother. I don't remember us owning a home – we always rented. We moved a lot. I went to five high schools. We didn't have roots, as they say. So I guess that's why, when I got old enough, when I was sixteen, and my dad had left, I just felt I had to get out.'

Hackman appears to have left Danville with no other purpose in mind except escape. His chosen means of flight was to lie about his age and join the Marines, although that was a spur-of-the-moment decision.

'I joined the Marines when I was sixteen, just to break out a little. It was ridiculous really how I joined up. I'd had a row with the basketball coach at school, and passed a Marine recruiting centre on the way home. So, out of pique, I signed on! And my parents let me go, though I was under-age. I dropped out, that's the truth of it. I was literally in high school in the middle of the week and in training at the Marine base on Parris Island, South Carolina by the end of the week. I hated the Marines but loved the travel and freedom.'

Hackman has subsequently acknowledged that his small-town upbringing instilled a restlessness and feeling of wanderlust in him. As a teenager he had no clear impression of what he might make of his life but was certain that a mundane blue-collar job would not satisfy him. 'I once had a summer job at a steel mill,' he recalled. 'I think I could have gotten stuck in my hometown and ended up unhappy with a common job.'

The prospect of being a journalist failed to inspire him sufficiently to want to stay in school as he was impatient for some excitement, and besides, as he has drily noted, 'When I learned in school that I couldn't write, I figured that it might hinder any newspaper career.'

The possibility of pursuing a career as an actor may have been a dim and distant notion, but there would have been little in Danville to help him substantiate it. However, like any youngster, Hackman enjoyed the thrills and spills of the escapist entertainment purveyed by his neighbourhood movie theatre. In an interview with Pete Hamill for *Film Comment* he admitted, 'In my early days as a kid, I was bananas about all the swashbuckling guys, Errol Flynn and that kind of thing. Not really understanding what it was they did, but just being attracted to the adventure. I had a terribly high fantasy life in terms of movies. I think I really had my acceptance speech for the Academy Awards when I was about twelve. But strangely, I had a real split about going off and doing something about it. Because I wasn't in the Glee Club, or the chorus, or the community players. I was terrified, just terrified. But I still had this Walter Mitty thing in my head that said, "Oh, I can do that if I want to, but, ah, you know, it makes me a little nervous, so I'll wait a while." ' And he did.

In the interim Hackman travelled the world with the Marines, journeying to Hawaii, Okinawa and Tsingtao in

China. During his stay in China, Hackman's unit needed a disc jockey for their radio station and he volunteered. As a young man Hackman was shy and admits he 'did not fit the Marine stereotype.' However, his work with the Armed Forces Radio Service was one step towards breaking down his natural reserve. His faltering style of presentation was neither slick nor confident – he would often dry up when reading the news – but he reckoned that the experience was valuable, and 'Besides, what better place to practice than on a station where 90% of your audience is Chinese and can't understand a word you're saying anyway?'

Hackman spent four years in the Marine Corps, completing his service at Camp Pendleton near Oceanside in California. His service life was abruptly terminated when he was involved in a motorcycle accident and broke both his legs. The injuries he sustained rendered him unfit for duty and can still cause discomfort, especially if he is called upon to enact an arduous action scene or an exhausting chase. At the time, the accident prevented him from being posted to Korea. Having been reared on fantasies of what Errol Flynn could achieve in combat, he probably resented his direct exclusion from the field of battle. However, of the men from his battalion who served in Korea, only one in ten returned alive.

At the age of twenty Hackman was discharged from the Marines as a disabled veteran. A tall (6' 2"), well-travelled and experienced young man, he felt confident, almost cock-sure, about his potential. 'I felt years older than my contemporaries. I had spent four years in the Corps and I thought I knew just that bit more than the other guy. I didn't, of course.'

Readjusting to civilian life, Hackman made a further attempt to acquire the rudiments of journalism but still lacked the concentration or patience to persevere with the subject. If the written word was not to prove his forte, then perhaps he could make use of his Marine Corps experiences and try a different medium of reportage. He duly travelled to Manhattan and enrolled at the School of Radio Technique.

The big city, however, soon brought him down to size. 'I really didn't know anything about the city. All I could think of was Times Square. So when I arrived at the Port Authority Bus Terminal, I got in a cab and very authoritatively told

[3]

the driver to take me to Times Square – which was, of course, only a block away. The cab driver knew he had a live one.'

As he settled into New York life he began studying painting at the Art Student League, and thus began a hobby and form of relaxation that has remained constant and fulfilling over the past thirty-five years.

It was also around this time that Hackman met the woman who would later become his wife – Faye Maltese, a trim and sometimes volatile Italian with whom he was instantly smitten.

'It was in 1951 in New York, at a YMCA dance. I'd just come out of the Marines and I was staying at the Y, going to a school that taught you how to be a disc jockey, and I'd actually been locked out of my room for not paying the rent. They'd stored all my clothes. Faye says that the first thing she noticed about me was that I wasn't wearing any socks. I was a real hick.'

However sartorially inelegant he may have appeared, Hackman created a favourable impression, and credits their romance as 'a case of the attraction of opposites. Faye is a New Yorker, from a large Italian family. I'm from the mid-West from a small family and a small town.'

Faye worked as a secretary in a bank, and over the next few years her support and encouragement were vital in convincing Hackman to pursue a career as an actor. After studying radio technique he used his basic broadcasting skills to move over to television, and spent a period as a floor manager and assistant director for a succession of television stations in Danville, Florida and California.

Eventually, however, he chose to become an actor. He was wary at first about committing himself to such a course; looking in the mirror he was painfully aware that his rugged-looking but ordinary mug in no way lived up to his old Errol Flynn fantasies and that he could probably never expect to be a leading man in that tradition. Furthermore, he had squandered a good deal of time in other pursuits, time that he could never reclaim in a very competitive field that always seemed to favour the young and the beautiful. His close friends may have doubted his sanity, but his own modest ambition only extended to the hope that he might make a living from a precarious profession. However, with Faye's

[4]

rock-solid support, he knew that he could become an actor of some description.

Hackman has always been reluctant to analyze his reasons for becoming an actor. As late as 1986 he stated, 'I don't really know why I became an actor. I haven't examined that decision closely, because it's a little mystery I like to leave unsolved.' Nevertheless, on another occasion he admitted, 'I really started in the business because of Brando, I suppose. I saw in Brando some kind of kinsmanship, not because of the way he looked but something inside him that let me say: "I can *do* that." I'm sure that's why he has such a following. People see in him some kind of strength that *could* be an everyday attitude. Although he's not a common man at all. He's not your ordinary off-the-street guy. I mean, there's a lot more to him than that.

'When I first saw him in films – I guess it was *The Men* – I'd already started to work as an actor, but then that *really* convinced me that I could maybe *do* it, that maybe there really was an area for me . . .'

In California, he enrolled at the Pasadena Playhouse to study drama. His early experiences were chastening, as his fellow students were all younger or better looking or more confident or a lethal combination of all three. At the end of the year he shared with a fellow classmate the dubious distinction of being dubbed the student least likely to succeed. The other fellow was seven years his junior and would become one of Hackman's closest friends within the film industry. His name was Dustin Hoffman. The alarming misjudgement of the Pasadena Playhouse alumni was for both actors a minor irritant and perhaps some kind of incentive to succeed and prove their contemporaries wrong.

Hackman's public debut at the Pasadena Playhouse came in a production of *The Curious Miss Carraway* with Zasu Pitts. After a year in California he returned East and made his professional debut in summer stock at Bellport, Long Island. Back in New York, his relationship with Faye Maltese blossomed and the couple were married on New Year's Day, 1956.

Faye continued to work at the bank to supplement the family coffers, and as the years passed, it seemed as if Hackman's earnings as a smalltime actor would never be sufficient to support the couple, never mind the large family that they hoped to raise. Hackman grabbed any available short-term, stop-gap form of employment in order to keep earning during the inevitable round of auditions and rejections that are the lot of any aspiring actor. At various times he was a soda jerk, truck driver, shoe salesman, furniture mover and counterman. He was also a doorman, and one memorable encounter in that capacity provided a blow to his self-esteem that is vividly recalled to this day.

'They were having a big convention in New York and they wanted a doorman at Howard Johnson's to kind of posh the place up a bit. So, they got me a white uniform with green piping on it and I stood in front of the building, opening the door for all these people to go in and have ice-cream and sandwiches. One day, I'm outside there and here comes this guy down the street in dress blues, a marine. I thought, "Hmm, he looks familiar." He happened to have been my first sergeant. Well, he got about twenty feet from me and recognized me and I wanted to die, shrink into myself, but I gave him a snappy salute and a big grin. He stood there looking at me and he finally said, "Hackman, you're a sorry son of a bitch." He walked on and I had to finish my day bathed in sweat.'

Mr and Mrs Hackman continued to eke out a moderate living from their base in a sixth floor, $22–a-month apartment in the East 20s of New York. Hackman was a modest actor, content with his slow progress towards a greater understanding of his craft and uncomfortable with the business aspects of a profession where it is important, at least initially, to sell yourself and be noticed by the right people. Asked why he persisted with his career through the long, lean years of anonymity, Hackman has replied, 'I was lucky enough to get tiny breaks at opportune moments; they were enough to keep me encouraged. I never thought it would happen to me. When I looked at others making it, they seemed to have a glamour about them that I lacked. I began to just hope for work. I figured if I could be a working actor that would be enough. Let others have stardom. I'd be content to make a living at my craft.'

Dustin Hoffman, struggling just as valiantly against stereotypical notions of leading men, was now also in New York and providing Hackman with further encouragement. 'I

[6]

knew Gene was going to make it by the way he walked into a room,' Hoffman later averred. 'No matter how shy he was, as soon as he entered he was noticed. There was something about him – a presence that was unmistakable.'

One of the 'tiny breaks' that sustained Hackman was his first major television role in a segment of the dramatic anthology series *The US Steel Hour*. This segment, called *The Little Tin God*, was broadcast on 22 April 1959 and marked the beginning of what would become a burgeoning career as a television guest star. In the decade between 1959 and 1968 Hackman appeared in some of the better TV shows including *I Spy*, *FBI*, *Iron Horse*, *Hawk* and *The Trials of O'Brien*. He appeared more than once in *The Defenders*, a superior drama series that ran from 1961 to 1965 and featured E. G. Marshall and Robert Reed as a father-and-son lawyer team. The series gained distinction for tackling social and political issues like euthanasia, blacklisting, civil disobedience and abortion. Even more remarkable for a prime-time series was the fact that the lead characters were occasionally seen to lose a case. Hackman appeared in the 'Quality of Mercy' episode in 1961 and the 'Judgment of Eve' in 1963. Filming took place in New York, and the now impressive roll-call of guest performers included Dustin Hoffman, Robert Redford, Martin Sheen and Jon Voight.

Hackman also had been making appearances in off-Broadway productions, including Valgrem Massey's *Chapparal* and John Wulp's *The Saintliness of Margery Kempe*, and had been working with an improvisatory show in Greenwich Village. However, his unexpected appearance on the *US Steel Hour* gave a real boost to his self-confidence. One friend noted that, 'when Gene started to work on the dramatic shows on TV he began to gain confidence, and it made him change a great deal. His shyness remained but his face seemed to say, "I know what I'm doing." '

Hackman himself felt that he was acquiring some valuable acting experience through his television work and continuing his education as a performer. 'We used to do things like *The Defenders* and *Naked City* and that kind of stuff in New York, and I would maybe have only five or six lines. But man, I was Mister Tension. And I'd come on and blaaaaghh, God-I-hope-I-can-get-these-things-out-in-one-thing so I can go *home!* Until finally you realize what you're doing and you say, "Wait a minute, why do I want to be an actor if I want to go home? It just doesn't make any sense." So, as soon as you start relaxing, the more apparent it is that the process is not one of driving against the lines, but of absorbing what's there. I'm a great believer in relaxation in terms of any creative work. I think you can't really think unless you relax. Acting is thinking *and* feeling.'

As his career began to take shape, Hackman received another boost with his film debut in the 1961 gangster picture *Mad Dog Coll*, directed by Burt Balaban. A predictably tough-talking, raw-edged bloodbath, it was advertized in screaming headlines as the 'blistering story of Vincent Coll, the maniac with a machine-gun who terrorized New York'. Offering pat psychological insights into Coll's penchant for mayhem, the film has highly effective staccato bursts of gangland violence as Coll lives up to his nickname, attempting to become the toughest underworld figure of them all. An interesting supporting cast of future luminaries included Telly Savalas, Jerry Orbach and Vincent Gardenia. Hackman's participation as a cop was strictly limited, but clearly far from enjoyable, as he would later refer to *Mad Dog Coll* as the least favourite of all his films. The sensibilities of genteel British audiences remained protected from *Mad Dog Coll* for over a decade, but the film finally surfaced, albeit briefly, in 1973.

The combination of employment off-Broadway and on screen was modest but tangible evidence of the progress Hackman was making in his career. Certain of a slightly healthier degree of financial stability, the Hackmans decided to embark upon a family. A son, Christopher, was born in 1960 and was followed, in due course, by Elizabeth in 1963 and Leslie in 1966. Friends were quick to spot the changes in Hackman, the family man, and one of them noted that 'Gene's pride was spectacular. He walked around ten feet tall. I never saw a father as happy as he was, and Faye was as completely fulfilled as a woman has a right to be. Gene just talked about having a big family, and Faye smiled her quiet smile.'

Despite a happy home front and a slowly but surely advancing career, the acting profession still offered Hackman a generous share of hard times and periods of euphemistic 'resting'. He now enjoyed the friendship of several colleagues who shared his plight. Together they provided mutual encouragement and a camaraderie that allowed him to face whatever adversity might arise. The struggling thespians among Hackman's contemporaries included Robert Redford and his close acquaintances Dustin Hoffman and Robert Duvall. Looking back from the perspective of stardom, Hackman had bittersweet but affectionate memories of the early 1960s.

'No one can ever understand what happens inside an actor – and no matter what you see outside, inside he trembles. For me, the knowledge that I wasn't alone and the fact that other actors felt exactly the way I did made life easier. No one starts at the top in the theatre – and the bottom is a very ugly place. To look back, other than at the friendships, is painful a great deal of the time.'

Dustin Hoffman once recalled, 'Gene never lost his sense of humour, and in those days that was a feat. We were all getting turned down for jobs left and right, there seemed to be no end to our rejections. When we would meet for coffee, we would all crack jokes to keep from crying, but Gene won the award for unflagging good humour. I think that terrific wife he had at home was the reason. He was so far ahead of the rest of the world by having her.' Hackman has frequently confirmed that it was having Faye by his side that was the crucial factor in his good-humoured survival. 'Without Faye, it would have been unbearable,' he said once. 'To come home every night and find her there made me want to go on. The children gave me the sense of belonging that I think all men need.'

Those early days definitely did not consist of unrelenting gloom and despondency. Hoffman is a renowned practical joker and could always be counted upon to devise some outrageous stunt. One Christmas he was working at the toy department in Macy's. Acting as Christopher's minder one day whilst Hackman attended an audition, Hoffman embarked upon selling the bemused toddler as a life-size doll for the knockdown bargain price of $16. A concerned father returned before his friend applied the wrapping paper and string to the 'doll'. Reminiscing for Mike Bygrave in the *Mail on Sunday* in 1982, Hackman stated, 'Even though I know they're stars, I still can't picture Bobby and Dusty except as living in those little cold-water flats in New York that I lived in too. I remember Dusty living with me and my wife when he was out of work one time. In those days it was a question of which one was the more broke right then, and the other two would help him out.'

Sheer persistence brought results in the cases of Hoffman, Duvall and Hackman, yet in the early days the greatest hindrances to their careers were perhaps their own attitudes. Hackman subsequently recalled, 'Bobby and I were very similar in that we were very self-conscious about selling ourselves as actors. We had our pictures and our résumés and we would make the rounds of the agents and the producers, but we never got in to see anybody. We used to slip our photos under their doors, stuff like that. It was ridiculous. We both knew we could never get a job, but it was like paying lip service to the process.' Hoffman has endorsed this view, adding, 'We were not salesmen. We would back into a spotlight rather than walk directly into it.'

Of the trio, Hackman was the most painfully self-effacing and determinedly realistic; in one interview he claimed never to have suffered any anxiety about the possibility of stardom because it seemed such an unobtainable goal. His aim then was merely to advance a rung up the ladder from off-Broadway to Broadway and perhaps, one day, establish a certain reputation as a reliable character actor. Looking back after the success of *The French Connection*, Hackman reflected, 'It's very confusing to me, even now, to really discern where I was then, and was I really ready to do any more than I was doing when I got there. Or could I have gotten there earlier? Or was I superseding my talents? One never knows. I keep wanting to stretch, at least within the context of my ability. But you just don't know how much of yourself you're using. At least I don't.

'But I was strangely philosophical about my work. Or defensive. Because I never really felt I was being held back. I built up a kind of defense that said, "If I get it, fine; if I don't, that's fine too".'

Increasingly, Hackman found himself in employment as an actor rather than a soda jerk trying to be an actor. Another of his encouraging 'tiny breaks' came when he secured a supporting role in the original production of the Neil Simon comedy *Barefoot in the Park*. Robert Redford played the lead, opposite Elizabeth Ashley, but Hackman had made it to Broadway and thus attained one of his goals. 'In those days I had only small goals,' he said in retrospect. 'To go from $45 a week off-Broadway to $90 a week as a supernumerary on Broadway seemed like stealing. I missed one step – I went straight into a supporting part on Broadway. Life was simpler then and full of wonderments.'

Hackman is one of many actors to express genuine delight and surprise that he should actually be receiving some form of remuneration for his work at all. If a role did not fully stretch his capabilities then the payment was always to be considered 'stealing'. *Barefoot in the Park* brought rewards beyond the mere financial – an opportunity to hone his comedy technique before an audience, the chance to explore a character at greater length than ever before, and the challenge of constant daily exposure to audiences, critics and talent spotters. His involvement in the show certainly resulted in some offers of work. 'I began to feel like I really had a future, and the nightly audience response served to reinforce my hopes. It never occurred to me that I could play the lead – that was for glamour types like Redford – but a career as a character man seemed perfect for me.'

With his career gaining momentum, Hackman was cast in Irwin Shaw's *Children from Their Games* as the stolid football player Charles Widgin Rochambeau, 'a kind of flashy role that I had a great time with.' He moved on to Howard Teichman's *A Rainy Day in Newark* and then, most important of all, Muriel Resnik's *Any Wednesday*.

Any Wednesday is a lightweight farce in which a millionaire industrialist cheats on his wife each Wednesday by spending the day with his young mistress in a New York apartment that is charged to one of his corporations as a business expense. His blissfully parallel-running lives are irrevocably complicated when a young associate is accidentally sent to make use of the company apartment and falls in love with the mistress. Jason Robards played the industrialist, Sandy Dennis the mistress, Ellen Gordon, and Hackman portrayed the juvenile lead of Cass Henderson, the ardent young suitor.

There were many influential people who had not considered Hackman the ideal choice to play Cass. In her

[11]

book *Son of Any Wednesday*, Muriel Resnik wrote that the director found it hard to imagine who might be less well suited to the part. An audition with Sandy Dennis failed to display the best of either actor, and according to Resnik, Dennis found her potential co-star 'repulsive . . . She almost died when he came into the room and she had her first look at him.' However, the one person who was in Hackman's corner was Resnik herself: 'I got an enormous charge out of hearing my lines when they were read properly, and when Gene Hackman read the first Cass-Ellen scene I was beside myself. He was so good and so right. I said I wanted him but they all told me to calm down and not make up my mind until we'd read everyone on the list. But I knew then that no one could be better no matter how many we read.' Hackman may have been 'replusive' to Sandy Dennis but to Resnik he was 'exactly the man I meant – warm, funny, mature and very nice.'

Resnik's lone dissenting voice held sway and Hackman duly joined the case of *Any Wednesday*, which opened at the Music Box theatre on Broadway on 18 February 1963. It was an immediate hit and Resnik's sixth sense about Hackman was vindicated by the critical and popular reactions to his performance. According to Richard Watts Jnr of the *New York Post*, 'The angry young man, who knows what he is up to, is expertly and likeably played by Gene Hackman,' whilst Walter Kerr of the *New York Herald Tribune* wrote, 'Gene Hackman . . . is an exceedingly nimble performer who can put a finger in your eye before you have quite noticed your eye is open, and he has a wonderfully light-footed habit of stepping off a joke before it begins to complain.'

The play ran for 938 perormances and was filmed in 1966, with only Jason Robards repeating his stage role; Jane Fonda was brought in as Ellen and, to Hackman's disappointment, Dean Jones was Cass.

The success of *Any Wednesday* established Hackman as much more than a Broadway supernumerary and served as the first major breakthrough of his career. Underlining his newfound good fortune, he found himself the recipient of the Clarence Derwent Award for his performance in *Children from Their Games*, which had survived the minimum amount of time any play can on Broadway – just one performance. Despite closing on its opening night, the play was highly regarded by the select few who had witnessed it. Hackman might never have heard of the Clarence Derwent Award; but he welcomed both the recognition of his abilities and the cash prize of five hundred dollars designed to provide practical encouragement to young actors.

One of the people who saw *Children from Their Games* was the director Robert Rossen, who was then engaged in casting the smaller roles in his latest film, *Lilith*. Hackman was offered, and accepted, the brief, eighth-billed role of Norman, one of the patients at a mental institution.

Rossen was one of the most talented and tortured directors to emerge from within Hollywood during the post-war years. A former boxer and writer, he arrived in Hollywood in 1936 and worked as a scriptwriter at Warner Brothers during their peak years. His directorial career began in 1947 and included the hard-hitting boxing drama *Body and Soul* and the Oscar-winning *All the King's Men*, an excellent study of how absolute power corrupts, based on the life of Senator Huey Long. In the 1950s, Rossen became involved in a protracted and agonizing series of skirmishes with the House Un-American Activities Committee. He had been a member of the Communist Party between 1937 and 1947, a fact that he finally admitted to the Committee in 1953, naming the names of fellow sympathizerrs.

According to his closest associates, Rossen never recovered from the traumas invoked by his blacklisting by the industry and his decision to testify. His subsequent work became increasingly personal, with the protagonist an often neurotic and self-destructive man in search of some kind of peace, love or understanding. Prior to *Lilith*, he had completed *The Hustler*, featuring Paul Newman in one of his best roles as the pool shark Fast Eddie Felson.

J. R. Salamanca's novel *Lilith* seemed ideal material for Rossen. Set in Maryland after the war, it deals with a young man taken on as a trainee therapist at an asylum. He falls under the spell of a beautiful patient named Lilith and is keen to enter her special world constructed from the insights and desires of the schizophrenic. His love turns to hate when he fails to comprehend the complexities of her promiscuity and his subsequent actions lead to one patient's suicide

[13]

and Lilith's total withdrawal from the 'normal' world. He tries to run away but returns to the asylum seeking help for himself.

Although it was only Salamanca's second novel, *Lilith* was greeted with widespread acclaim on its publication in June, 1961 and went into five hardback reprintings before selling over 500,000 copies in paperback. Its early reputation grew as it became the Book-of-the-Month Club's August choice and was serialized in *Good Housekeeping*. Rossen acquired the film rights and became the director, producer and co-writer of a project that began production on 6 May 1963 in Great Falls, Maryland.

Filming proceeded over three months, mostly on location and largely in continuity. Only two weeks of studio filming were deemed necessary, and those took place at the then brand-new Long Island Studios facilities that had been converted from old aerodrome hangars at Roosevelt Field. The major location for *Lilith* was Killingworth in Locust Valley, Long Island. The former summer home of the late Myron C. Taylor, Chief Executive of the US Steel Corporation and Envoy to the Vatican, Killingworth served as the grounds and buildings of the tranquil Poplar Lodge.

Throughout the filming there were rumours of disharmony between star Warren Beatty and his colleagues Jean Seberg and Peter Fonda, with the latter threatening physical retaliation at the slightest further provocation. Rossen reportedly found much of the process unpleasant and *Lilith* was to be his final film. On its release the film was generally disliked by the critical fraternity, partly because of the subject matter, partly because many of its attitudes were ahead of the times and partly because of the painful personal links between Rossen and his work.

There is an unsettling and uncomfortable mood to a film exploring the lure and fascination of a mad person's world and demanding who is the more culpable, Lilith for her calculating displays of affection to one and all or Vincent Bruce (Beatty) for his self-regarding actions and complicity in their disastrous tryst. In subsequent analyses of Rossen's work *Cinema* magazine noted, 'The protagonists in Robert Rossen's films are blind people struggling for sight' whilst *Film Quarterly* observed, 'In all of his major works Rossen was concerned with the search of a young man for something he does not recognize as himself, his identity.'

Beatty's Vincent Bruce is the most complex variation on Rossen's central preoccupation, and as he is ultimately able to face his own need to seek treatment at Poplar Lodge, his final despairing plea of 'Help me . . .' provides some satisfactory degree of climactic resolution to both the film and the director's career.

Although neither a critical nor commercial success upon its release, *Lilith* was more characteristic of the type of film fare that would attract Hackman than the run-of-the-mill material that would be his lot over the next few years. As time passed and critical re-assessments were undertaken, opinions regrouped in favour of *Lilith*, still an underrated and well-acted film. In 1966 Jean Seberg told *Cahiers du Cinema* that people had often reproached Rossen 'with being heavy, with being the elephant in the china shop; *Lilith*, on the contrary, is a magnificent crystal, so clear and so pure that it can only break itself. Madness is often sordid: he knew, in this last film, how to go beyond appearances, towards something very beautiful, in which all his personal unhappinesses were buried.' In 1986 the *British Monthly Film Bulletin* re-evaluated the film, concluding that *Lilith* was 'one of the finest films about madness ever made'.

Hackman's participation in *Lilith* was minimal; with just a few minutes on screen his work on the film did not entail a great deal of commitment in terms of time or acting concentration. However, he was convinced that his professional future lay on the stage, and *Lilith* was probably a welcome but minor summer diversion from the more pressing matter of how to capitalize on his status as the year's Clarence Derwent Award winner. The critical and public reaction to the finished film probably confirmed his ingrained prejudice against the medium. One person begged to differ with him, and Warren Beatty later magnanimously declared that Gene Hackman was the best thing about *Lilith*. Ultimately, Beatty's opinion was the one that mattered.

Chapter Two

Hackman remained with the Broadway company of *Any Wednesday* for one season before choosing to leave the security of a long-run success to explore the numerous offers now coming his way. As a mark of his rising status he shared above-the-title billing with Robert Preston in Jean Kerr's *Poor Richard*, and his other theatrical work at this time included *The Natural Look* with Brenda Vaccaro. Unfortunately, *The Natural Look* shared with *Children from their Games* the dubious distinction of closing after one night, although on this occasion there would be no awards to compensate for the hard work and frustration entailed in a one-performance run.

Now becoming a more readily recognizable name among the casting agencies and producers' offices, Hackman found himself increasingly under consideration for guest roles on television and small supporting parts in films. For such a thoroughly professional performer his attitude towards any form of acting on celluloid was singularly blinkered and dismissive. 'I always thought of films in those days as just a way to make some money, so I could live,' he has frankly confessed. 'A lot of New York actors at that time considered film to be something less than good acting . . . that it was a way to steal some money – so many weeks in California, hotel expenses paid and back home again. Great! Nobody would ever see the film and you'd come back to New York and go on with your life. I did not know anything about film technique and I did not much care.'

Hackman's disparaging view of the film world must partially reflect the minimal demands that the medium initially made on his talents and the preconceptions he shrewdly held of how film can limit and typecast an actor within certain rigidly defined parameters. On Broadway he

[16]

was beginning to be recognized as a skilled and adroit interpreter of comedy roles; on film his physique and physiognomy would probably consign him to a life of playing gruff sergeants and tough cops – muscle-and-bone, low challenge roles. Nevertheless, the realistic business man in him was happy to make guerrilla raids on the film world and then scurry back to the superior climes of Broadway and some 'proper' acting.

In 1965 he was cast in *Hawaii*, his first brush with mainstream Hollywood filmmaking. James Michener's massive 937-page tome had been purchased as a potential screen property during August 1959 from the publisher Random House in a deal reportedly worth $600,000. The epic novel went on to sell some four million copies and was announced as the next project for Oscar-winning director Fred Zinnemann after he completed *The Sundowners* (1960).

Zinnemann worked on the preparation of the film for three years before encountering a number of insurmountable obstacles that precipitated his withdrawal from the enterprise. Zinnemann had sought to encompass the whole, wide-ranging sweep of Michener's novel and thus envisaged a big-budget, lengthy film that might run for four hours or even wind up being two films, such was the scope of the material. The substantial budget required would be somewhere in the region of $17 to $18 million.

Nowadays, of course, *Hawaii* would probably become a sprawling television mini-series shown over consecutive evenings as primetime viewing. In the early 1960s a four-hour, $18 million film was not something to be embarked upon lightly, and thus United Artists placed a budgetary ceiling of $10 million on the film and Zinnemann left, citing a suitably vague reason of 'differences of opinions'.

Scaling down their aspirations for *Hawaii*, the Mirisch Corporation chose to concentrate on just a few chapters of the book, concerning a 19th-century Calvinist missionary's attempt to bring Christianity to the natives of one Hawaiian isle. The noted scenarist Dalton Trumbo spent eighteen months working out a satisfactory script before the film was finally put into pre-production. Although now more modestly proportioned, *Hawaii* was still to be a formidable undertaking requiring the cooperation of the Hawaiian state authorities and the American Army, Navy and Marines, and

[17]

involving the reconstruction of the 1850 Honolulu waterfront at Pearl Harbour, the construction of several seagoing vessels (specifically whaling ships and seventy-five foot double canoes) and the re-creation of an entire village. Filming was scheduled to take place in four phases, beginning with two weeks in Norway during February of 1965. This would be followed in April with work in New England, then four weeks in Hollywood and four months in the Hawaiian Islands. Filming was scheduled to finish in September 1965, and the movie to be on the cinema screens by the summer of 1966.

The relatively inexperienced George Roy Hill was assigned the directorial chore of guiding and shaping this daunting production. As a form of insurance against the calculated financial risk involved, it was perhaps inevitable that major stars were deemed essential to play the three main roles. Julie Andrews, with *Mary Poppins* (1964), *The Sound of Music* (1965) and an Oscar to her credit, was currently considered the top female box-office attraction in the industry, and at an estimated salary of $700,000, was the first star to be signed. Richard Harris and Max Von Sydow followed. For the less significant roles, George Roy Hill insisted upon actors who had 'as little previous identification as possible' to make it 'easier for the audience to accept them not as themselves but as the characters they are portraying.'

Hackman's appearance in *Hawaii* is brief. He plays John Whipple, a missionary-doctor friend of Von Sydow's religious fanatic Jerusha Bromley. On this evidence one can sympathise with Hackman's apparent disdain for the specific demands of screen acting. His importance in the overall production of *Hawaii* was undoubtedly negligible, and it is understandable and inevitable that he would arrive at some point in the six-month schedule, perform his lines and then, equally unceremoniously, depart. It is hard to display loyalty or concern when you are so patently labelled as a small cog in a giant industrial wheel. Filmmaking at this level, for a supporting player of Hackman's then modest stature, is probably an unavoidably impersonal act and received the degree of detached commitment that it merited; no more, no less. (Another future star was employed as an even smaller cog in *Hawaii;* the redoubtable Bette Midler was a Hawaiian extra.)

When *Hawaii* was released in 1966 it met with barely suppressed yawns and generally unenthusiastic reviews. A long and sober examination of the unbending, righteous zeal of a Calvinist missionary, *Hawaii* could scarcely be termed exciting. Bereft of some fifty minutes of the original American running time of 3½ hours, the film still opened in Britain to critical notices like the *Daily Express*'s succinctly damning description, 'formidably dull'. The *New Statesman* was more sympathetic, saying, 'As it stands, it isn't the threatened epic at all, but rather the tale of an American Calvinist missionary who comes to an Hawaiian isle around 1820 and there lives through twenty heartbreaking years. The effect is of a portrait of bigotry and intransigence in some depth, with fire, pestilence, high winds and pagan weddings providing visual relief or sideshows.'

The final budget of *Hawaii* was estimated to be as much as $14 million. However, in both 1966 and 1967 Julie Andrews was voted America's top box-office draw and her loyal fans turned out in force to accumulate an American gross of $15,500,000. Her popularity elsewhere probably ensured that the film eventually returned a modest profit on its investment. *Hawaii* also went on to secure a tiny niche in the film history books, winning an Oscar for special visual effects. Hollywood returned to Michener's novel a few years later for *Master of the Islands* (1970) with Charlton Heston.

Moving from one end of the Hollywood spectrum to the other, Hackman next appeared in two routine bread-and-butter Warner Brothers productions which can only have confirmed his notions about celluloid typecasting. One of them, *Covenant with Death*, was the first feature film by television director Lamont Johnson. Set in the 1920s, it revolved around a murder trial.

Bryan Talbot (Earl Holliman) is arrested and sentenced to death for the murder by strangulation of his wife. The convicting evidence is flimsily circumstantial, but his reputation as a hotheaded, hard-drinking man prone to jealousy and violence had won him few friends and he is duly led to the gallows. Vehemently protesting his innocence, he grabs the hangman and their struggle results in the latter's death.

The second strand of the plot involves Ben Lewis (George

[19]

Maharis), a half-breed judge who is torn between a white girl and the Mexican, Rafaela, whom his mother would prefer him to marry.

The complicating twist arrives when the local police chief, Alfred Harmsworth (played by Hackman), discovers a suicide note from someone else confessing to the murder in question. Talbot is acquitted of murdering his wife, but is immediately re-arrested for the death of the hangman. Lewis has to sit in judgement on the case, despite previous personal animosity between the two men. He pronounces Talbot innocent on the grounds that 'an innocent man has the right of self-defence against a society that has been mistaken, including the right, the obligation, to save his own life.' Talbot is released, and Lewis resolves his personal dilemma by asking for the hand of Rafaela.

Hackman's function in *Covenant with Death* was a secondary one, merely to move the plot along by viewing the wife's body, arresting Talbot, escorting him to the gallows, discovering the suicide note, etc. He basically carries out the legwork to allow the principal stars to take centre stage. Although a not totally undistinguished second feature, the film was intended merely to pad out some value-for-money double bill and consequently it received little attention. In *The Warner Brothers Story*, author Clive Hirschhorn considers the film, ultimately, 'an uneasy mélange of melodrama and tedium'.

First to Fight was a more strictly conventional exercise in uncritical World War Two heroics, no doubt intended to inspire the youth of a nation heavily involved in an altogether different kind of war in Vietnam.

The film focuses on the momentary doubts and fears that afflict the brave Jack Connell (Chad Everett). Awarded a Congressional Medal of Honour and promoted to second lieutenant after displaying exemplary heroism on Guadalcanal, Connell marries and becomes an instructor at a Fleet Marine camp in California.

Recalled to active duty in the Pacific, Connell is met by a platoon who are proud to hail a decorated veteran as their new leader. However, under fire once more, he is unable to command. As he witnesses the slaughter of his men, his own life is saved only by the intervention of Sergeant Tweed (Hackman). Other events serve to underline Connell's cowardice and lose him the respect of his men. On further anti-Japanese manoeuvres the ever-reliable Tweed is wounded. The men prepare to retreat but, under stress, Connell controls his fears and leads the platoon to a strategic victory. Discussing events with Tweed, he is able to admit that all men, even heroes, experience fear but now that he has learned to conquer his, he will once again be proud to be the 'first to fight'.

Nauseatingly all-American, *First to Fight* displayed no ambitions to be anything other than the cannon-fodder patriotic production it clearly was. As Sergeant Tweed, Hackman plays the familiar figure of right-hand man, offering moral support and strength to the top man in his momentary self-doubt. It was another case of taking the money and running back to Broadway.

In Britain, both *First to Fight* and *Covenant with Death* were unhesitatingly earmarked as second features and were shorn down to their bare essentials, involving a loss of around twenty-five minutes in each case.

Of the Hackman-Duvall-Hoffman trio, Gene was not the only one to be acquiring some much-appreciated living expenses from the film world. Robert Duvall had made his film debut as Boo Radley in *To Kill a Mockingbird* (1962) and was now a not infrequent performer before the cameras. Hoffman resisted the lure of easy money for the longest time, although perhaps he wasn't asked. However, in 1966 he appeared in *Madigan's Millions*, a low-budget gangster comedy, before hitting the jackpot with the lead role in *The Graduate* (1967), a part that had been rejected by Robert Redford on the grounds that no one would believe he ever encountered problems attracting girls. Utilizing his newfound power as a leading man, Hoffman secured a role for his friend Hackman. The latter's gratitude was short-lived, however. Whether through inexperience, or a situation in which his disregard for film technique found him out, Hackman was fired by director Mike Nichols.

Reflecting on his dismissal almost fifteen years later, Hackman calmly observed, 'That was a painful experience. I was supposed to play Mr Robinson and I was fired during rehearsals. I think it was my own fault. I just wasn't capable then of giving the director what he wanted. That's why I believe it takes ten years to become an actor. Doesn't matter what age you start. There's no substitute for experience.'

If Hackman was at all dejected by his brief interlude on *The Graduate*, solace was at hand in another film that would prove equally significant and durable. When this film was released in 1967, Alexander Walker of the *London Evening Standard* noted, with characteristically unequivocal prescience, 'Make no mistake: *Bonnie and Clyde* is a film from which we shall date reputations and innovations in American cinema.'

Like many of the best Hollywood offspring, *Bonnie and Clyde* had to struggle to be born. The film was first conceived in 1964 by Robert Benton and David Newman, who were then employed on *Esquire* magazine as art director and editor respectively. The two men shared a passion for the movies and any lull in the day or coffee break would be filled with conversation about the great directors and the exciting new discoveries to be found amongst the 'New Wave' European directors like François Truffaut and Jean-Luc Godard. Eventually, one conversation came around to the subject of making a film of their own, and thus began a course that resulted in *Bonnie and Clyde*.

The most direct inspiration for the film came from the chance discovery of a book by John Tolland entitled *The Dillinger Days*. Tolland's gangster chronicle incorporated a rogue's gallery of the principal characters to blaze their way across the American continent during the years of Prohibition and the Great Depression. Benton and Newman were especially intrigued by the occasional references and footnotes alluding to Bonnie Parker and Clyde Barrow. William Witney's punchy *The Bonnie Parker Story* (1958), with Dorothy Provine, had already attempted to recreate the exploits of the female half of the team, but the two writers felt that the story of Bonnie and Clyde contained enough raw material to allow them room to explore a number of questions about celebrities, folk heroes and the all-American need for achievement and recognition. Suitably inspired and emboldened, they began to work on a script.

Heavily influenced by a month-long season of Alfred Hitchcock films at the Museum of Modern Art in New York, they wrote a seventy-page summation of their project with the banjo-strumming music of the Foggy Mountain Boys playing in the background as they worked, and images from their favourite François Truffaut films flitting through their minds. One Truffaut film that they particularly admired was *Jules et Jim*; it seemed to achieve a rare combination of re-creating times past whilst embodying a contemporary relevance. *Bonnie and Clyde* would similarly attempt to refract the present through the past.

Once their ideas were done on paper, Benton and Newman decided to approach Truffaut and ask if he might be interested in directing their work. Helen Scott, an acquaintance at the French Film Office in New York, passed on the script to Truffaut with a unique personal endorsement urging him to read the material. One month later, Truffaut was in New York discussing the project. A former critic whose opinions had been unmerciful and forcibly couched, Truffaut had mellowed over the years until he evinced a natural concern and empathy for anyone who had somehow surmounted all the obstacles and made a film of some description, regardless of its merits. His attitude towards the American team was one of unselfish generosity.

Truffaut sent the two men to watch a number of relevant films, including Joseph H. Lewis's *Gun Crazy*. He discussed how they might improve their script. He encouraged, he approved, but he could not give them a guarantee that he would direct the film. Firstly, he was heavily involved in trying to raise an adequate amount of finance to film several projects of his own, most pressingly Ray Bradbury's *Fahrenheit 451*. Secondly, he argued that his command of the English language was insufficient to warrant his directing such quintessentially American subject matter. Truffaut thus demurred and returned to France, whilst Benton and Newman commenced their embellishment and revision of the script in the light of Truffaut's comments as well as extensive researches of their own into Bonnie and Clyde's life and crimes deep in the heart of Texas.

Truffaut read the new, improved Bonnie and Clyde script and expressed his appreciation of what the two writers had managed to achieve. However, he had not obtained the elusive finance for *Fahrenheit 451* and was thus unavailable, neatly resolving any debate over his suitability. As a further favour, though, he had passed on their work to Jean-Luc

Godard, who was similarly impressed and would soon be able to meet them in New York.

Godard is hardly a director to remain hidebound by convention or practicality. In New York, he decided that his wildfire enthusiasms should be channelled into direct and immediate action, consequently he would be ready to start filming within three weeks. Unfortunately, Benton and Newman had signed a contract with two friends who had agreed to act as the film's producers. Not surprisingly, these two gentlemen were intent on cooling Godard's ardour with a few questions about petty but niggling concerns like location scouting, a cast, a budget and some form of pre-production. They also had the temerity to suggest that the current Texas weather might not be entirely favourable. A crestfallen Godard retorted, 'We can make this film anywhere; we can make it in Tokyo. I am speaking cinema and you are speaking meteorology.' There was little common ground to be found between such diverse sensibilities and Godard left for France, advising Benton and Newman to make contact when they had re-established ownership of the script.

Eighteen months were to pass before *Bonnie and Clyde* would be returned to its rightful owners. In the interim, Truffaut would make *Fahrenheit 451* and Godard would complete *Alphaville* and *Pierrot le Fou*, whilst Benton and Newman would leave *Esquire* and write a book and a broadway musical about Superman. *Bonnie and Clyde*, meanwhile, was rejected by most of the major studios and was fast receding towards the horizon as something that might have been.

In observing the filmmaking process it is important not to forget the elements of chance and luck. On numerous occasions some of the most important films ever made have been salvaged from oblivion by unforeseen circumstances – for example, Claudette Colbert's indisposition bringing Bette Davis into *All About Eve*, or the last-minute introduction of Vivien Leigh to David O. Selznick as his Scarlett O'Hara. Just when it seemed that *Bonnie and Clyde* might never reach the screen, fate lent a hand by arranging a Parisian lunch between François Truffaut, Leslie Caron and Warren Beatty. Afterwards, nobody could quite recollect how the subject had been broached, but the *Bonnie and Clyde* script was

[24]

mentioned. Caron felt that it might make an excellent vehicle for the two of them and Beatty was sufficiently enthusiastic to track down the writers upon his return to New York.

Benton and Newman were flattered by Beatty's interest, but prepared themselves for a swift rejection on his part. The two men had envisaged Bonnie and Clyde as heroically anti-establishment figures, heedless of the prevailing restrictions and mores within the rest of society. Thus, in early drafts of the script, Clyde Barrow's sexuality was explored in some detail and complexity, suggesting not only a relationship with Bonnie but also a homosexual involvement with a third member of the gang. Judging Beatty by his very public image of heterosexuality and not by his actor's instinct for a good script, Benton and Newman anticipated a polite 'thanks, but no thanks' from the young star. To their surprise, Beatty liked the script, was willing to pay $10,000 for an option on the material and would not only act in but also produce the film. *Bonnie and Clyde* had journeyed from near oblivion to almost certain reality within an extremely short time, and all thanks to some post-prandial chit-chat between friends.

In a subsequent interview with *Cinema* magazine, Beatty explained what elements had originally attracted him to *Bonnie and Clyde*:

'The Freudian nature of their own relationship puts me to sleep. I've seen too much of that. I'm more interested in the kind of pathetic things they did. The absolute non-existence of any regard for their society. The public's treatment of them. The love/hate that the public felt for them. The desperation for the little guy to get out of the crowd. That interests me. Clyde wanted to *be somebody*.'

Clyde Barrow wasn't the only person who wanted to be somebody; Beatty wanted to shed his pretty-boy image and gain the artistic respect of the film industry. He also wanted to advance his career to a point where he could gain full control over every aspect of the increasingly rare films in which he would choose to appear. Producing *Bonnie and Clyde* was the first step on the road to becoming an all-round filmmaker of note.

As *Bonnie and Clyde* advanced towards the filming stage casting became all-important. Although Jean-Luc Godard had rekindled some interest in the project, Beatty and his

[25]

writers agreed upon Arthur Penn as their choice for director. Penn's work, including *The Left-Handed Gun* (1958) and *The Miracle Worker* (1962), had displayed a predilection towards featuring the loner and those at odds with the mainstream of society. He had previously directed Beatty in *Mickey One* (1965), an undervalued study of a nightclub entertainer seeking some direction in his life. Penn's guiding hand would prove invaluable in refining and honing the basic elements that would make *Bonnie and Clyde* so successful.

Having amicably agreed upon a director, Beatty and the writers next had to find an actress who might play Bonnie Parker. Contrary to her own opinion, Leslie Caron was clearly inappropriate for the part. Among the ladies given more serious consideration were Natalie Wood (who had been Beatty's co-star in *Splendor in the Grass* (1961)), Carol Lynley, Tuesday Weld and even Beatty's sister Shirley MacLaine. *Lolita* star Sue Lyon was about to be signed for the role when Penn suggested a young stage actress whose work in *Hogan's Goat* had impressed him. Her name was Faye Dunaway, and although she was under contract to Otto Preminger she was allowed to accept outside engagements and was duly offered and accepted the role.

Bonnie and Clyde involves a relatively small but crucial nucleus of main characters, so further casting was undertaken with due consideration and caution. The diminutive and puckish Michael J. Pollard was assigned the part of C.W., a hick hanger-on who represented all the sidekicks that had travelled with the Barrow gang. Stage and television actress Estelle Parsons was chosen to play Clyde's sister-in-law Blanche. Jack Nicholson had been mentioned for the part of Clyde's brother Buck, and there is now some confusion as to how Hackman was eventually chosen instead. In a not always reliable 1975 profile in *Films in Review,* Hackman recalls not having any contact with Beatty since their professional association on *Lilith* and recollects, 'I was in a New York hospital with blood poisoning, laid up for six weeks. Warren dropped in to see me. I was not only surprised, but touched. He said he had a film role he wanted to discuss with me. It was Buck Barrow in *Bonnie and Clyde.*'

The profile goes on to explain that Beatty had been driving around Hollywood shortly before and had noticed Hackman standing on the corner of Hollywood Boulevard and Vine

[26]

Street. This passing glimpse supposedly brought Hackman back to his attention and caused him to offer Gene the role. Other accounts indicate that Hackman's friend Estelle Parsons alerted him to the film and suggested that he enquire after the part of Buck. In one 1980s account Arthur Penn stated, 'Warren Beatty suggested Gene for the part. He had worked with him on *Lilith* and I had seen Gene in a play in the Berkshires with Estelle Parsons and knew they'd be great together.'

Regardless of how Hackman came to be cast in *Bonnie and Clyde*, it is sufficient to note that he was, and that it proved to be his most influential screen role thus far.

A large portion of the credit for the success of *Bonnie and Clyde* must go to Warren Beatty, who toiled incessantly to ensure that the film was made and seen. It was Beatty who finally found a major studio willing to back the project and even then he literally embarrassed Jack Warner into parting with the needed $2,500,000. Warner couldn't stand to see a grown man beg and eventually succumbed to his imploring. Beatty may have been desperate, but he was not foolish; he retained a personal stake of 40 per cent of the film's commercial fate.

As Beatty worked on every aspect of the production, Penn and the scriptwriters hammered out a final draft of the screenplay, paying particular attention to the simplification and clarification of Clyde's sexuality. Faye Dunaway prepared for the film by losing twenty pounds in weight to help her capture the pinched, strained nervousness of her character. Hackman reluctantly worked on his Southern accent. Michael J. Pollard's laid-back quality and other personal characteristics were incorporated into the persona of C.W. As a team spirit grew, everyone was fulsome in their praise of Beatty.

Penn, who is not a man prone to showbusiness exaggeration, hailed him as a 'perfect producer' who made everyone 'demand the best of themselves. Warren stays with a picture through editing, mixing and scoring. He plain works harder than anyone else I have ever seen.'

An equally laudatory Hackman commented, 'Warren is an amazing man. He has this playboy image, but underneath he's a shrewd, busy film-maker.' There were to be

[27]

many occasions on which Beatty's tenacity would be sorely tried, but it was never found wanting.

At long last, filming began in Texas in towns on the outskirts of Dallas that had remained virtually unchanged since the Depression. Great care was taken to ensure a faithfulness to the spirit of that time; those who had known the real Bonnie and Clyde were welcome witnesses to the filmmaker's re-creation of their actions, and three of the banks that the gang had once raided were re-opened after having lain derelict and disused since the Depression.

Hackman needs the stimulus of constant challenges and fresh horizons. He found playing the character of Buck Barrow irksome. 'I got terribly bored with the character by the time the film was over because of the accent. It was so heavy that it depressed me. I had been working for several years in New York and I had been working to try to say my ING sounds, and I had suddenly gotten back to where I was saying goin' and comin' and that kind of thing, and you get tired of a character.'

However tiresome Buck Barrow may have been in the short term, he was part of a valuable learning process that began with *Bonnie and Clyde*. That film was a revelation to Hackman and can be said to have irrevocably altered his attitude towards working for the screen. It marked the first time that he portrayed a character with any depth or complexity and the first time he had to develop a form of characterization that worked specifically for the medium of cinema. Doing this taught him the differences between work that involved adapting to the unpredictable daily rhythms of a live audience and work that dealt with the small details and gestures of a flesh-and-blood human being – the kind of acting that meant reacting to the events and people around him with a minimum of flamboyance and a need for quiet conviction.

Arthur Penn is one of the best film directors that Hackman has ever worked with, and proved a perfect teacher to a willing pupil. In an interview with *Cinema* Penn had this to say about his approach to actors:

'I guess there are two things I try to work for. One is to address the actor to what the scene requirements are, to fulfil whatever the story requires at that point, with sufficient relaxation and sufficient ease to permit accidents to occur.

[28]

The other is to keep them feeling that an accident is not a mistake. The accidents are human behaviour. Most actors come on a movie set and have the lines and the marks and the action clearly in mind and they do them, and if there is any variation from that, they stop or they come apart. I hope that slowly we are learning about each other enough to admit the unexpected. The unexpected is what makes for good acting.'

Hackman greatly admired Penn's philosophy and the fluidity of a working atmosphere that left room for the actor to make his own contribution. *Bonnie and Clyde* finally allowed him to respond to the creative demands of film acting and feel an important member of a team, not merely an insignificant cog.

Bonnie and Clyde has justifiably come to be regarded as a highpoint of American cinema in the 1960s. Benton and Newman's script captured the special quality that they had perceived in Truffaut's *Jules et Jim:* that of defining the present while evoking the past. It illuminated the rebelliousness of the Sixties through the medium of two hell-for-leather gangsters from the Thirties. The characters of gangsters elevated to folk heroes, ordinary people with a desperate desire to stand out from the crowd, were as relevant to the Thirties as Andy Warhol's claims of instant celebrity were to a later generation. Both the performances and the direction in *Bonnie and Clyde* brought out the universality of the story, lauding an unconventional code of bloody morality and skilfully juxtaposing humour and death.

The acting throughout is flawless, with Hackman employed to present a rougher-hewn and less charismatic foil to his screen brother Beatty. Hackman's Buck Barrow is one of life's followers, not one of the leaders; an ordinary man intent on the practicalities of life with little regard for the judgement of posterity or the attainment of immortality. Torn between the qualms and worries of his genteel wife and his sly admiration for his brother's bravado, he represents the majority who are torn between conformity and individualism and fail to make a clear-cut choice between them.

The struggle to bring *Bonnie and Clyde* to the world did not end when the last reel of film was exposed in the Texas sunlight. When a print of the fully complete, edited film was screened for the top executives at Warner Brothers, their reaction could hardly have been less favourable. One member of the audience is alleged to have dismissed it as 'a piece of shit'. Consequently, it was decided to release the film in a manner that reflected their opprobrium: as a minor feature in their less esteemed theatres. However, they had failed to consider the celebrated tenacity of Warren Beaty. Quite apart from his 40 per cent stake in the film, Beatty was painfully aware that his credibility as more than a pretty face rested on the success of *Bonnie and Clyde*.

Beatty's earliest victory in the first of many skirmishes with his studio over the handling of the film's release was to secure a prime date in the summer schedule of 1967. This achieved, he still felt that Warner Brothers would be inclined to put their promotional muscle behind the studio's own production *Camelot* and neglect *Bonnie and Clyde*. Partly for the publicity, partly to sound out unbiased opinion, and partly because he was persuaded against his better judgement, Beatty allowed the film to be made the opening night presentation at the 1967 Montreal Film Festival.

By chance, that August, Bosley Crowther of the *New York Times* was covering the event and saw the film. What the police perpetrated on the bullet-ridden corpses of Bonnie and Clyde was small beer compared to his review. He wrote, 'It is a cheap piece of baldfaced slapstick comedy that treats the hideous depredations of that sleazy, moronic pair as though they were as full of fun and frolic as the jazz-age cut-ups in *Thoroughly Modern Millie*. . . . This blending of farce with brutal killings is as pointless as it is lacking in taste, since it makes no valid commentary on the already travestied truth. And it leaves an astonished critic wondering just what purpose Mr Penn and Mr Beatty think they serve with this strangely antique, sentimental claptrap.'

Shortly after the Montreal Festival, *Bonnie and Clyde* went on release in America. The initial critical reaction was mixed, with many of Crowther's distinguished colleagues echoing the substance, if not the vitriol, of his comments. In *Newsweek*, Joseph Morgenstern crushingly described the film as 'a squalid shoot-'em-up for the moron trade.' However, no one can ever second-guess the public. They liked the film and weren't too partial to being called morons. Soon, debate over the film's merits raged in the letters pages of the most noted journals in the land.

In Britain, the film was scheduled to open during the first week in September. Box-office receipts were expected to be low and the mood of those entrusted with launching the film was not buoyant; Warner Brothers had allocated a promotional budget of less than a third of the sum they intended to spend on *Camelot*. One executive felt that the names Bonnie and Clyde would lack significance for British audiences and complained that the title 'sounds like two Scottish football teams'. Apparently, concern over the film being misconstrued as some panegyric to the river Clyde in Scotland was genuine. With that in mind, the nervous London distributors suggested a title change to *Bonnie and Clyde Were Killers*. Via a telegram, Beatty responded with his own alternative: *Bonnie and Clyde Aren't Rivers*.

Pre-release jitters were speedily dispelled when the film opened at the Warner Theatre on September 7th; over four hundred eager customers were waiting in line outside and the establishment enjoyed the best first-day takings in its thirty-three year history. *Bonnie and Clyde* was a European hit.

Armed with sheaves of laudatory reviews and vindicated by the escalating box-office figures in New York, Beatty and the public begged the home critics to re-examine the film and cajoled Warner Brothers into a re-launch. Bosley Crowther remained adamant that the film was a cruel distortion and a burlesque of the truth. In response, Penelope Gilliatt wrote in the *New Yorker* that '*Bonnie and Clyde* could look like a celebration of gangster glamour only to a man with a head full of wood shavings.' Joseph Morgenstern won respect for re-reviewing the film and retracting his earlier comments, now marvelling at 'scene after scene of dazzling artistry' and a film that 'knows perfectly well what to make of its violence'. *Time* magazine reversed its uncomplimentary remarks and devoted a six-page cover story to what their critic termed 'not only the sleeper of the decade but also, to a growing consensus of audiences and critics, the best movie of the year.'

Beatty's tireless efforts had ultimately been rewarded with all that he had really wanted – a fair hearing. Bonnie and Clyde was one of the most talked-about films of the year and now perfectly able to stand on its own, independent of its star's protection. He had enjoyed the exhilaration of being the underdog and valiantly scrapping for his space in the market place. In conversation with Sheila Graham he remarked, 'Bosley Crowther has been very helpful to us. His misguided moralizing about the film has made the other critics determined to be heard.'

The supposed 'moron trade' for *Bonnie and Clyde* would prove both bountiful and durable, with the film eventually providing a tenfold return on its initial investment. *Camelot*, in contrast, enjoyed one brief, shining moment of glory and then faded away.

Chapter Three

The worldwide impact of *Bonnie and Clyde* staggered even those who had been closest to its success. The characters, as portrayed in the film, were accepted and hailed around the globe as symbols of the age: Bonnie's beret became an indispensable fashion accessory; the 'Thirties look' was deemed the next major trend; Beatty and Dunaway, in gun-totin' pose, sold thousands of posters; and even Cartier's on New York's Fifth Avenue decorated a window display with fake bullets and the trademark beret.

Everyone connected with the triumph of *Bonnie and Clyde* benefited in some specific way. Beatty earned the respect for which he had been striving; Dunaway was flavour of the month and the world's most important new female star since Julie Andrews; and all the supporting players were elevated from relative obscurity to some measure of fame. Everybody was now a somebody who sported a recognition tag for their peers and the public marked 'Bonnie and Clyde'.

Hackman was unprepared for the way in which *Bonnie and Clyde* would change his career. His experience working on the film led him to formulate a more responsible attitude to screen acting and now, because he was a 'name' to the public, it was less likely that he could pocket the money and flee after any future assignment.

His higher public profile resulted in a deluge of offers, some flattering, others easily rejected. In the former category was a co-starring assignment with Burt Lancaster in a new John Frankenheimer production tentatively titled *The Fall Guys*. The length of time before that was scheduled to commence allowed him to slot in a couple of other films; after years of scraping around for a full schedule of work he wasn't about to remain idle unless forced to.

Thus, with one film, Hackman had become a sought-after

supporting actor with a healthy-looking future career. For someone whose last decade of existence had rested precariously on the uncertain prospect of the next small job, the security of full employment was an alien and unsettling mode of life. In a 1978 interview with *Films Illustrated*, he recalled, 'It was the first time in my career that I could see my life mapped out in front of me. I should have been delighted, but in fact I went through a very depressing period. I had subsisted on a day-to-day level for so long, quite liking the idea that I didn't know what I was going to do next. Suddenly I had a good salary, three firm jobs and a future – I found that surprisingly tough to adjust to.'

For someone who had endured years of rejection and often a part-time only livelihood from his chosen profession, a certain basic insecurity is never eradicated, regardless of the magnitude of later successes. Having at last attained a small niche within the film industry, Hackman found it hard to convince himself that he wasn't merely enjoying some transitory, short-lived peak that would soon dissolve into another round of unemployment.

'Film acting was still just a way to make some bread, but when *Bonnie and Clyde* opened it was an enormous hit. One day I was walking through Greenwich Village and a group of people started shouting across to me, calling me 'Buck', which was the name of the character I played. I can't tell you how startling that was to me. I had never realized the true power of motion pictures until that moment. But after *Bonnie and Clyde* burst, I grabbed everything that came along. I was terrified the bubble was going to burst and it was all going to end.'

As Hackman became more intensely involved in film work, he finally began to acknowledge the special skills that the medium required and actually enjoy the discipline and precision that it demanded of him. In *Film Comment*, he expounded on his responses to the film medium and made comparisons with the comedy work he had done on stage.

'I really didn't appreciate movies until I got into pictures myself,' he admitted. 'Until I really understood what it was to be a motion picture actor, and what it takes, and what nuances you can use, and about underplaying. I never really appreciated it until then. It was like comedy. I wasn't really aware until my last two years in New York, when I started doing a lot of comedy, how much more expertise and real judgement it takes to do real comedy, rather than drama. Because drama in many ways is arbitrary: you can choose not to cry in a scene where everyone else is crying, and that's a *choice*. And you can defend that choice to your death, saying that it's a character who is cut off, a character who is doing a whole different number. That's defendable. But in comedy, if the laugh doesn't come, there's no way you can defend that.'

Prior to the release of *Bonnie and Clyde*, Hackman had completed a smallish role in the plush soap-opera *Banning*. Set amidst the denizens of an exclusive Los Angeles golf club, the film starred Robert Wagner as a professional golfer trying to live down a shady past and fight off the advances of several of the female members of the club. Hackman contributed his tuppence worth as the immoral golf pro Tommy Del Gaddo.

In January of 1968 he began work on the first of his 'three firm jobs', *The Split*. Professionally engaged during nearly every waking hour, he worked on the one film whilst being fitted for the wardrobe on his next one, and still found time to do the rounds of press interviews and talk shows to continue the promotion and spin-off from *Bonnie and Clyde*. The principals involved in *Bonnie and Clyde* were now all considered newsworthy; Faye Dunaway made the covers of both *Newsweek* and *Life* magazines and the straight-talking Michael J. Pollard wondered aloud what the public would have made of the original script in which 'Bonnie was a nymphomaniac, Clyde was a homosexual transvestite and I was supposed to have been picked up to keep 'em both happy.' Hackman's concerns were less abstract and again reflected his discomfort at lacking the handsome good looks that, he felt, distinguished the true film stars. 'I worry about my double chin,' he told one interviewer. 'I know I'm not a leading man, but I still worry.'

The Academy Award nominations for the films released in 1967 were declared during the production of *The Split*. In the run-up to the announcement *Bonnie and Clyde* had been in contention with *In the Heat of the Night*, *The Graduate*, *Cool Hand Luke* and *Guess Who's Coming to Dinner?* for the major critical accolades of the year. Robert Benton and David

Newman were honoured by the New York Film Critics with the Best Screenplay Award. A similar citation was bestowed by the National Society of Film Critics, who also named Hackman as the year's Best Supporting Actor – his first award for film work.

Bonnie and Clyde was nominated for ten Academy Awards, a distinction shared with *Guess Who's Coming to Dinner?*. There were seven nominations for both *The Graduate* and *In the Heat of the Night*. Hackman received his first Academy nomination as Best Supporting Actor, an honour he shared with Michael J. Pollard. The other nominees were Warren Beatty, Faye Dunaway, Estelle Parsons, Arthur Penn, Robert Benton and David Newman, Burnett Guffey for his cinematography and Theadora Van Runkle for costume design. *Bonnie and Clyde* was also amongst the five films selected as the year's Best Pictures, the others being *The Graduate*, *Guess Who's Coming to Dinner?*, *In the Heat of the Night* and, incomprehensibly, *Doctor Dolittle*, which had benefitted from an expensive publicity campaign targeted specifically at Academy Award voters. *Banning* received a single nomination in the Best Song category for 'The Eyes of Love' with music by Quincy Jones and lyrics by Bob Russell.

The fortieth Academy Awards ceremony was scheduled to take place on 8 April 1968 at the Santa Monica Civic Auditorium. Anticipation within the industry was high, as there appeared to be few predictable winners and the spread of nominations ranged from stalwarts like Rod Steiger to sentimental favourites like the late Spencer Tracy and a slew of representatives from the new generation like Dustin Hoffman and Katharine Ross.

The speculation, rumours and gossip all paled into ghastly insignificance when Dr Martin Luther King Jnr was assassinated on April 4th. The funeral service was scheduled for April 9th and several of those involved with the Oscar claimed that they would not attend the ceremony if the Awards went ahead as scheduled. On the *Tonight* show Sammy Davis Jnr explained, 'I asked President [Gregory] Peck to postpone the Awards to show that someone cares. I certainly think any black man should not appear. I find it morally incongruous to sing 'Talk to the Animals' while the man who could make a better world for my children is lying in state.'

Gregory Peck assembled the Board of Governors and a decision was taken to postpone the ceremony until April 10th. The annual Governors' Ball was cancelled and what had been planned as a four-decade celebration of the Oscars became a sober and tense evening with the entertainment community at its most self-consciously dignified; master of ceremonies Bob Hope was warned not to overdo the light-hearted quips and gags.

There was still an excitement and feeling of anticipation about the Oscar evening for the stars of *Bonnie and Clyde*, many of whom had never been considered important enough to be invited before, never mind having a personal stake in the outcome. Warren Beatty escorted Julie Christie and Faye Dunaway arrived with Jerry Schatzberg. Gregory Peck had graciously agreed to appear at the Tony Awards in return for David Merrick allowing Estelle Parsons a night off from her Broadway play *The Seven Descents of Myrtle*. Hackman attended with his wife Faye and fellow nominee Michael J. Pollard.

Hackman's buddy Dustin Hoffman had been nominated as Best Actor for *The Graduate* and thus the two friends were able to make their Oscar debut together. Hoffman escorted Ellen McCarthy, the daughter of Senator Eugene McCarthy, and was to present the Best Cinematography Award with Katharine Ross.

Gregory Peck opened the proceedings and declared, 'Society has always been reflected in its art, and one measure of Dr King's influence on the society in which we live is that two of the five films nominated for the Best Picture of the Year deal with the subject of understanding between the races. It was his work and his dedication that brought the increasing awareness of all men that we must unite in compassion in order to survive. The lasting memorial that we of the motion picture community can build to Dr King is to continue making films which celebrate the dignity of man, whatever his race or colour or creed.' With Hollywood so sorely feeling its responsibility to underscore the mood of the country, there was little hope that *Bonnie and Clyde*, a zestful, blood-stained underdog, could occupy the winner's enclosure.

Peck then handed over to 'a man who pricks the balloons of pomposity' – Bob Hope. Hope joked about Lyndon

[37]

Johnson, Edith Evans's mini-skirt, the youthfulness of Dustin Hoffman ('he made a picture he can't get in to see') and *Bonnie and Clyde* ('Warren Beatty arrived in a truck with Faye Dunaway behind in a getaway car'). Then, the serious business of revealing the winners commenced.

After Carol Channing had presented the Best Sound award to *In the Heat of the Night*, Patty Duke stepped forward to present the first acting award of the evening: Best Supporting Actor. Hackman and Pollard had been nominated alongside John Cassavetes for *The Dirty Dozen*, Cecil Kellaway for *Guess Who's Coming to Dinner?* and George Kennedy for *Cool Hand Luke*. There has been a tendency throughout the Academy's history for two actors nominated from the same production to split the vote for that particular film and this will have contributed to the outcome in this case. When Duke opened the envelope, George Kennedy was the winner. Hackman's disappointment can only have been mild; to have won this early in his career would have been even more unnerving than the thought of secure employment, and besides, he probably genuinely did not regard his performance as worthy of the award.

As the evening progressed, Katharine Hepburn, Olivia De Havilland, Grace Kelly and Anne Bancroft presented a potted history of the four decades of the awards. It was not to be a historic evening for the *Bonnie and Clyde* party; Beatty lost to Rod Steiger, Dunaway to Katharine Hepburn, Arthur Penn to Mike Nichols and *In the Heat of the Night* was named Best Picture. From the ten nominations Bonnie and Clyde was successful in only two categories, Burnett Guffey's cinematography and Best Supporting Actress. Receiving her award from Walter Matthau, Estelle Parsons commented, 'Boy, it's heavy. I have to thank David Merrick, who let me out of my Broadway play so I could be here this evening. Little did he know what he would mean to me, really. Thank you, it's really a great moment.' Asked by reporters if she had felt disappointment for her colleagues, Parsons responded, 'I felt sure that we'd get Best Picture but then nobody likes Warren Beatty. I like Warren very much, but he is not the kind of guy people say, "Gee, he's a great guy".' According to *Newsweek*, Beatty's reaction to the evening was a muttered, 'We wuz robbed.' The most level-headed and dismissive response came from Faye Dunaway,

[38]

who stated, 'Martin Luther King had just been assassinated, it was no time to worry about a piece of gold statuary.'

Unperturbed by any of the Oscar hoopla, Hackman returned to work on *The Split*, a fashionably brutal heist thriller slickly directed and peppered with thoroughly amoral characters played by an auspicious cast of solid actors and future stars. Among the luminaries were Donald Sutherland, Warren Oates, Jack Klugman, Diahann Carroll, Ernest Borgnine, Julie Harris and James Whitmore. Jim Brown starred as the criminal mastermind who assembles a gang to rob the Los Angeles Coliseum during a football match. The robbery goes like clockwork, but his ingenious scheme has included no provision for a psychotic killer and the interest of a crooked detective, Lieutenant Walter Brill (Hackman), who had decided to muscle in on the proceedings.

In truth, *The Split* is not a very good film. Producers Irwin Winkler and Robert Chartoff had enjoyed a tremendous success with the film *Point Blank* and decided to film another novel by the same author, Richard Stark. Alas, *The Split* is no *Point Blank* and director Gordon Flemyng is no John Boorman. Whilst *Point Blank* is a taut, dazzling revenge story, *The Split* is an altogether more familiar one of a falling-out amongst thieves, violent and nasty although distinguished by the calibre of the cast and the splendid colour camera-work of Burnett Guffey. *Esquire* magazine gave the film a reasonably sympathetic ride, nonchalantly remarking, 'The Split is a breakthrough, with a Negro hero (Jim Brown) and a black heroine (Diahann Carroll) who gets killed by a white sex nut, and that's all you can reasonably ask for. You can't expect a breakthrough and a great movie too.' *Variety*, however, was more specific in its criticisms, bluntly stating, 'Hackman lacks authority in a poorly developed role.'

Continuing his movie marathon, Hackman reported for work on *Riot*, a bloody melodrama in the tradition of *Riot in Cell Block Eleven* with a few points of interest to its credit.

The Riot, a first novel by Frank Elli, was published in 1966, selling more than a quarter of a million hardback copies before its first paperback printing in January of 1968. Elli could genuinely claim to have undertaken exhaustive research into prison life, as he had been an inmate of various penal establishments over a period of two decades. Whilst serving a long sentence in Stillwater Prison, Minnesota, he took a correspondence course in writing. His professor, Harold J. Alford of the University of Minnesota, was taken by a particular composition of Elli's in which he described a prison riot. Alford urged him to expand the material into a novel and helped him to find a literary agent on his parole in 1965.

The manuscript of *The Riot* was sold for the tidy sum of thirteen thousand dollars, became a Literary Guild selection and won Elli the Thomas R. Coward Memorial Award for Fiction. Popular acclaim, judged by the book's position in the best-seller charts, was matched by critical enthusiasm and the *Los Angeles Times* noted, 'Elli recreates the violence and excitement that only a witness could record. . . . In this remarkable first novel the author, for twenty years an inmate of prisons from Stillwater to San Quentin, has written simply the best book available about American prison life.'

Interest in the film rights to *The Riot* developed swiftly and Paramount was the eventual purchaser. Veteran producer-director William Castle, then filming *Rosemary's Baby*, was placed in charge of the screen version and James Poe was hired to write the screenplay. Buzz Kulik was selected as the director and set about adding a sense of immediacy and individuality to a project heavily burdened with stereotypes witnessed a thousand times during the era of screen gangsters in the 1930s. His most influential decision was to make the film entirely within the walls of an active prison and to cast real convicts in all but a handful of the roles.

The institution chosen for the venture was the Arizona State Penitentiary, presided over by Warden Frank Eyman, one of America's top penologists for over four decades, who had gained renown by clapping the handcuffs on John Dillinger in 1934. Eyman was a key figure in smoothing the way for the filmmakers' activities and was recompensed with the warden's role in the film.

Before the start of production, Castle and Kulik visited the prison to reconnoitre their main location and begin the casting process. Kulik stressed that authenticity was to be the keynote and noted, 'Seeing those prisoners you realize that they represent a cross-section of society – Hollywood has created and perpetuated the myth that most convicts resemble Bogart or Cagney. There is no "convict" type;

[40]

switch most of these men from prison denims to civilian clothes and outside they pass for doctors, merchants, bankers, labourers – which many were before they came here.'

On a subsequent visit to the penitentiary, Kulik was accompanied by Hoyt Bowers, Paramount's casting director. Four hundred convicts were interviewed and eighty of those were selected to read for various roles. The troupe of eighty underwent a five-week course in acting under Paramount's drama coach Bob McAndrews. William Castle sent two hundred copies of the novel to be circulated throughout the prison to let the inmates know the intentions of the filmmaking unit that was about to descend upon them. Kulik then returned to announce his final choices for the speaking and featured roles.

McAndrews was proud of the progress of his unique drama class and revealed, 'They worked like beavers. They did improvisations and rehearsed one another; some of them really caught the acting bug – wanted to know who'd be a good agent to look up when they got out.' The convict actors were to be paid Actors' Guild salaries. Some of the money would go towards the financing of a regular theatre group within the prison.

Riot would employ eight professional actors, the most prominent of whom would be Jim Brown and Hackman. The difficulties of filming within a community of seventeen hundred criminals and staff posed unique problems for the actors and crew as well as necessitating an extremely cautious security policy. Every outside worker was required to carry an ID card at all times and nobody could leave the prescribed filming area without a security guard as escort. No one was permitted to give or accept gifts or mementoes of any kind from the inmates. A long list of restrictions was rigidly enforced and Dona Holloway, one of William Castle's closest associates, wasn't allowed on the set of his production because of the rule prohibiting female visitors within the prison.

Thanks to the unprecedented regard for security, filming passed without incident and the company received a generous degree of cooperation from both the inmates and the guards. One convict, serving a sentence for burglary, was dismayed to learn that his parole hearing would inter-

[41]

fere with his participation in the film and asked his lawyer that it be postponed.

The filmmakers responded to such unsolicited self-sacrifice by staging *Riot*'s world premiere in the recreation hall of the Arizona State Penitentiary in December of 1968. Jim Brown, several Paramount executives, newspaper reporters and some two hundred and fifty convicts sat down for the film's maiden screening with the approval of Warden Eyman. 'I know the movie depicts a mass escape attempt,' he conceded, 'but it shows nothing new, nothing that hasn't been used before. In fact as so many of them get killed in the process I think it will do them good to see it. It may help get some of that nonsense out of their heads.' A print of the film remained at the prison and was screened over five consecutive nights to allow all the inmates a chance to view the fruits of their labours.

Unfortunately, Eyman proved a fair critic of *Riot*'s failings. It does offer nothing new, and the combination of pace, violence and an authentic setting can do little to erase images of *Brute Force*, *Each Dawn I Die* and similar examples of the genre. In the film, thirty-five of the toughest cons choose the warden's absence to stage a break-out in a maximum security penitentiary. Their leader and spokesman is Red Fletcher (Hackman). Cully Briston (Jim Brown), who is serving a five year sentence, does not want to become involved in the actions of his compatriots but is inadvertently drawn into the events.

The cons seize eight hostages, including the deputy warden, and what began as a sudden expression of their frustration soon escalates into a potentially more dangerous situation. Red informs the media that the hostages will remain unharmed only if the prison authorities are willing to negotiate over their grievances. However, Red's ability to control the impulses of his fellow inmates weakens when a batch of moonshine is brewed and the drunken convicts want to exact revenge on their hostages. Looking out for their own best interests, Red and Cully decide that Red should stall for time in the negotiations whilst Cully and a group of the cons dig an escape tunnel.

The warden returns and immediately sets about restoring his authority. In the ensuing mayhem, Red, Cully and ten others attempt their breakout. Only three members of the group manage to reach the final tower wall that separates them from the possibility of freedom – Red, Cully and Joe Surefoot, a psychopathic killer. As Cully leads the way over the wall Joe attempts to knife him in the back, but is stopped by Red. Cully drops down to the outside world but when Red follows him the dying Joe slices his fingers and the escape rope and he plunges to his death. Cully is the only one to escape and there is speculation that his freedom will be short-lived.

Although quite tense and arresting, *Riot* is still entangled in the clichés of its particular genre, with Hackman and Jim Brown left to ring the changes on the type of partnership portrayed by the likes of George Raft and James Cagney thirty years earlier. The violent content of the film may seem unremarkable to contemporary audiences, but the nastiness of it caused a stir in 1968, with *Time* magazine noting, 'Even in these bloody times, the violence in *Riot* is rather extravagant: when cons are shot in the chest, gore gushes from their mouths, and throats are slit with slashing abandon. Director Buzz Kulik shot the film entirely in the Arizona State Prison, more for the sake of novelty than authenticity. He never once manages to capture the claustrophobic frustration of prison life. Although *Riot* aspires to be reformist social criticism, it is about as effective – and moving – as a convict chorus of "Don't Fence Me In".' Across the Atlantic the British *Monthly Film Bulletin* was more impressed, hailing *Riot* as 'one of the most striking prison dramas since *Riot in Cell Block Eleven*'.

Hackman's personal notices for *The Split, Riot* and other work around this period began to set a pattern for how he would come to be regarded during his years as a supporting and character actor. Generally his work was liked, regardless of the viewer's opinion on the merits of the film in which he was appearing. The more people saw of him, the more they realized that he could be relied upon to give a performance at least equal to, if not superior to, his material. Gradually, he was gaining a reputation as an always dependable actor whom it was a pleasure to encounter. *Time*, however, in reviewing *Riot*, sounded a note of warning: 'Gene Hackman, a fine character actor, deserves better parts than the one he is given here, and audiences deserve better than the careless ease he brings to it.'

By July of 1968 filming was ready to commence on the John Frankenheimer project that had now been retitled *The Gypsy Moths*. As well as offering an opportunity to work with one of the most accomplished American directors of the Sixties, the film was also something of an acting class, affording firsthand observation of two veteran film actors, Burt Lancaster and Deborah Kerr, at work together for the first time since *From Here to Eternity* (1953). Several years later Hackman talked to *Film Comment* about the abiding impressions made on him by his first encounters with a major and powerful Hollywood star like Lancaster and the lessons he had learned.

'I found a lot of people would defer to him in ways that – I was from the theatre, you know – that I'd wonder, "Why don't they argue with him a little bit? What, is he gonna punch them out or something?" No, not necessarily, because he's a bright guy. But it's just that you reach a certain level and people get frightened of your money or your power, or both, you know. And when I found *myself* doing that, when I found myself getting my way without somebody really pushing against me, I really started getting worried. Because I think that's one of the really dangerous things, when you get in a certain position of being able to say just anything, and people say: "Yeah, right, bring it in." That's bad.'

Lancaster and Frankenheimer had enjoyed a fruitful partnership throughout the Sixties that had resulted in films like *Birdman of Alcatraz* (1962), *The Train* (1963) and *Seven Days in May* (1964). *The Gypsy Moths* was to be their last film together and proved an uncharacteristically tender and probing drama of life in small-town America.

The Gypsy Moths of the title are a trio of skydivers who tour the small towns of the American mid-West with a show of death-defying stunts. Rettig (Lancaster), Browdy (Hackman) and Webson (Scott Wilson) arrive in Bridgeville, Kansas early one July in preparation for their performance. It is typical of the places they visit, containing 'a college and missile base', but holds a special significance for Webson as it is the town where he was born and raised by his aunt Elizabeth (Kerr) and her husband V. John Brandon (William Windom). The men visit Webson's relatives and are invited to stay.

*

[44]

During their stay each man becomes romantically involved: Webson with college girl Annie (Bonnie Bedelia), the ebullient Browdy with a topless waitress and the dour, world-weary Rettig with Elizabeth, who responds to his physical charms but is unwilling to forsake her arid-seeming marriage when he asks her to leave with him.

Rettig's philosophy has always been, 'To face death is hard, but to face life is harder'. At the climax of the following day's airshow, he performs the dangerous 'cape stunt' and chooses not to open his parachute; instead he plummets to his death. Browdy and Webson stage a memorial show to pay for the funeral at which Webson's nerve is tested as he attempts the 'cape stunt'. The jump is a success but Webson claims it will be the last. Browdy seems equally relieved that their skydiving days are over and suggests that he will try his luck in Hollywood as a stunt man. The Brandons resume their cosy lifestyle, with Elizabeth confessing to her husband that the prospect of jeopardizing their careful routine had terrified her.

John Frankenheimer described *The Gypsy Moths* as a film about 'choice and self-destruction'. Filming in Wichita, Kansas during the summer of 1968 can only have evoked Hackman's memories of his own early background as the film attempted to capture the small-town rhythms of stale but secure marriages, colourful interludes with exotic strangers, ladies' social clubs and cheap bars as the backdrop to Frankenheimer's larger preoccupations. Of the three main male characters, Scott Wilson's Webson is the most conventional – a young man still enamoured of Rettig's charisma and still to develop his individuality as an adult. Lancaster's interpretation of the enigmatic Rettig is a deliberately muted and disturbing one as he paints a man who seems to have run out of reasons for living. His death robs the film of its watchability, yet his characterization is so low-key that it fails to elicit our sympathy. Hackman is quietly left to walk away with the acting honours. His Browdy appears the most 'regular' of the trio, a grinning, brawling hustler intent on good times with booze, broads and boodles of money. However, the screenplay allows Hackman to flesh out what could have been a stereotype, as Browdy is also a man who attends church every Sunday, enjoying the pleasures of the flesh during the week and repenting at the weekend. He is

[45]

a man who has learnt his limitations, performing the 'cape stunt' once to prove he can do it but careful not to repeat the act for the good of his health. He is also a man with dreams for the future. 'I'm not going to be doing this forever, I have plans,' he boasts to Sheree North's admiring waitress.

Hackman captures the dual nature of Browdy by playing up his back-slapping, life-of-the-party image yet undercutting it with numerous quick gestures of impatience and concern to show the tension underlying his bonhomie and the nervous edge to his life. It is a neat and thoughtful piece of characterization.

The Gypsy Moths was not a commercial success on its release in 1969, and Lancaster later admitted that it might have appeared pretentious. Almost twenty years later it stands as a refreshing and sensitively-acted portrait of emotional turmoil as the unusual and the conventional interact. As befitted his growing reputation for dependability, Hackman was singled out in some quarters for specific praise. *Time* magazine said, 'The interrelationships of the characters make sense but have little emotional resonance, a handicap that only Gene Hackman manages to surmount. His brassy characterization of a free-living skydiver adds a poignant dimension of reality to a film that, like skydiving itself, is an exciting but slightly dubious exercise.'

As the demand for his services grew, Hackman phased out his work for stage and television. In 1968 he appeared in a *CBS Playhouse* special 'My Father, My Mother' and was the guest star in an episode of the popular *I Spy* series with Bill Cosby and Robert Culp. His last dramatic appearance on television came in the film *Shadow on the Land* which was transmitted on 4 December 1968. In the film, America is in the grip of a totalitarian government and two men lead a secret underground force fighting for the restoration of democracy. A promising idea and an interesting cast (John Forsythe, Carol Lynley, Jackie Cooper) were wasted on an underdeveloped script, although playing the Reverend Thomas Davis gave Hackman a change of pace after two years as gangster, brutal jailbird or crooked cop. His own political stance could be described as liberal, and he has been a caring and concerned member of the wider community, but he has never aligned himself with a

[46]

particular candidate or a specific issue in the manner of many of his showbusiness contemporaries. He once explained, 'I loved the Kennedy idea and I really don't know why. I just like the idea that there was a young man who seemed to care about us. Then I met Bobby Kennedy a couple of months before he was killed and I was so impressed. After he was killed I felt I didn't want to get involved politically any more.'

For the cinema Hackman moved on to *Marooned*, a timely but sluggish space melodrama directed by John Sturges. The star was Gregory Peck, although Hackman's contact with him would be minimal. Hackman plays one of three astronauts who have been in orbit for five months of a planned seven-month mission aboard a space laboratory. Displaying symptoms of severe fatigue, the trio are ordered to cut short their mission and return to earth. However, the retro rockets of their craft fail to ignite and the men are marooned in space with only forty-eight hours of oxygen. Back on the ground, controller Charles Keith (Peck) anxiously monitors the men's fate as a rescue mission races to their aid.

Of the three astronauts in the film, Hackman's smallish role as Buzz Lloyd marked him out as of lesser importance than colleagues James Franciscus and Richard Crenna. The film's greatest asset was the realistic-seeming special effects, which received an Oscar. The film itself was unable to compete with the real-life Apollo moon landings and its excessive length of 2¼ hours undermined the innate urgency of the fictional drama. *Time* gave the film scant consideration, stating that '*Marooned* rates about one-half out of a possible 2001.' Peck didn't rate the film too highly either, feeling constrained by his deskbound character. He told his biographer Michael Freedland, 'I've found that technical types, engineers and people who have to have total control don't make interesting parts. You can't show the inner emotion that the man feels because he has to be supremely efficient.'

It was while Hackman was filming *Marooned* that he was approached by novice director Michael Ritchie and offered a more interesting supporting role in a further film, *Downhill Racer*. The film was a particularly personal project of its star Robert Redford, as he explained in David Downing's biography:

'It wasn't supposed to be a picture about skiing, although the studio never got that through their heads. . . . I wanted this movie to be the portrait of an athlete, of a certain kind of person in American society. It annoyed me the way athletes were portrayed in films. They were always clean-cut, middle-American types who came off the farms and had great wives behind them and great moms and dads. It was a Norman Rockwell depiction of America and that's not the way I saw it. I said, "What about the athlete who's a creep?" We do tend to tolerate creeps who win. Who remembers who came in second? I wanted to see that in a film and it only happened to be skiing because I was into it at that time and thought it was something very beautiful and visual that hadn't been dealt with in film before.'

Redford's interest in the self-destructive pursuit of success as an end in itself has been a theme that he has returned to at frequent intervals throughout his career. *Downhill Racer* was his first self-controlled exploration of the topic and was first mooted as a project for Paramount Pictures over the winter of 1966–1967, with Roman Polanski mentioned as the likely director. At the time Redford had a contract to appear in a Paramount western entitled *Blue*. One week before shooting was scheduled to begin he changed his mind and was replaced by Terence Stamp. Paramount sued him, he countersued and the studio's enthusiasm for his skiing project evaporated. Some time passed before matters were amicably resolved and *Downhill Racer* became a joint effort, for Paramount release, between Redford's Wildwood and his agent Richard Gregson, who was then married to Natalie Wood.

When *Downhill Racer* was finally given the go-ahead, Redford cast about for a suitable director and chose the thirty-year-old Michael Ritchie, whose television work had impressed him. Working in unison, the two men decided on a very definite approach to the film that would be based on naturalism and realism. In *Action*, Ritchie explained that he had 'wanted the picture to look accidental' and stated, 'I did not want the audience to feel that a director was "designing" what they were seeing. We were aiming for a documentary feeling, as though cameras happened to be around while something real was happening.'

Ritchie would use many basic techniques to achieve his *cinema-verité* ambience, including overlapping dialogue, entirely location filming and an insistence on controlled, low-key performances. The casting of the film would reflect this decision too, utilizing largely unknown or non-professional actors. The one exception was the actor required to play the ski-team coach, a part Ritchie felt was only 'half formed' in the script. 'It needed an extraordinary actor to bring it to life,' Ritchie said.

During discussions over who might be suitable, Ritchie and Redford kept arriving at the conclusion that what was needed was someone like Gene Hackman. Ritchie eventually decided, why have someone *like* Gene Hackman when you can hire the genuine article? Therefore, he met with Hackman on the *Marooned* set, and they discussed their knowledge of skiing, which was virtually non-existent, and some of the planned script rewrites. Hackman accepted the role.

The film would be made on location in Colorado and throughout the Swiss, Austrian and French Alps with a British technical crew who offered the best value for money. An inflexible starting date was announced to coincide with the start of the European ski-race season. Then, and only then, Paramount chose to cancel the picture, claiming that an estimated production budget of three million dollars was too costly a risk for a film with dubious commercial appeal. Ritchie and company argued their case with the Paramount accountants and won the day at a revised figure of one million eight hundred thousand dollars.

Downhill Racer was scheduled for seventy days of principal photography, with a further twenty-five days of second-unit work to capture the authentic world of the ski championship. Ritchie ruefully reflected that his longest previous schedule had amounted to twenty-three days on a television show and that he had never employed more than eighty extras in a single day. *Downhill Racer* would use up to 750 per day, of whom the bulk spoke no English. For a novice to the cinema, *Downhill Racer* was a baptism by fire.

Filming on a modest budget in Europe entailed numerous logistical problems: the exposed film was being processed in London and therefore no one knew if their work would be technically acceptable, an early spring thaw necessitated a seven day working week lest all the snow disappear, and cameramen had to deal with the technical difficulties of filming ski scenes. Joe Jay Jalbert was trained to ski whilst holding a camera and helped surmount the problem of acquiring genuinely exhilarating unfaked ski footage. As Ritchie remarked, 'We were not after pretty pictures, but rather to get the hard, gutsy type of footage that emphasizes the dangers of speed.'

Redford had been so closely involved with the development of his character that his only need for direction came on questions of emphasis and shading. Hackman was exactly the conscientious, ever-ready professional that Ritchie had expected. The director has written, 'Whether on a ski slope or in a hotel lobby, Gene quickly breathed life into his character. He brought such strength and authority to the part that the only problems we had were over those scenes where Redford was supposed to leave Hackman bewildered and plowed under.'

In subsequent recollections, Hackman chose to concentrate on the financial aspects of the film: 'I remember we were shooting *Racer* in Switzerland on a tiny budget, and alongside was the costly Bond film *On Her Majesty's Secret Service*. We used to see crates of champagne hauled up the mountain. Still, in the end we did well out of the opposition. It was a mild winter, and the Bond lot had flown in fake snow. As soon as they left, we moved in and used their spare "snow".'

The deliberately casual, throwaway style of *Downhill Racer* irritated some viewers and critics, but the film is a vividly-etched portrait of someone obsessed with the attainment of success. David Chappellet (Redford) is a tough, undisciplined skier from Colorado who earns a place on the American ski team after another member withdraws through injury. He has the talent, but perhaps lacks the temperament to prosper, and although marked out as a future star he is soon at loggerheads with the team coach, the gruff, no-nonsense Eugene Claire (Hackman). Through seasons of training and competitions Chappellet's renown grows to rival that of his teammate Johnny Creech (Jim McMullan), a less hot-headed and more experienced skier.

Ruthlessly single-minded in his pursuit of the Olympic challenge, Chappellet exploits and disregards anyone he encounters, unwilling to cooperate in the team spirit and intent only on being champion and finding fame. When he risks Creech's life in a dangerous mountain race he is reprimanded by Claire who tells him, 'You never had any education, did you? All you ever had were your skis – and that's not enough.'

In the final pre-Olympic race Creech breaks a leg and is denied his shot at glory. Chappellet wins the Downhill event and should be savouring the high point of his life, but his victory has been close-run and as the hollowness of it strikes home he is left to ponder how fleeting his moment will be.

Cast against type, Redford's blonde, all-American persona adds an edge to his dissection of an all-American heel. Hackman as the coach restates the quality evident in *The Gypsy Moths* of presenting a character who operates on more than one level. In this instance Hackman's skiing coach is a man whose love of his profession makes him resent Chappellet's cavalier disregard for sporting ethics, yet he must still support and share the glory of a winner regardless of personal distaste.

Ritchie felt that this mixture of attraction and repellence provided Hackman with one of his best moments: 'At the end of the picture, Redford has seemingly won the big ski event and Gene tries to take the credit. But as news of another possible winner drifts through the crowd, Gene slowly, unconsciously moves away from his "student". Then the challenger falls, and like a victory machine unplugged and then replugged, Gene is again slapping Redford on the back, shouting, "I knew we could do it." This kind of ambiguity and even outright duplicity is seldom found in parts for "leading men". After all, how could such double-dealers deserve the girl? But it is very human, and it's at the core of Gene Hackman's greatest performances.'

Downhill Racer had been a film that Redford wanted to see made because the subject matter was something he felt deserved wider exposure. However, given a choice between the Redford of Butch Cassidy or the Redford of *Downhill Racer*, audiences expressed their preference via the box-office. Redford personally was unperturbed by their choice, philosophically observing, 'It took two years of my life, but

[51]

it wasn't very successful commercially. Really, the films I've wanted to make and have really been behind haven't made much money. That's the way it is. But you end up with the satisfaction of doing something on film that you have a kind of passion for.'

Chapter Four

In a perceptive essay for Danny Peary's book *Close-Ups*, Michael Ritchie suggested that the key to understanding Hackman's career is his frustration about never 'getting the girl'. In Ritchie's *Downhill Racer* he had frequently felt like a 'high-priced extra' and even the most challenging of supporting roles still hadn't stretched his talents to the full. Now that he was committed to a full-time cinema career it was only logical that he should crave the 'star' roles, not just for the sake of his ego but because they offered the most scope for a full and detailed exploration of an individual character.

Hackman's frustration at not being able to advance beyond the ranks of the reliable character men was grounded in a realistic assessment of his own romantic appeal. By his reckoning, which concurred with the general consensus, male stars needed charisma, good looks and a romantic aura that would never leave in doubt their right to 'get the girl'. Hackman knew that he had the acting ability to meet the challenges of large, demanding roles, yet these roles were the exclusive province of the stars and when he looked in the mirror he still saw an 'old potato face' that could provide no adequate latter-day substitute for the Errol Flynn-inspired fantasies of his youth.

The question of age was also a contributory factor to his impatience. His 40th birthday was now just around the corner – on 30 January 1970 – and time was surely running out if he were to make the promotion from supporting character actor to star character actor. A glance at the established box-office attractions of that period would reveal the allure of Steve McQueen (40), Clint Eastwood (40) and Dustin Hoffman (33). Elliott Gould, at 32, was the newcomer to the ranks and the likes of McQueen and Paul Newman had consolidated their star status some time ago. In Hackman's case time was not on his side. Neither, it transpired, were the studio executives. He had enjoyed the experience of working with John Frankenheimer on *The Gypsy Moths* and the director was keen for him to play the lead in his latest project, *I Walk the Line*, a rural drama in which a sheriff ruins his public and private life by falling in love with a moonshiner's daughter. Columbia Pictures are alleged to have overruled Frankenheimer's selection and insisted upon the more conventional choice of Gregory Peck.

A chance for Hackman to display more of his emotional range came when he was cast in the film version of Robert Anderson's *I Never Sang for My Father*. Ironically, the film was more akin to the work one would have expected to see Hackman perform on stage than to his recent brusque and bruising film characters.

Like *Bonnie and Clyde*, *I Never Sang for My Father* had endured a long and torturous passage from the page to the screen. Director Gilbert Cates outlined the slow progression in an article for *Action* in 1970. He recalled that the project had begun in 1962 when Robert Anderson wrote an original screenplay about the relationship between an elderly man and his grown son. It was entitled *The Tiger* and Anderson's friend, director Fred Zinnemann, was keen to film the work if Spencer Tracy could be persuaded to play the old man. Tracy's failing health restricted his film activity during the last years of his life and the part was deemed too demanding for him.

Elia Kazan, another of Anderson's friends, was then in the process of establishing a theatrical repertory company at the Lincoln Center. Kazan liked *The Tiger* and asked Anderson to turn it into a play for his new company. Ultimately, however, the company failed to include anyone with the maturity or stature to tackle the role of the old man. Meanwhile, John Frankenheimer had read the script. He was then filming *Seven Days in May* and enjoying one of the best director-actor relationships of his career with Fredric March. Frankenheimer passed on the script of *The Tiger* to the actor and a tentative agreement was reached whereby Frankenheimer would direct the film co-starring March and his wife Florence Eldridge. The prolific Frankenheimer was then called to the rescue of the Burt Lancaster film *The Train*, assuming the director's chair after the dismissal of Arthur Penn. Heavily involved with this and other projects, he suggested that Anderson look elsewhere.

Anderson decided to follow Kazan's advice and *The Tiger* became a play called *I Never Sang for My Father*.* Gilbert Cates had been the Broadway co-producer of Anderson's *You Know I Can't Hear You When the Water's Running*. He had read *Father* at the same time and went on to produce the Broadway version. Directed by Alan Schneider, *I Never Sang for My Father* opened at the Longacre Theatre on 25 January 1968 and ran for 124 performances. The British actor Alan Webb played the old man, Lillian Gish his wife, and their children were portrayed by Hal Holbrook and Teresa Wright (Anderson's real-life wife).

Cates was immediately struck by the cinematic potential of what he saw on stage and became the guiding influence behind a film version, securing the permission of those concerned to undertake the dual functions of producer and director. As the play's stage producer Cates had been closely involved with the problems of casting the old man. Among the many to decline the role were Edward G. Robinson, Fredric March, Ralph Richardson, Melvyn Douglas and Alfred Lunt. Much as Cates admired Alan Webb's stage performance, he wanted an American actor for his film and thus the problems of suitability and availability arose once more. Cates decided to try and win over Melvyn Douglas, whose prime reason for rejecting the stage version had been his lack of enthusiasm for playing the character night after night. The film-making process could eliminate that obstacle. Douglas responded to Cates's simple logic and accepted the role of the cantankerous Tom Garrison.

Other elements of the cast now fell into place for a film project that was briefly known as *Strangers* before reverting to its original title. None of the four stage performers would survive the transition to the screen; Dorothy Strickney played Margaret Garrison, replacing an otherwise gainfully employed Lillian Gish, whilst Hackman and his friend and *Bonnie and Clyde* co-star Estelle Parsons were cast as the brother and sister.

---

* Murray Schisgal had written a one-act, two-character play entitled *The Tiger*, hence the title change for Anderson's play.

I Never Sang for my Father was allowed the comparative luxury, for a film, of a rehearsal period of one week, a valuable time for director and actors to adjust to each others' rhythms and resolve potential problems that can hold up the very expensive process of actual filming. Production began with a few days on location at Kennedy Airport and then proceeded at the Biograph Studio in the Bronx and a specially-selected house owned by the Mayor of White Plains in New York. As a director with little experience of the film medium, Cates was somewhat in awe of Melvyn Douglas, whose screen work stretched back over four decades. Cates admitted, 'Part of me was always prepared for the day Melvyn might say, "That's not the way Lubitsch would do it." It never happened. Not because he didn't have cause, but because Melvyn Douglas only draws from the past, he does not live it.'

The filming was an exhaustive and fulfilling process for everyone concerned, but not a particularly happy one. *I Never Sang for My Father* deals with a serious emotional divide within a family and offers little by way of light relief. Hackman has said, 'Making the film wasn't gratifying; the script was tight and the material was depressing. It only worked because of what people brought to it.'

In the film, Hackman plays Gene Garrison, a kindly young widower who enjoys an uneasy relationship with his irascible old father Tom, an egotistical, domineering patriarch. Whilst his parents have been on holiday in Florida, Gene has visited California and fallen in love with Peggy Thayer (Elizabeth Hubbard), a divorcee with children. He now faces the dilemma of whether to marry and move west or stay east near his parents. It is a problem he feels unable to discuss with his parents, particularly his father, who seems to demand much of him yet bestow very little in return.

The matter is complicated when his mother Margaret (Dorothy Strickney) suffers a heart attack and dies. Gene feels his responsibility to his father more acutely than ever, yet resents the old man's selfish reaction to his mother's demise.

Gene's sister Alice (Estelle Parsons) arrives from Chicago to attend the funeral service and to discuss their father's future. Alice has been banished from the family home since she married a Jew. Time and distance have not diminished the hurtfulness of Tom's actions, and therefore she is detached and unsentimental about Gene's problem, advising him to marry Peggy and move to California. However, he retains a lingering hope that some understanding might still be reached with his father.

At a subsequent meeting with his son, Gene's father pours scorn on his children's concern about his future, rejecting out of hand their suggestions of a nursing home or a full-time housekeeper. Alice tries to convince Gene that his father will never change his arrogant, petty-minded attitudes but Gene is unable to accept that there can be no emotional bond between a father and son.

Peggy arrives from California for a convention and is taken to meet Tom. She is charmed by his gentlemanly display of old-world manners and courtesy. However, when Gene invites him to move in with them he reverts to type, rudely refusing. Hurt by yet another rejection of his love, Gene finally accepts the unbreachable gulf that exists between them and decides to marry Peggy and move to California.

An admittedly depressing excursion into the terrain of Eugene O'Neill, *I Never Sang for My Father* is an arresting and moving cinema piece largely due to the superlative performances of those involved. Melvyn Douglas is uncompromising in his portrayal of the vain, bullying family dictator, and the film reveals the gentle vulnerability of Hackman's playing for really the first time. The emotional complexity of his character is well handled, capturing the torment, frustration and self-inflicted guilt of a normal, caring child whose attempts at conciliation and understanding are thwarted by the self-absorption of a father who cares for no-one but himself. Gene is caught in a web of filial loyalty and anguished incomprehension, and it is with relief rather than exultation that one witnesses his eventual release.

Critics who had generally been supportive of Hackman, berating the kind of role in which he was cast, now had cause for celebration. In the *New Yorker*, Pauline Kael noted that 'Gene Hackman has his best screen role thus far; he's a fine, naturalistic actor, and though he isn't particularly handsome, he has an interestingly expressive face. He's believable and compelling in what could be a drag of a role.'

In Britain, Gavin Millar of *The Listener* wrote of Hackman

'emerging as one of the current screen's great character actors', and said, 'Perhaps the best thing he has done to date is the tough manager in Michael Ritchie's *Downhill Racer* last year. Gilbert Cates's direction is less gifted than Ritchie's and the load on Hackman is correspondingly greater. But, uneasily affectionate, confused by his hatred, he is well up to it.' Nina Hibbin of *The Morning Star* summed up the majority view in her notice: 'Gene Hackman, too often in the past tucked away in secondary parts, plays the difficult role of the son with immense feeling and conviction. Through small gestures and tiny flickers of pain across the face he conveys the conflicts, doubts and indecisions of a man of gentle nature striving to achieve emotional maturity.'

I Never Sang for my Father received three Oscar nominations; Robert Anderson was cited in the category of Best Screenplay based on material from another medium, whilst, in a somewhat surprise reversal of the on-screen emphasis, Melvyn Douglas was honoured with a Best Actor nomination while Hackman was relegated to the Supporting Actor category. Still preoccupied with his lack of star status, Hackman ruefully commented to Michael Ritchie, 'I think the Academy is trying to tell me something.'

The business aspect of winning an Oscar provokes a good deal of jockeying for position amongst the major studios based on expensive advertising and promotional campaigns within the trade journals, special screening facilities and other legitimate ploys to woo the voting populace of Academy members. An Oscar win gives an unrivalled boost to a career and can mean additional millions at the box-office. Therefore it is understandable, if not always laudatory, that it should bring out the competitive instinct in all but the most hardened cynic. Actors who have built a reputation for being reclusive, or whose relations with the press are considered strained, will suddenly become freely available, effusive and revelatory at the mention of an Oscar nomination. It is a frequently undignified but irresistably fascinating phenomenon.

Even an Oscar win could not be expected to transform *I Never Sang for my Father* into a box-office blockbuster. As an Oscar competitor it was too small, too serious and too intimate a specimen. Sentiment was not on its side as no one involved had suffered traumatically, and although Melvyn

Douglas was of the suitably venerable age that attracts awards, he had already won an Oscar for *Hud*. It seemed inevitable that *I Never Sang for my Father* would be outflanked by its more glamorous and more popular competitors. The nominations were in recognition of work well done, the actual awards could be guaranteed to go elsewhere.

The Academy Awards ceremony took place on 15 April 1971 at the Dorothy Chandler Pavilion in Los Angeles. The evening held the promise of controversy. George C. Scott had been nominated as Best Actor for his thunderingly compelling portrayal of Patton. His antipathy to the Award was widely known and long established – he had refused a Best Supporting Actor nomination for *The Hustler* (1961). Scott told reporters, 'The ceremonies are a two-hour meat parade, a public display with contrived suspense for economic reasons.' He made it bluntly apparent that he would not accept the award should he be named the winner.

Scott's fellow nominees were canvassed for their opinion on the actor's stand. Melvyn Douglas responded, 'Scott's position doesn't affront me. I'd accept the Oscar because there is gratification in getting an award.' Ryan O'Neal, nominated for *Love Story*, optimistically stated, 'If I win it will be because Scott backed out. I think Scott made an admirable stand, but for me the nomination is a great honour.' The two other nominees seemed cheerfully resigned to the inevitable, with Jack Nicholson (*Five Easy Pieces*) unashamedly announcing, 'I'm voting for myself though I don't expect to win it. Scott already has it sewn up, whether he likes it or not. But the Oscar is as valid as any award around.' James Earl Jones (*The Great White Hope*) concurred: '*Patton* was great and I think Scott deserves to win. I don't feel my life depends on winning the Award – but I love receiving trophies.'

The Scott issue dominated the 1971 ceremony, with everyone on tenterhooks to discover whether the Academy had the temerity to give an award to such a vocal dissenter. Hackman, at least, did not have to wait long before hearing his fate. After a few preliminary remarks from Academy President Daniel Taradash and the announcement of the Best Sound winner, Maggie Smith relieved the tension among the Best Supporting Actor nominees, all of whom were present. Hackman faced competition, in alphabetical order, from Richard Castellano for *Lovers and other Strangers*, Chief Dan George for *Little Big Man*, John Marley for *Love Story* and John Mills for *Ryan's Daughter*. Smith revealed the winner to be her fellow Briton Mills, for his enthusiastic portrayal of the mute village idiot in David Lean's stupendously overblown romance. 'I was not expecting to be standing here with Oscar' declared the winner. 'I was thrilled to be in the building. I was speechless for a year in Ireland and I'm utterly speechless this moment.'

Robert Anderson lost to Ring Lardner Jr for his adaptation of *M*A*S*H*. Melvyn Douglas was called upon to present an Honorary Oscar to Lillian Gish, but bowed to the unstoppable force of that year when Goldie Hawn ripped open the relevant envelope and shrieked, 'Oh, my God! The winner is George C. Scott.' In New York the unimpressionable Best Actor of 1970 claimed that he had passed the evening watching a hockey game and was in bed by the time of the Californian commotion over his victory.

Hackman found it difficult to capitalize on either the alleged value of an Oscar nomination or the quality of his work in *I Never Sang for my Father*. The American film industry was going through one of its periodic bouts of depression as a new wave of contemporary and adult features like *Midnight Cowboy* and *Easy Rider* made their impact. In a state of upheaval and uncertainty over the next big trend, and experiencing the financial doldrums, studios cut back their production rosters and stuck to the most crass and marketable commodities, brutal violence and explicit sex, in the hope that nothing succeeds like excess. Faced with the diminished scale of job opportunities and increased competition for the quality assignments, Hackman accepted whatever came along. Bills have to be paid, one assumes, and that can be the only justification for his appearance in two unmitigated junk films that he wisely claims never to have seen.

Doctors' Wives was a lethal and ludicrous cocktail of medical melodrama, murder and steamy sex. The nonsensical plot does not warrant summarizing here except to mention that Hackman's minor and comparatively straightforward character is reconciled with his wife (Rachel Roberts) after she confesses that her own psychiatric problems stem from a lesbian encounter several years before. Other plot strands include a doctor found shot in bed alongside the corpse of a colleague's wife; a brilliant brain surgeon held for this murder whose unique operating skills are required to save the life of a nurse's stricken son; a suicide attempt; and the inevitable adultery and blackmail for light relief.

Critical reaction to the film varied from outrage to a sly regard for the giddy absurdity of a film that couldn't possibly be meant to be taken seriously. Pauline Kael labelled it 'Jacobean soap-opera', whilst the *Time* reviewer appeared to have enjoyed the film against his better judgement:

'By most standards, *Doctors' Wives* is a terrible movie,' he wrote. 'This does not, however, prevent it from being fun. In fact, it is an enormously entertaining slab of Hollywood kitsch because of, not despite, its outrageous plot turns, its hyperthyroid acting and its determination to out-sex and out-suds even the seamiest TV soap opera. It is an example of assembly line, bit-studio moviemaking at its grotesque best.'

Christopher Hudson in Britain's *Spectator* was in a far less charitable mood, tartly observing, 'In appealing unashamedly to vicious morons the film will no doubt find a permanent place in the affections of its makers.'

If the 'vicious morons' found *Doctors' Wives* appealing, then they probably felt in seventh heaven when they saw *The Hunting Party*.

The production notes on *The Hunting Party* promote it as 'probably the first psychosexual western, stressing as it does the connection between sex and violence all the way through the story.' It certainly sounded a winner to the Levy-Gardner-Laven production trio who agreed to film the original script on the day it was offered to them. Screenplay writer Lou Morheim explained the scenario's development thus:

'Originally, I was only interested in writing a story about an outlaw who desperately wants to learn how to read, and who kidnaps a teacher to help him. The idea expanded into a hunting party that turns into a manhunt after the kidnapper.'

Oliver Reed read the script whilst on holiday in Barbados and agreed to play the illiterate cowboy, Candice Bergen was engaged as the kidnap victim and Hackman completed the triumvirate by accepting the thankless task of playing a one-note character described as a 'sadistic, sexually deranged bully'.

Having rejected Mexico as a substitute for the Old West, the producers settled on Spain as their stand-in, utilizing locations around Madrid, the Almeria hinterland and Andalusia. The filming commenced on June 22nd and wrapped on September 5th after eleven weeks in an area where midsummer temperatures rise to the 115 degree mark.

The plot of *The Hunting Party* is brutally simple. Surly outlaw Frank Calder (Oliver Reed) has designs for better living and kidnaps Melissa Ruger (Candice Bergen), whom he believes to be a schoolteacher who may teach him to read. Melissa is unfortunately the wife of millionaire cattle baron Brandt Ruger (Hackman), who is not a forgiving man and regards Melissa as personal property akin to his ranch and railway stock. Although Melissa attempts to escape from Calder's clutches, she is strangely drawn to him and is far from happy with Ruger, who is hardly the most tender or solicitous of husbands. Ruger leads a posse after Calder's band of outlaws and a cat-and-mouse game ensues through the mountain ranges as both parties suffer casualties.

Ruger is relentless in his pursuit and unperturbed when his men grow weary and refuse to follow him. In a final showdown he kills Calder and then turns the rifle on his wife, firing one clean, fatal shot.

Hackman is visibly ill-at-ease with the demands of an exercise in outright sadism and sneering brutality. He is too diligent an actor to indulge in the lip-smacking, moustache-twirling black villainy that the part requires and is thus left to his own devices. Reed was easily pleased by the mere offer of a part in a western and Bergen was casually off-hand in her remarks: 'All I do in this film is get raped and have orgasms. But I've got the orgasms down pat now. It's your token ten seconds of heavy breathing followed by my baroque expression, eyes heavenward.'

Ten seconds of heavy breathing seems an apt description for *The Hunting Party*'s impact on the wider public. The critics were justifiably unimpressed, although *Films in Review* bravely distanced itself from the majority, claiming the film to be 'widely misunderstood in its attempt to teach mankind not to live by the law of the gun.' Hackman's recorded recollection of the film is a more personal and trivial one; he told *Woman* magazine in 1972, 'Boy, did I get it in the neck from my wife when I made that film! There was an actor who looked a lot like me in it, and a magazine used a photo of him with half-nude girls from the film on his knee. Everyone, including Faye, thought it was *me*. Ouch!'

Matters improved for Hackman with his participation in *Cisco Pike*, the first feature directed by UCLA film graduate Bill Norton and the film debut of Kris Kristofferson. Arriving late in the day amidst a cycle of films involving the drug scene (*Panic in Needle Park*, *Born to Win*, etc.) *Cisco Pike* has tended to be overlooked, but has a distinctive flavour of its own and a superb cast that also includes Harry Dean Stanton and Karen Black.

Norton's career had so far encompassed 'a couple of TV commercials, some rock-and-roll shorts and a couple of short films at UCLA' when he was advised by his father that the best means of becoming a director was probably to write a decent script and hope that someone would let him direct his own material. He took this fatherly advice to heart and after starting, but never finishing, three other scripts he completed one entitled *Dealer*, 'loosely based on my experiences and the experiences of a friend of mine who made his living as a marijuana dealer.'

The *Dealer* script was presented to Alan Howard, who was then assistant to Gerry Ayres, the vice-president of Columbia Studios. Howard liked the material and passed it on to Ayres, who agreed to produce, much to the relief of the poverty-stricken Norton, who was surviving on unemployment benefit.

Norton asked if he might direct *Dealer*, entertaining little hope that his request might actually be granted. Ayres took the comparatively rare step of personally financing a short test which Norton would direct as a form of evidence for the Columbia top brass that he could pass some film through a camera and present them with usable, coherent footage. The test was acceptable and Norton was welcomed as a new member of the Hollywood hyphenates: a writer-director.

Retitled *Cisco Pike*, Norton's script was filmed in Los Angeles, with Norton experiencing great trepidation over his big-studio debut. As he balanced the differences between the enthusiasm of a modest student crew and the alternate pressures and professionalism of an extensive Hollywood film unit, he was receiving a crash course in film technique; learning that time is measured in dollars and that 'improvisation only works well when you have a well-structured, well-written script to fall back on.'

In the film Kris Kristofferson plays the title character, an over-the-hill rock star awaiting trial on his second drugs-related offence. Hackman is fanatical narcotics cop Leo Holland, who decides to turn his expert knowledge to his own ends when a heart ailment threatens to bring about his enforced retirement on an unsuitably modest pension. He hijacks a consignment of Mexican marijuana and offers Pike a deal whereby if the singer sells the dope he will use his contacts and outstanding favours to guarantee a lenient day in court.

The film then follows Pike's odyssey through the flotsam and jetsam of downtown Los Angeles as he attempts to unload the consignment. He journeys through a downbeat milieu of contrasting customers (from wealthy executives and radical lawyers to burnt-out musicians and junkies), just another loser in an overpopulated world of no-hopers.

Kristofferson had previously auditioned for *Two Lane Blacktop* before being cast in Cisco Pike, which he unjustly described in one 1972 interview as a 'contrived, crappy movie'. He told *Rolling Stone* about his feelings on becoming an actor: 'I'd never even been in a school play, but I read the script and I could identify with this cat, this dope dealer. People said, "Don't do it, take acting lessons first!" But it seemed t'me that acting must be just understanding a character, and then being just as honest as you possibly can be. I shoulda been scared, but then I shoulda been scared the first time on that Troubadour stage and I wasn't.'

Hackman's work on the film was generally much appreciated, with the *New York Times* describing him as 'quickly becoming the most important and versatile actor in American films,' adding that 'although the role of the cop is rather sketchily written, Gene Hackman gives it surprising depth.'

Although it was made first, *Cisco Pike* was released after Hackman's next film. Again, he was cast as a compulsive and brutish narcotics cop and there are other similarities between the two characters. However, both audience and critical reaction would ensure that Leo Holland was overshadowed by his fellow officer, a far from 'gentle' gentleman by the name of 'Popeye' Doyle.

Chapter Five

'The first things that count about me are as follows: I drink beer, I lay broads and I bust heads.' Those words, whether apocryphal or not, were reported to be the first uttered by Eddie Egan to director William Friedkin. Egan was a tough, passionately dedicated New York cop who had been responsible for tracking down one of the biggest narcotics hauls ever. Friedkin was the man who was going to film his story as *The French Connection*.

In October 1961, Egan and his partner Sonny Grosso had stumbled across an ambitious drug-smuggling ring that stretched from an original source in Turkey through Lebanon and the South of France to Montreal and finally to New York. Four months of painstaking surveillance work resulted in the seizure of heroin with a street value of $32 million. The drugs had been secreted into America within the bodywork of a car belonging to a French television star. To understand the scale of the case it should be noted that the shipment could have supplied New York addicts for two years.

Some years later Robin Moore, who had written *The Green Berets*, turned Egan's remarkable drugs bust into a book which was then optioned by producer Philip D'Antoni with a view towards making a film. D'Antoni had recently produced *Bullitt*, a hugely popular cop film whose success rested squarely on the personal magnetism of star Steve McQueen and a brilliantly-staged car chase up and down the hills of San Francisco. D'Antoni felt that *The French Connection* contained a similar mix of elements, and that the only outstanding ingredient it still required was a great chase sequence. The chase in *Bullitt* had been hailed as the modern-day equivalent of Ben-Hur's chariot duel and would perhaps stand as the definitive example of its kind.

Although he might be unwilling to admit it, D'Antoni was in competition with himself to improve upon his best.

The prolific young director William Friedkin was assigned the task of bringing *The French Connection* to the screen. He foresaw two main challenges: to explore and make understandable the mentality of a tunnel-vision cop like Egan, and to stage one stupendous car chase. On the latter aim he was completely in accord with D'Antoni, and he subsequently recalled, 'What we needed most of all was a powerful chase. In fact, our thinking frankly followed formula lines: A guy gets killed in the first few minutes; checkerboard the stories of the cop and the smuggler for approximately twenty minutes; bring the two antagonists together and tighten the screws for another ten minutes or so, then come in with a fantastic ten-minute chase. After this, it was a question of keeping the pressure on for another twenty minutes or so, followed by a slam-bang finish with a surprise twist.'

Reducing a complex task to such basics gives the erroneous impression that *The French Connection* was a fairly straightforward project to assemble and film. It was to be anything but easy.

Initially, D'Antoni was developing *The French Connection* as a project for National General Pictures. Two unsatisfactory scripts were presented within the space of a year and both were summarily rejected. The material then gathered dust for ten months as Friedkin made *The Boys in the Band*. The two men faced general industry opposition to the film as studio executives found the lead character unsympathetic, were worried by the lack of female interest in the story and were hesitant over the commercial prospects of a cop film in which the criminal mastermind ultimately evaded apprehension. Friedkin and D'Antoni knew that the material should work, but held personal reservations about capturing the rhythms and nuances of New York street dialogue and about how they could legitimately integrate their cherished chase into the screenplay.

As a successful producer,* D'Antoni regularly received various missives and manuscripts for his attention. One such document was the galley proofs of a novel by Ernest

---

* *Bullitt* had grossed $19 million in America.

Tidyman entitled *Shaft*. D'Antoni read the book and passed it on to Friedkin, who concurred with his decision that they contact Tidyman and ask him to collaborate with them on a script. Tidyman had never written for the screen before, but he had spent twenty-five years as a working journalist including a spell as a crime reporter for the *New York Times*. His pertinent knowledge and writing ability, as discerned from the pages of *Shaft*, made him an ideal partner.

As Tidyman worked on an entirely new version of the *French Connection* script, Friedkin and D'Antoni focused their attention on the car chase. They spent an afternoon together, intent on solving the crucial problems of how it might be staged, what vehicles it might involve, where it would take place and how they could make it more exciting, more dangerous and more real than anything previously seen on screen. Inspiration finally dawned as they strolled along Lexington Avenue in New York and began to work out a scenario in which the Egan character was the victim of an assault on his life. They have him decide to pursue the sniper. Neither man can reach his car, but the sniper boards a train. Egan commandeers a car and the chase ensues; a mad desperate scramble with one man in an elevated train and the other careering through the main thoroughfares of New York in ardent pursuit. After excitedly walking and talking for fifty blocks, the two men had solved their problem and a firm plan for the famous chase was in the works.

Tidyman incorporated all their work into a draft screenplay which was accepted by Richard Zanuck and David Brown at Twentieth Century Fox. The new script was a considerable improvement on what had previously been offered around Hollywood, but the Fox executives were still taking a substantial risk because, as Friedkin noted, 'every studio in the business turned the picture down, some twice.'

Friedkin considered the chase in *The French Connection* as 'the most important element in the film' and consequently concentrated his energies on liaising with the Metropolitan Transit Authority of New York City and examining the nuts - and-bolts practicalities of what he intended. At the same time pre-production work progressed and casting considerations were gaining top priority.

Eddie Egan and Sonny Grosso had now been fictionalized

as Jimmy 'Popeye' Doyle and Buddy Russo. Roy Scheider, the Obie award-winning stage actor, who also had some film experience, was cast as Russo, but finding an actor who was willing to portray the uncompromising ruthlessness of 'Popeye' was more time-consuming. D'Antoni had apparently approached his *Bullitt* star Steve McQueen. Jackie Gleason was another major name mentioned in connection with the role. Friedkin worked with columnist Jimmy Breslin, coaching him for an assault on the role, but as Scheider recollected in a 1983 interview, 'In the action stuff he was great, but when he had to say "pass the sugar" not too good. Desperate . . .'

As it became clear that the Paul Newmans and Steve McQueens of the profession were not falling over themselves in the rush to play 'Popeye', the possibility arose of whether Eddie Egan himself might not be the most appropriate choice to portray his fictionalized counterpart. But for whatever reasons, Egan proved to be unacceptable, although he did mention that his choice for the part was Rod Taylor.

Working their way through the casting directories, Friedkin and D'Antoni called Hackman and asked him to come to New York to discuss the part. His reaction to it was immediately positive. 'When I first read the part,' he recalled, 'it seemed like a chance to do all those things I watched Jimmy Cagney do as a kid.' The prospect of his first starring role was both flattering and exciting. To the filmmakers he had the physical presence for the role – big, burly, not conventionally handsome. He had lived in New York before and would have an instinctive feel for the neighbourhoods that were 'Popeye' Doyle's beat. Most importantly, he was an actor and not a star; he would be more likely to place the requirements of the character before his 'image'. Hackman could be relied upon to play 'Popeye' as written and not dilute their intentions.

After meeting Hackman, Friedkin and D'Antoni had only one major reservation over casting him as 'Popeye' – he was too nice. They had discussed the character of a brutal, ruthless, streetwise cop with a soft-spoken, gentle-natured teddy-bear of a man. Actor and character were the complete antithesis of each other; yet, Hackman's profession was one of make-believe, and you don't have to be tough to act tough. The actor's fine track record and general suitability outweighed any concern about his innate gentility, and after a nail-biting weekend in a New York hotel awaiting his fate, he received a telephone call informing him that he was indeed to be 'Popeye' Doyle.

Although the fantasy of Jimmy Cagney was appealing, the reality of the film's violence upset and disturbed Hackman. 'Violence was a great problem to me in the picture,' he said in 1972. 'In the opening scene I have to beat up a black pusher in the street. We shot it more than twenty-seven times – my beating up this kid, and I really had to hit him. Between takes he kept saying it was all right and he'd smile and we'd do it again. I don't know how he could stand it, I felt horrible. I almost couldn't go through with it. I personally could not be a cop. I just couldn't do that. It was something to do with being brought up in a more gentle atmosphere. I've just never had the kind of New York intenseness, the push, the competitiveness.'

Friedkin had decided that, within the limits of a dramatic entertainment, *The French Connection* would accurately reflect the working environment and often unpleasant methods that were commonplace practice for the members of the New York Police Department. He immersed himself in the detectives' lifestyle, absorbing their attitudes and vernacular and storing any scrap of information or insight that might prove useful. He also enlisted the assistance of some rather less upright citizens, telling the *Sunday People*, 'I filmed *The French Connection* in eighty-six of the hardcore drug locations in New York. I was led to them by a man known as Fat Thomas, who is a wheelman (driver) to dope-running gangs. He's been arrested fifty-two times – but always wriggled free for lack of evidence.'

In preparation for the film, Hackman and Roy Scheider spent several weeks travelling at night with Eddie Egan and Sonny Grosso, participating in police raids and noting down fragments of dialogue that were later incorporated into the script. For Hackman, especially, the experience was an eye-opener.

'I watched Eddie Egan and I tried to do the physical stuff. There's a certain New York street guy, you know, the way he walks, the way he talks, the way he bounces. It was very, very tough for me. People think I'm like that, but nothing could be further from the truth. I was amazed at the violence in those men's lives. It would scare the hell out of me.'

This close involvement with the defenders of the law changed attitudes about cops and demolished many of the prejudices that 'liberals' like Hackman and Friedkin had previously held. Promoting the finished film in Britain in 1972, Friedkin told *The Guardian*, 'I went into the movie with the usual attitudes. I was against any kind of police violence but I came out thinking it was all too easy to criticize this guy. It was quite another thing to be him, to go into the streets alone and fight against the drug racketeers. They would stop at nothing, and he discovered that he could only do his job if he didn't either. He is just a product of his environment and the film for me is not so much about the case as about him.'

Hackman developed an uneasy admiration for the boys in blue based on the sheer demands that society made upon them. 'Being around cops changed my mind immensely about them,' he admitted. 'You can't walk in there like Mr Nice Guy and get people's attention. It's an enormous job. I'm all for those guys. More people should know the kind of work cops have to do and they'd respect them a great deal more.'

His opinion of the specific personality of 'Popeye', however, remained unchanged. 'I didn't have any sympathy with him at all. He was a sort of composite and I am sure his sort of violent cop does exist. New York is a pretty violent place and I suppose you've got to have violent cops. Some people will see this movie and see some social significance in it. The only social significance as far as I can see is that we have allowed tough cops like the one I play to grow up.'

Hackman researched, analysed and virtually breathed the character of 'Popeye' Doyle until he felt it was 'under my skin'. Scheider later said, 'We didn't know how good it would be, but we did know it'd be the most authentic cop movie made up to that time.'

Filming was scheduled to take place on seventy shooting days from December 1970 through to March of the following year. They would be working in the cold of winter, snatching scenes and time at the indulgence of the local authorities, filming on the streets with the inherent drawbacks of co-ordinating the massive crew of a major film with the innocent bystanders of the curious general public.

The budget was an extremely modest $2,200,000 and the leading actor, who had never before carried the burden of a starring role, still felt qualms about his ability to convincingly replicate the sense of seething inner violence that was the key to his character. In 1986 he told British chat show host Terry Wogan, 'I was pretty much in over my head. As a matter of fact on the second day of shooting I asked the director to replace me because I just didn't feel I could do it. I was popping these guys in the mouth and playing this tough guy and I had never played a role quite that demanding. However, after a while, if you punch someone long enough you get used to it. So, I kind of came around a bit.'

Filming *The French Connection* was a gruelling and exhausting process. The New York winter of 1970–1971 was not mild and Hackman found himself working in sleet, rain and even snowstorms. People were felled by colds and flu, union problems caused headaches, equipment even froze in the severe cold. Friedkin had been rather looking forward to the prospect of inclement weather because he felt it would contribute to the gritty reality of what would appear on screen, but even he baulked at some of the conditions.

'It was painfully cold through most of December and January when the chase was filmed. Very often it was so cold – sometimes five degrees above zero – that our camera equipment froze, or the train froze and couldn't start. One day, the special effects spark machine didn't work, again because of the cold. Once the equipment rental truck froze. We seldom had four good hours of shooting a day while inside the train.'

The chase scene, filmed out of sequence and intermittently over a period of five weeks, presented Friedkin with the biggest logistical problems. His consultations with the Transit Authority had resulted in a longer chase and one that more accurately reflected what would happen if such an event were actually to transpire. They advised him on safety precautions and technical devices like the deadman's brake and the trip-lock, and generally 'their suggestions were more exciting than what we had conceived'. The Authority gave Friedkin permission to use one section of the express track on the Stillwell Avenue Line on the understanding that its use would be restricted to the period between 10:00 a.m. and 3:00 p.m., well outside the passenger rush hour.

Friedkin tried to simplify the chase scene by filming, wherever possible, separate sequences with the train and with 'Popeye's' car. Every shot, every stunt, every moment involving pedestrians was meticulously planned to minimize risk and maximize the film-making possibilities. Five individual stunt scenes within the overall chase were planned, involving collisions, narrow avoidance of a woman and a baby buggy, driving the wrong way up a one-way street, and all this against the backdrop of a seemingly normal Brooklyn day.

The car chosen as 'Popeye's' vehicle was a brown 1970 Pontiac four-door sedan, equipped with a four-speed gear shift. Stunt driver Bill Hickman was enlisted to man the wheel during the most dangerous moments, but Hackman himself was to be in the driver's seat as much as possible, and according to Friedkin, 'drove considerably more than half of the shots that are used in the final cutting sequence'. It is Hackman behind the wheel when the car is thundering along at speeds of between seventy and ninety miles per hour.

The potential for accident or injury was high throughout the five weeks of filming the chase. The events of the first day did not bode well as a stunt driver mis-timed his cue and smashed into the Pontiac, almost destroying it on the driver's side. Fortunately, no one was injured, but Friedkin relied heavily on the co-operation of city officials and the grace of God. Quite often his principal safety precautions were to pray a lot and keep his fingers crossed.

The final shot of all was the most dangerous and is described in full by Friedkin in the magazine *Action:*

'For one particular shot, we used no controls whatever. This was a shot with two cameras mounted, one inside and one outside the car. The inside camera was on a 50mm lens, shooting through the front window; the outside camera was on a 25mm lens mounted to the front bumper. I was in the car. Bill Hickman drove the entire distance of the chase run, approximately twenty-six blocks, at speeds between seventy

[73]

and ninety miles an hour. With no control at all and only a siren on top of his car, we went through red lights and drove in the wrong lane! This was, of course, the wrap shot of the film.'

Hackman finished work on *The French Connection* in March 1971. He headed back to Hollywood and the April Oscar show. Such was the moribund state of the film industry that, in spite of his nomination for *I Never Sang for my Father* and his first lead role in *The French Connection*, he was unemployed with no future plans.

Friedkin's involvement with *The French Connection* continued unabated as he embarked on the essential postproduction work of sound mixing and editing prior to the film's scheduled release during the closing months of 1971.

The final shape of *The French Connection*, which is reputed to have grown and prospered at the editor's table, runs very much according to the simplistic formula that Friedkin had outlined at the beginning of the project. The film opens in Marseilles. A French detective is shot by Pierre Nicoli (Marcel Bozuffi), who pockets his gun and walks away. The scene fades out.

In Brooklyn now, a drug pusher is cornered by two detectives. He lashes out at Buddy Russo (Scheider) and cuts his arm, but is beaten into submission by the brutish Jimmy 'Popeye' Doyle. The pusher is booked, Russo receives treatment for his wound and the two men officially end their shift. Doyle, however, is a man who never goes off-duty and he persuades his partner to accompany him to a club on the East Side. The prospect of a relaxing drink soon vanishes when Doyle spots a couple with known drug connections spending lavishly. The detectives follow the couple through the streets of lower Manhattan, across the Brooklyn Bridge and into Brooklyn. The trail ends at an unprepossessing candy store, apparently operated by the couple.

In Marseilles, businessman Alain Charnier (Fernando Rey) and his wife Marie (Ann Rebbot) are about to embark on a transatlantic voyage to New York. Among their fellow passengers are Nicoli and Henri Devereaux (Frederic de Pasquale), a popular television star who is visiting America to film a documentary special.

Doyle and Russo continue their surveillance of the Brooklyn candy store and are convinced they have stumbled onto something when the owner Sal Boca (Tony Lo Bianco) travels to the Manhattan apartment of Joel Weinstock (Harold Gary), one of the chief bankrollers of illicit narcotics importation.

Upon his arrival in New York, Devereaux is besieged by reporters and closely scrutinized by Charnier and Nicoli as he drives away in his custom-made Lincóln, specially shipped over on the French liner.

Doyle and Russo have now persuaded their superior to let them concentrate exclusively on the Boca case and two Federal Narcotics Officers are assigned to assist them. Meanwhile, Charnier is given a guided tour of Ward's Island, which includes a fire training school, a deserted asylum and the New York Police Automobile Auction.

Accompanied by Bill Mulderig (Bill Hickman) and Phil Klein (Sonny Grosso), Doyle and Russo observe Boca entering a top Madison Avenue hotel and meeting Charnier and Nicoli. The round-the-clock surveillance operation is extended to cover the activities of the two Frenchmen.

Several days later, whilst walking home, Doyle comes under fire from a roof-top sniper. A bystander is killed by one of the shots. As Doyle races to the opposite building he catches sight of Nicoli sprinting to the subway and boarding a train. Doyle commandeers a passing car and sets off in desperate pursuit, zig-zagging through the traffic whilst trying to keep the elevated carriage within sight. On the train Nicoli unhesitatingly kills a motorman and transit cop before disembarking at another station, breathless but free. However, he has not reckoned on Doyle's persistence and he is met by the waiting cop, his gun drawn.

Police surveillance now places suspicion on the contents of Devereaux's Lincoln, which is impounded. Hidden inside the splash-pans are one hundred and twelve pounds of heroin. No public announcement is made of the find but an increasingly nervous Devereaux reneges on his deal with Charnier, leaving him to drive the Lincoln to the Ward's Island rendezvous with Boca and Weinstock.

The police are lying in wait at the island. Weinstock and another man surrender immediately, but the others choose to shoot it out. Russo kills Sal Boca whilst his brother Lou and Charnier dash towards the abandoned asylum. With the scent of the chase in his nostrils, Doyle's reactions are fast and unthinking, his momentum unstoppable. Warily making his way through the gloomy interior of the asylum, Doyle is fired upon and retaliates instantly and instinctively by shooting his unseen assailant: in the shadowy asylum he has killed narcotics officer Mulderig. His colleagues are horrified by the shooting, but Doyle pauses only momentarily before rampaging onwards in search of an elusive quarry who has now made good his escape.

When *The French Connection* was released in America it opened to sensational reviews and smashing box-office success. The *New York Daily News* raved, 'Pure dynamite. Its trigger-fast explosive scenes and high-tension chases (the one in *Bullitt* pales in comparison) will have you literally gasping for breath.' The *New York Times* hailed it as 'a sensationally crafty, cops-and-dope-smugglers melodrama that sees New York as it really is.'

Hackman's personal notices were of the type an actor dreams of writing himself. In the *London Evening Standard*, Alexander Walker wrote, 'Just as happened with Lee Marvin, the film makes a star out of a character actor who is no beauty but a force of flesh, bone and blood who takes over a role and lives it.' Dilys Powell in the *Sunday Times* lauded, 'Gene Hackman, savage exasperated gestures and the mad ill-assembled features of a puppet carved from packing-case wood, gives a performance of devoted, inexorable vindictiveness.' Nina Hibbin in the *Morning Star* would brook no arguments over the success of the film: 'The unabating inner fury with which Gene Hackman brilliantly portrays this uncouth character becomes the main driving force of the film.'

As the queues snaked around cinema pay desks, industry pundits began to analyze the hit-making ingredients of *The French Connection*. Firstly, the icy recreation of the New York milieu could not be faulted. Egan and Grosso had advised on every aspect of the film and both played minor roles, Egan appearing as Doyle's boss Lieutenant Simonson, head of the New York Police Department Narcotics Squad. The quest for authenticity had extended to the smallest possible detail, and even the original mechanic who had found the heroin in the car played himself. Secondly, the car chase was a frenetic, furious, bravura classic, brilliantly conceived and endlessly improved upon in the editing process.

However, authenticity and a superb chase cannot entirely account for the unusual popularity of the film, and the final conclusion was inescapable: *The French Connection* succeeded because of the overpowering conviction and dominating presence of Gene Hackman.

Hackman's 'Popeye' Doyle is a completely consistent creation from the crummy pork-pie hat on his head to the plodding flatness of his copper's feet. His compulsive crime-busting marks him out as a seedy, low-life soul mate of Clint Eastwood's Dirty Harry. He is a man so dedicated to eradicating the criminal fraternity that he has grown danger-ously close to embodying all that he seeks to conquer: brut-ality, violence, sledgehammer inhuman callousness.

The role had not been easy for Hackman, especially the physical elements of the violence and the chases. The injury from his marine days had resulted in the placement of a plastic and steel knee in his left leg, making any form of running painful, yet in the *French Connection* he runs frequently to portray a character who is an overwound mechanism that never relents. The actor's attention to detail is particularly noticeable in his delineation of 'Popeye': every visible aspect of the man, from his unkempt mop of hair to his torn coat and sloppy eating habits, indicates a lack of vanity and a total disregard for the image that he presents to the world. It doesn't matter that he looks shabby, it is irrelevant that you wouldn't want him as a neighbour, the only thing of importance is his effectiveness. He fights fire with fire, a bull-in-a-chinashop approach that cleans the scum off the streets with no questions asked about the methods.

In his analysis of Hackman, director Michael Ritchie considered *The French Connection* in terms of its impact on the actor's career and his own pet theory about Hackman's frustration at never getting the girl:

'His "Popeye" is a haunted man who has no private life, whose work is an obssession, who treats all "germs" equally, regardless of race or nationality. It's "up against the wall" for everybody. There is no sacred institution, not even Santa Claus.

'Hackman's "Popeye" Doyle is not the common man. [He]

is the common man's ideal of what he would like to be in a crowded, frustrating, unjust world. No leading man I can think of could have played that part as well. The ultimate tribute that can be paid to both Hackman and director William Friedkin is this: not only doesn't "Popeye" get the girl (there is no girl to get), he doesn't even get his man. Fernando Rey goes free and "Popeye" is left in existential limbo.'

With Steve McQueen as 'Popeye' we would have rightly expected there to be a girl; with Hackman the question never arises. *The French Connection* stands as a rare instance of actor and character in perfect unison.

Chapter Six

As Hackman slowly unwound from the intensity of playing 'Popeye' Doyle, he began to search around for further work. The industry had yet to recover from its temporary slump and the options were sparse. Thus, in the late summer of 1971, he embarked upon a secondary role in a Lee Marvin film entitled *Kansas City Prime*.

Ever the clear-eyed realist, Hackman recognized the film for what it was – employment:

'It had been five or six months since I had finished *The French Connection* and nobody knew about that, so it was a matter of a job at that point. It wasn't especially rewarding, it could have been a good experience I suppose, but it turned out not to be terribly exciting. I'm not trying to put the picture down, it works on a certain level. I didn't expect it to work in any other way. It's just that sometimes your working experiences are very exciting, sometimes they are not.'

Director Michael Ritchie noted that Hackman's six weeks of work on the production were marked by 'all the professionalism and conscientiousness that the industry has come to associate with its fine character players.' *The French Connection* had apparently been just another job of work and not something that was about to turn Hackman's head or inspire delusions of grandeur. Well, not yet, anyway.

Retitled *Prime Cut*, the film was released in the Summer of 1972. An uproariously sleazy and black-comedy gangster drama, its unsettling tone never appealed to a mass audience, although Ritchie claims that his version of the film was only shown in Minneapolis where it was a success. Lee Marvin plays Nick Devlin, a tough underworld enforcer who journeys to Kansas to collect half a million dollars owing to Chicago mobster Jake (Eddie Egan). The last man dispatched on a similar mission has just been returned to Jake as a package of frankfurters.

The sausage-maker had been 'Mary Ann' (Hackman), who runs a slaughterhouse as the legitimate cover for a variety of illegal activities including drug-running and prostitution. In his Kansas barns the cattle pens are filled with nude teenage girls kept in a permanently half-drugged condition.

Devlin arrives in Kansas with three gunmen and a small arsenal of weaponry. He refuses an offer to join 'Mary Ann's' operation, demands the half million dollars and abducts one of the girls as insurance against non-payment. Eventually, after much carnage, Devlin and his sub-machine gun resolve any outstanding business disagreements by shooting 'Mary Ann', who topples into the pen of a prize boar. Devlin frees all the girls and tenderly puts his arm around his former hostage Poppy (Sissy Spacek), who asks where they are going. He replies, 'Chicago. It's windy – and calm, and peaceful as anyplace, anywhere..'

Because of its Kansas setting, Ritchie was prone to describing *Prime Cut* as his *Wizard of Oz* movie, although he later admitted that neither he nor Hackman were especially proud of their efforts in this instance. It can only really be appreciated by those with a strong stomach and a ghoulish sense of humour, otherwise it is ever so slightly distasteful. In Britain, George Melly commented in *The Observer*, 'As to why I disliked the film quite so much, I think it is because it gloats so hypocritically over what it pretends to condemn.' Alexander Walker of the *London Evening Standard* sadly noted, 'It is the outstanding achievement of this film to smooth over Lee Marvin's rough edges and to make Gene Hackman's well-rounded gutsiness perfectly flat.'

Hackman's gangster, 'Mary Ann', was a typical 'good ole boy' villain, full of greasy goodwill and backslapping bonhomie until the time comes to put another opponent through the mincing machine. The success or failure of *Prime Cut* was largely immaterial to him by the summer of '72, for by then *The French Connection* was a hit, and for better or worse, he was being acclaimed as one of the oldest new stars in the industry.

The enormous popularity of *The French Connection* had taken everyone by surprise. William Friedkin suggested that perhaps it retained a universal appeal because it had refused to be judgemental towards its central character.

'I could have made the film into a paean of praise for the cop, or a condemnation of him and his methods,' he told journalists. 'My own feelings were up the middle. I saw both sides of it. So, I guess the movie is capable of satisfying everybody, though that's not what I was after. Those who think the police are brutal will go on thinking that. Those who feel they have a hopeless job and ought to be thanked will carry right on saying so. I'm happy about that because I don't think a film has to persuade or propagandize. It is better to state facts.'

Hackman was more bewildered, and typically self-effacing, when it came to recording his reactions to the film's success.

'I thought the film would either be received by the critics and stand as an example of that kind of film or that it would be an audience movie. I didn't think for a moment that it would become *both*. I had no idea it was going to be such a good film when I accepted it. I didn't think the characters would be as well-rounded. It is a brilliantly edited film. The cutting did a great deal to help. I can't take too much of the credit for my performance.'

Whilst Hackman was able to share in the glory of *The French Connection*'s success, he did not participate to any great extent in the profits that were now flowing in. He had played 'Popeye' Doyle for a flat fee, lacking the foresight or stature to insist on any potentially more lucrative arrangement. Furthermore, he was soon under contract to reprise the character should a sequel be required, and that was one commitment that would stick in his throat in subsequent years.

For the moment, though, he could savour his elevation to stardom as critics praised his acting, audiences lined up to see the film and the general public increasingly began to stop him in the street, just wanting to say hello to 'Popeye'. He also became adept at the art of public speech-making as the numerous award-giving bodies recognized him as the actor of the year. The National Board of Review named him as the Best Actor of 1971 and he received a Golden Globe as the Best Actor in a Drama. During the balloting of the New York Film Critics there was a dead heat between

[81]

Hackman and Peter Finch (for *Sunday, Bloody Sunday*). Hackman won on the second count and was presented with his citation by Paulette Godard in a special New York ceremony.

An Oscar nomination, his first as Best Actor, seemed a certainty, and when the nominees were announced, *The French Connection* had been mentioned in eight categories: Editing (Jerry Greenberg), Sound (Gordon K. McCallum and David Hildyard), Cinematography (Owen Roizman), Adapted Screenplay (Ernest Tidyman), Supporting Actor (Roy Scheider), Director, Best Picture – and, as expected, Best Actor. Hackman was in contention for the Best Actor trophy with Finch, Walter Matthau (for *Kotch*), George C. Scott (for *The Hospital*) and Topol (for *Fiddler on the Roof*).

The ceremony took place on 10 April 1972 at the Dorothy Chandler Pavilion in Los Angeles, with Helen Hayes, Alan King, Sammy Davis Jnr and Jack Lemmon as hosts. The evening was to be a sentimental and significant one as it marked Charlie Chaplin's return to the Hollywood film community after a self-imposed exile of thirty years. Hollywood appreciates nothing better than an aged performer accepting an Honorary Oscar, and the air of mutual forgiveness for past neglects guaranteed some emotional scenes. To enhance Chaplin's importance to the evening it was decided that no other Honorary Awards would be presented that year.

Hackman attended the ceremony and was to act as co-presenter of the Best Supporting Actress Award along with Raquel Welch. The task served as a minor distraction from the more pressing purpose of the evening, although as the awards were announced it did not look like shaping up as *The French Connection*'s night; Best Cinematography want to Oswald Morris for *Fiddler on the Roof* and the Best Supporting Actor was Ben Johnson for *The Last Picture Show*. However, the omens improved as Jerry Greenberg accepted the Best Editing Award, making sure to thank the New York subway system, and Ernest Tidyman won in his category. Friedkin had been the Director's Guild of America choice for the year and he continued the trend by taking an Oscar from presenters Natalie Wood and Frank Capra.

To the strains of the theme tune from *Cabaret*, Liza Minnelli came forward to announce the Best Actor. Excited by the prospect, she read the nominees, tore open the envelope and paused to enquire, 'Are you as nervous as I am?' She then screamed out, 'The winner is Gene Hackman in *The French Connection!*'

Nothing can really prepare a performer for the full force of an Oscar win – a potent moment in which tension is relieved and a mixture of shock and exultation forces its way to the surface. Hackman made his way to the podium and examined Minnelli's envelope just to check that no mistake had been made. 'This is what it says,' he assured the audience, and there was no doubt that the unknown actor from a coldwater apartment in New York tonight grasped the film world's highest accolade. He thanked Friedkin, he thanked Faye and had even greater cause for celebration when Jack Nicholson announced *The French Connection* as the year's Best Film. The ceremony ended with the tribute to Chaplin, all the winners going on stage to sing his composition 'Smile'.

Years later Hackman was able to reflect on the Oscars with a degree of objectivity and told Mike Russell, the publicist on *Eureka*, 'The Oscars as such . . . the evening itself . . . is a tremendously high evening, at least it was for me. But since then, the Oscar *per se* doesn't mean that much to me. What does mean a great deal to one after the Oscar is your career. And sometimes it can affect it adversely – especially in supporting categories. An actor will immediately try and move up several notches, or beyond where they're saleable . . . and that's a real detriment to them. The whole business to me, once you can stand off from it and look at it objectively, is fairly ugly. There's a lot of hype. I've often thought, and this is nothing new, that the nominations are nice. To be nominated with four other people is quite a tribute. When it gets down to the best of any one category, who the hell is to say? We'd all have to play the same role! I don't have my Oscar any place where I can look at it all the time, but – yeah – it's nice to have. It's kind of special.'

As Hackman rightly observed, the Oscar can be a blessing or a jinx to its winner. Film stardom and success had arrived at a relatively late age for him; he was 42 and resolutely realistic about what might be possible in the future. He openly admitted that any number of equally proficient actors could have played 'Popeye' and that his interpretation of

[83]

the part did not mark him out as uniquely gifted. However, since it had fallen to him to play the part, he felt entitled to reap the rewards. To the press he talked of *Klute* and *Fat City* as the kind of films that he would like to make and apologized for not resembling what he regarded as a movie idol. 'I know I'm not the conventional handsome star but just because I don't happen to resemble Tab Hunter or Ryan O'Neal doesn't mean I'm not virile. There's a lot of romance in all of us.'

In the 'Rambling Reporter' column of the industry paper *The Hollywood Reporter*, a caustic Hank Grant noted that in 1972 Hackman 'has had more pic offers this year than any other male hero in Hollywood, which is darned good for a guy who, before he copped the Oscar award, was turned down so many times he was beginning to look like a bedspread.' Hackman was announced as the star of several films, including *The Big Wild Red* for David Foster and Mitch Brower, who had produced *McCabe and Mrs Miller*, and *Dunn*. Dirt-track racing, one of Hackman's favourite off-screen pursuits, was the subject of *Dunn* but in May of 1972 he declared that the film had been shelved indefinitely.

One of Hackman's ambitions was to play a romantic role because, he reckoned, 'You can't become a really big star unless you have played a romantic hero of some kind. After that you can do anything and the public will play along with you. It was exactly the same in the old days of Hollywood. You didn't have to be good-looking to be a star, but you did have to have a romantic aura.' Part of the dreamer in him may still have wanted to emulate Errol Flynn, but the business-like aspects of his character held sway and publicly he was wary of appearing too choosy or too exalted to still dirty himself in the marketplace. In Britain he told the *Sunday Mirror*, 'Many Oscar-winners or, more likely, their greedy agents price themselves out of business. They grab as much loot as they can. The bubble then bursts and often they find themselves on the "resting" list, trying to live up to their golden image with taxes catching up with them fast. They have to put on an act that they are out of work because they don't like the scripts offered them. The result is a reputation for being difficult. I've instructed my agent not to ask for the world when film offers come in.'

Hackman's desire for a grand, heroic role was partially

satisfied when he accepted the lead in the Twentieth Century Fox production of *The Poseidon Adventure,* a trend-setting piece of escapist entertainment that would stimulate an audience appetite for disaster films.

Based on the novel by Paul Gallico, which in turn had been inspired by a voyage the author undertook in 1937 aboard the liner the Queen Mary, *The Poseidon Adventure* was lavish-scale hokum with a star-studded cast in jeopardy on the high seas. Hackman was cast as an abrasive minister, and explained his interest in the film this way to *Show* magazine:

'I read a script twice, then I leave it alone for a while. The change of character in a role is the challenge I look for. I was interested in *The Poseidon Adventure* as a project rather than [in] the character. I wanted the experience and the tradition of a major picture being shot in a major studio. I want to achieve some kind of a combination of honesty and theatricality. Honesty alone isn't enough for me. I think that becomes very boring. What I like is the fusing of a real moment with a theatrical flip. If you can convince people that what you are doing is real and it's also bigger than life, that's exciting.'

The Poseidon Adventure is set aboard a luxury liner on her final voyage from New York to Greece. The weather during the voyage is atrocious, the seas are mountainous, but the passengers are determined to celebrate New Year's Eve in traditional style. At the height of their festivities the ship is battered by a freak tidal wave and turned upside down. It remains afloat and the survivors inside struggle against time and appalling conditions to reach the surface. Hackman is the Reverend Frank Scott, a man with an ebullient personality who leads the motley collection of survivors to safety, cajoling and bullying them on to greater exertions with his forceful message that God loves winners. His passenger list includes Ernest Borgnine and Stella Stevens as a surly cop and his wife, Shelley Winters as a nice fat Jewish lady who was once (conveniently) a swimming champion, Roddy McDowall as the injured steward Acres, Red Buttons and Carol Lynley as a couple who find each other during the tragedy, etc., etc.

The film was produced by Irwin Allen and directed by Englishman Ronald Neame. Neame admitted that the film was an 'unpretentious cliff-hanger' that he likened to *Airport*, but this was not going to prevent him approaching the project with complete professionalism. Paul Gallico's novel had been faithfully adapted for the screen by Wendell Mayes, but Neame insisted on a revised script that at least injected a modicum of characterization into the all-action proceedings. By then, Mayes was at work elsewhere and thus Oscar winner Stirling Silliphant was hired to complete the task.

The five-million-dollar production was filmed in continuity with location work on board the *Queen Mary* at Long Beach and the interiors at the Fox studios in Hollywood. A twenty-six foot minature liner was constructed for scenes in which the ship appeared to turn over, but in human terms, Neame tried to utilize as little trickery as possible. Working amidst oil slicks, fire and water made *The Poseidon Adventure* a hazardous and uncomfortable production, but if the cast could be persuaded to undertake as much of the stunt work as the insurers would allow, Neame could guarantee a better experience for the audience.

In a question-and-answer session with film students Neame enthusiastically praised his cast:

'The principals were marvellous. When you've got ten of them like I had here and they had to go through the agony that this lot had to go through. . . . What they have to do by the end is swim two decks underwater. They literally have to swim underwater to escape the flooding. They have to go up a vertical shaft where water is pouring down on them all the time. They have to go through the engine room, which is on fire. They have to climb up as high as thirty-five feet on upside down iron gantries.'

Neame received examplary support from his cast, particularly Hackman. As an actor he has been known to find aspects of the filmmaking process boring; unable to concentrate on anything else but often unable to work. He finds the amount of time spent waiting around a waste and a strain. Thus he has been inclined to choose roles that place physical as well as mental demands upon him.

'I choose physical roles because they are more satisfactory,' he told *Photoplay*. 'It's not enough for me to sit around all day waiting for a dialogue scene. As a performer I enjoy convincing people of the reality of the roles I'm playing.

When the juices begin to flow and the adrenalin pours into your system there's a feeling of wanting to do the stunts so close-ups can be filmed and the audience knows *you* are up there on the screen. One of the toughest and most exciting physical film scenes I ever did was in *The Poseidon Adventure*. I dropped twenty-five feet into a tank of water surrounded by flames for my final scene. It was exciting.'

On *The Poseidon Adventure*, Neame recalled, 'We were fortunate in having Gene Hackman, who will do anything. That man wouldn't have a double under any circumstances. Ernie Borgnine is just as tough. He wanted to do everything himself. So, you've got those two for a start. The moment that two of them did it, the third one didn't want to be left out. I must say, though, I was very cunning. I said, "Now, we could use a double. But, of course, the camera will have to be on your back". "Oh no, no, no," they'd say. I did play a certain amount of trickery on them. I said, "If you do it yourself, then we can have close shots".'

Neame, then in his early sixties, further shamed his cast into action by performing some of the climbs and stunts himself prior to filming. In the finished picture Shelley Winters, who had been encouraged to gain weight for her role, really does swim underwater, whilst Red Buttons and Carol Lynley worked against their fear of heights to climb gantries, giant Christmas trees and the like. Referring to Miss Lynley's bravery under stress, Neame commented, 'When you see her when she got to the top of the tree, that was fear on her face. That was not acting there. She was absolutely petrified.'

Perhaps it is the sense of commitment to the film on the part of everyone involved that makes *The Poseidon Adventure* work so well. The characters are cardboard, the plot is ludicrous and yet it succeeds as enthralling popular entertainment. The decision of Neame and his cast to treat the project with the same respect as they would something with a more noble intent paid substantial dividends. It is estimated that *The Poseidon Adventure* earned $160 million worldwide, much to the surprise of producer Irwin Allen, who said, 'I didn't know whether the public would go for *The Poseidon Adventure*. We were very concerned that we might lose money on it. I'd like to say, "Yes, I figured out the psychology of it." But I hadn't. I just kinda stumbled onto it.'

[87]

Success breeds many imitators, and soon cinema screens everywhere were filled with stellar casts under threat from earthquakes, burning buildings, air disasters and even great white sharks. Having had time to reflect upon the ingredients of *The Poseidon Adventure* and *The Towering Inferno*, Allen told an interviewer in 1975, 'I think the appeal of the disaster films is the vicarious thrill the public get from seeing others in deep trouble. It's true, isn't it? We all look at a fire or a road accident or some tragedy. But you have to make your stars ordinary so the public can identify. It's no good making them brain surgeons because there aren't many brain surgeons.'

Hackman's character did not survive the traumas of *The Poseidon Adventure;* he is able to lead his modest flock to the promise of safety but must sacrifice himself to insure their ultimate survival. In an interview, Hackman described the character as 'somewhat rebellious, a very strong man. He is more like a Unitarian minister. A person who believes in the will of one's soul, making progress in life, as opposed to prayer. So it is with that garland around him that he proceeds to become a leader when the ship meets with disaster.' It is through the sheer brute force of conviction that Hackman dispels the dramatic cobwebs from his character. His inspirational, life-affirming effervescence takes the character by the scruff of the neck and instills flesh-and-blood reality into it, whilst his edgy compulsiveness about never giving up reflects similar personality traits to those of the dogged, obsessive 'Popeye' Doyle. The admiring *Time* critic wrote, 'Gene Hackman, who seems to have the lion's share of the bad lines, nevertheless acquits himself very nicely indeed. There is one scene in which he is required to pray to God, pleading with him and admonishing him, that Hackman, against all odds, manages to make believeable.'

Retaining a sense of detachment from his involvement in *The Poseidon Adventure*, Hackman observed a certain irony in being cast as a leader and saw this as a way of art imitating life. Interviewed by Gavin Cort during filming, he said, 'The film allows me a quality of leadership which is not only true in the role, but in my role in real life now because I have the responsibility of the picture on me. Although there are lots of stars, the picture kind of depends on whether you

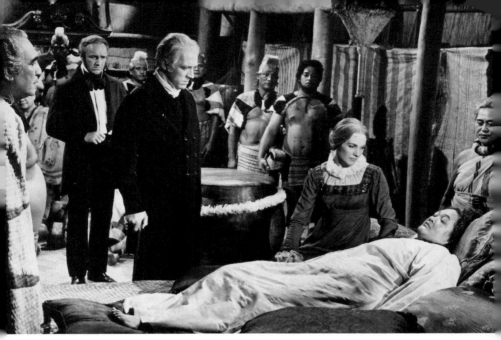

Hackman's first mainstream Hollywood movie role was in the 1966 adaptation of James Michener's novel *Hawaii*. In it he played the part of a missionary doctor (second from left), alongside Max Von Sydow and Julie Andrews. *(Kobal)*

Playing Clyde Barrow's brother, Buck, in *Bonnie and Clyde* brought Hackman his first Oscar nomination and earned him great critical acclaim. *(Warner-Pathe/Kobal).*

Marooned (1969) saw Hackman as astronaut Buzz Lloyd, adrift in space. The film had trouble competing with the real-life drama of the Apollo moon landing, as well as the far superior *2001*. *(Kobal)*

Hackman was Robert Redford's own choice to play the part of the American Olympic ski-team coach in *Downhill Racer.(Paramount Pictures/Kobal)*

Hackman won his second Oscar nomination in 1971 – again for Best Supporting Actor – this time alongside Melvyn Douglas in the family drama *I Never Sang for my Father.* (Kobal)

Jimmy 'Popeye' Doyle gets his man at the end of the most famous chase in movie history; and, at last, Hackman gets his Oscar – *The French Connection* (1971). *(Kobal)*

Hackman's Rev. Frank Scott has his hands full helping Shelley Winters in *The Poseidon Adventure* (1972). *(Kobal)*

Waiting for another free ride: Hackman as Max, the down-and-out with high hopes for the future, in *Scarecrow* (1973). *(Kobal)*

For Francis Ford Coppola who scripted and directed *The Conversation,* Hackman was ideal for the part of the surveillance expert 'because he's so ordinary, so unexceptional in appearance'. *(Kobal)*

The 1975 Western *Bite the Bullet* was, in Hackman's own words, 'the toughest film I ever worked on'. *(Columbia Pictures/Kobal)*

like my character. I've always played roles where I didn't have the responsibility of the picture, or anything else, other than doing my part as well as possible and going on to the next job. So the role is following life in a funny kind of a way.'

Life for Hackman was now considerably altered since his Oscar win. Personally he faced a whole new scope of demands upon his time; there were interviews to give, scripts to consider and career moves to contemplate. Before it had been a question of finding gainful employment. Now, he had a position and status to consider. Professionally, the whole business side of working for the cinema became more complex and presented a real dilemma for his future.

Hackman's best film work involves a very detailed and convincing depiction of a character within whose personality his own is completely submerged while he is playing that role. Stardom and the star system means that there are actors whose own personalities are what draw the regular paying public; actors who have developed a rapport with them and a mutual affection based on certain qualities that they project time after time and the public comes to expect. Hackman is perfectly able to realize the distinctions that people make and accepts that John Wayne or Cary Grant were movie stars in the true sense of that term, while he himself was a character actor first and a star second.

The problem of how to reconcile the professional demands of both labels was to dominate Hackman's career over the next few years. If he chose only the most demanding, most testing character roles he could win the respect of his peers and critics but alienate the public and forfeit his position as a bankable leading man. Alternatively, if he were to strait jacket his talents into a succession of conventional star roles, relying on his 'star' presence alone for their validity, then he could quickly grow bored with the whole business and lose his self-respect.

Already he was reacting against any attempt to pin him down and pour him into any rigidly defined mould, telling one questioner, 'I don't particularly want to go on playing violent parts. I don't want to be the Bogart of the Seventies. I wouldn't mind playing Bogart parts, of course. He was a very gentle man, you know, but had that great power of

[89]

implied violence. What I want to do is something different. Fewer films are being made all the time and an actor doesn't find all that many roles he is anxious to play. A lot of the parts are just plain dull and talky. You make your own drama by the kind of films you choose to make.'

For the immediate future he had been offered the script of *Scarecrow*, and within it there was a character that he *was* anxious to play. In the longer term he held some specific aspirations; he wanted to direct and had a vague notion of one day returning to the stage. However, the most important thing was to further explore the variety of substantial screen characters now being offered to him. As an actor he prefers to work on instinct, capturing the truth of a character through spontaneity:

'Generally to me it's kind of challenging to come on a set unprepared. I know there'd be some directors who'd go through the roof, you know. But I just like to work that way, unprepared. Knowing what the *character* is, but being like a sponge in some way. Being able to come on and meet your co-star or whoever you're gonna work with – maybe for the first time – as you do sometimes in film. Or the second or third time. Certainly not knowing a hell of a iot about the director, and how he works, unless you've worked with him before. And starting to build from there.'

Now that Hackman had the clout of a fully-fledged star, his ideal director would be someone who allowed him a comfortable space in which to make his contribution to the enterprise of putting a script on screen. He could work with someone whose idea of directing meant telling actors what to do, but he preferred not to and could work against someone placing unnecessary barriers on his freedom of expression.

In 1986 he told *American Premiere*, 'I rarely discuss the character with the director. Usually by the time they've made a firm offer for me to do the film, they feel that I can play it and they know what they're getting into and so do I. What I generally discuss with the director is if I have thoughts of how to make either my role or the film better. And that even isn't in great depth. I like to get a sense of who he is. I'm generally very concerned how a director operates, whether he gives the actor a lot of freedom or he's very rigid, or whatever. I can work either way, but with certain kinds of directors you need to have some kind of understanding before the film so that it's all pretty straight-forward about what you're going to do.'

Of course, Hackman now had the authority to ensure that any director would have to take account of his feelings and his working methods. That was one of the benefits of stardom. Other aspects of being a silver-screen luminary were less pleasing. People expected him to attend industry functions and socialize with the Hollywood set, yet he had always been someone who cherished his own privacy and was ill-at-ease attending parties where the talk circulated endlessly around the same topics of who was 'hot', who was 'cold' and how much a picture grossed during its opening weekend in Chicago. 'I guess I'm somewhat detached from the so-called glamour of the movies,' he has said. 'I'm philosophical about pictures. I do my best and let it go from there.'

He is not a gregarious man and his few close acquaintances within the entertainment industry, like Dustin Hoffman, Robert Duvall and Mel Tormé, had enjoyed his unswerving friendship and loyalty long years before the overdue triumphs of *The French Connection*. Now, however, everyone wanted to be his friend and bask in the reflected glory. He told Victor Davis of the *Daily Express*, 'You keep a little of yourself in reserve so that you are not hurt too much. The first thing about stardom is that you become a little paranoid: do people want you for yourself or for what they can get from you? Friends I had not seen for years came popping out of the walls waving movie scripts. I loaned an actor $3,000 so that the bank would not foreclose on his mortgage. He was supposed to repay in thirty days. That was three years ago. I lost a good friend who came on to the *Poseidon* set and said, "I need $8,000 right away." I said, "Don't we all!" '

Although he was at the very centre of what was happening, Hackman retained a clinical fascination with the consequences of stardom, pondering about both the differences in himself and the adjustments other people made to his newfound status. Interviewed on the set of *The Poseidon Adventure*, he was able to unburden himself of many of those observations, telling Gavin Cort, 'I think that the area that interests me more than any other right now is that of the

[91]

whole metamorphosis that has happened to me in the last six months. The change in people's attitudes, the advancements and the quality of the scripts now being offered to me. It's difficult to handle for a number of reasons. People change, but I have changed also. People feel they have to defer to you, which is somewhat uncomfortable. You find yourself with more juice, with more power, the handling of which is always a fascinating process. You use power for a number of reasons, to get what you want, to feed your ego, or to become a prick or whatever. It's a dangerous situation in some ways because one never knows quite how to read what is happening with you.'

The most immediate and apparent danger to Hackman was the effect of his 'power' on his home life. Months of hard work, meeting other people's demands and neglecting his wife and three children, brought the inevitable result – he was separated from Faye. Their estrangement did not last long and a happy reconciliation soon ensued, but the mere fact that it had happened was an early warning of the price Hackman might have to pay for the double-edged sword of stardom.

The most fascinating aspect of many actors' life stories is their early days, struggling against adversity and hardship to secure a lucky break and advance on the way to the top. The ensuing years are lived in the public eye; the major stars are, to an extent, public property; their every action public knowledge and thus fairly familiar reading. Hackman is almost the complete opposite. He had been around for a long time, had suffered the expected privations and setbacks, but his progression, from off-Broadway to Broadway to films to Supporting Actor Oscar nominations to stardom, is hardly remarkable. What is fascinating is what happened to him after that. Prodigious cinema historian David Shipman has judged his career thus: 'We lost an excellent character actor, but clearly didn't gain a star.' Others might disagree, but the tensions between the pressures of stardom and the need for integrity through his work would take their toll on him over the coming years.

Meanwhile, as 1972 slipped into 1973, Hackman had reached a peak in which every aspect of his life was in harmony and he was both busily employed and happy. He was reconciled with Faye and had overcome the hurdle of how to follow a major success like *The French Connection* by making an even more popular film in *The Poseidon Adventure*. The latter was the most popular film of the year in America and went on to join the list of all-time box-office champions, securing an incredible eight Oscar nominations. Further awards also came his way and the British Academy voted him the Best Actor of 1972 for his performances in both *The French Connection* and *The Poseidon Adventure*. As if that weren't enough, he also made his first appearance in the list of top box-office stars, coming in at a sensational third place behind George C. Scott and top attraction Clint Eastwood.

If the combination of work, acclaim and awards didn't offer him security and reassurance about his right to be considered a 'star', then nothing would.

Chapter Seven

At the Oscar ceremony in March 1973 Hackman could relax and savour the evening for its entertainment value. One year on from his own victory night, an entirely different collection of people were experiencing their personal anxieties whilst Hackman's sole responsibility was to announce the Best Actress winner along with his co-presenter Raquel Welch.

That particular year's festivities made headlines across the world for the acceptance speech given on behalf of the Best Actor recipient. Liv Ullmann and Roger Moore had opened the envelope to reveal Marlon Brando the winner for his performance in *The Godfather*. Brando himself was not present to accept his award, but his representative was there, and thus Sacheen Littlefeather made Oscar history when she came to the podium, announced herself as the President of the National Native American Affirmative Image Committee, and explained that Brando was refusing his award as a public gesture of protest against the treatment of American Indians by the film industry.

Miss Littlefeather's speech was greeted with some booing, a smattering of applause, and from most of the audience a stunned and disbelieving silence. Host Rock Hudson attempted to move the proceedings along, commenting that 'often to be eloquent is to be silent'. He introduced Hackman and Raquel Welch, who muttered her hope that none of the Best Actress nominees had a cause. The previous year Liza Minnelli had presented Hackman with his Oscar and now he returned the favour by announcing that Minnelli, for her performance in *Cabaret*, had been voted Best Actress of 1972. *Cabaret* was the evening's major winner, and *The Poseidon Adventure*'s eight nominations resulted in just one victory, for Al Kasha and Joel Hirschhorn as the composer and lyricist of the year's Best Song, 'The Morning After'. The film did, however, receive a Special Achievement Award for its visual effects.

Hackman's 'star' status was now bringing him the luxury of an exciting array of scripts that he was determined to make the most of, although he still harboured a residual qualm that his fame could be shortlived. A sequel to *The French Connection* now seemed inevitable, but the delays in finalizing a suitable storyline left him free to concentrate on other pursuits. His comfortable wealth even allowed him to enlist as a Broadway 'angel' when his friend Dustin Hoffman decided to make his debut as a stage director in 1974. The revue, *All Over Town* by Murray Shisgal, featured over sixteen major characters and encountered a good deal of indifference when Hoffman tried to raise the necessary finance for its staging. Exasperated by the continual round of rejections, Hoffman decided to acquire the money privately, and it has been estimated that in partnership with Hackman he sank some $300,000 into the show. Meryl Streep was among those who auditioned for the rare opportunity of being directed by Hoffman, and the final cast list was headed by Cleavon Little, Barnard Hughes and Zane Lasky. Unfortunately, their reviews were mixed and the production was only a limited success. However, Hackman's mere involvement in the enterprise illustrates his loyalty to an old friendship and the way in which he was free to take chances in whatever way he chose.

Hackman's next two films show him at his most daring as a professional gambler, momentarily uniting the integrity of his character acting with the larger-than-life demands of a star presence. *Scarecrow* and *The Conversation* represent some of the best work that he has achieved on screen.

Hackman has described *Scarecrow* as 'a combination of *Of Mice and Men* and *Midnight Cowboy*', and his character Max remains one of his favourites. A first script by playwright Gary Michael White, *Scarecrow* was brought to the attention of director Jerry Schatzberg, who was immediately impressed and willing to consider it as his next project. A successful fashion photographer, Schatzberg had turned director for *Puzzle of a Downfall Child* (1970), starring his one-time fiancée Faye Dunaway, and *Panic in Needle Park* (1971) with Al Pacino. His work had received serious attention and acclaim in Europe, but had failed to elicit any noticeable support from the paying public in his home territory of America. *Scarecrow* was a script that he wanted to film, but only if the studio, Warner Brothers, would guarantee him the casting that he felt most appropriate. To his surprise they consented to his choices without hesitation: 'I was expecting them to want totally wrong actors, but I was told: Gene Hackman and Al Pacino. They couldn't be more right for the picture.' The fact that Hackman had recently won the Oscar and that Pacino was the rising young star of *The Godfather* was probably more of an influence on the 'bankability' of the project than their undoubted suitability for the roles in question.

In the film, Hackman and Pacino affectionately play two no-hopers, gentlemen of the road, drifting and hitchhiking their way along the pothole-strewn highways of life. In preparation for filming they spent a week together, dressed in Salvation Army castoffs, working the streets of San Francisco seeking handouts from passers-by and getting the feel of their characters. Hackman was particularly enthusiastic about playing Max, declaring that the film was 'kind of a marvellous complement of a comedy and a look at life through the eyes of a couple of bums. It's a very exciting role for me, it deals with comedic elements and they are always a challenge.'

Scarecrow begins with some deliciously played and economically staged interplay between the two men. Max has just spent six years in San Quentin on an assault charge and is on his way to Pittsburgh, where he plans to open a car-wash with the money that he has saved from his prison wages. First, he wants to pay a visit to his only relative, a sister in Denver.

Lion (short for Lionel) has been away at sea for a roughly equivalent period, to escape the demands of a job with regular hours and the responsibility of providing for a wife that he abandoned when she was pregnant with their child.

The two men first meet on a deserted, windswept highway in northern California, each trying to secure a free ride to his destination. As they chase the same cars, warily shuffle from one side of the road to the other, shyly acknowledge each other's presence and begin to laugh at their mutual absurdity of non-communication, a tentative friend-

[96]

ship is broached and then sealed when Max offers Lion his last light.

As the two men travel together their characters are exposed and moulded by their unexpected closeness to a fellow human being. Max is a gruff, lusty, hot-tempered brawler who keeps the world at bay with two ever-ready fists and layers of camouflage-like clothing to prevent his detection as an amiable and even likeable fellow. 'I'm the meanest son-of-a-bitch alive,' he warns Lion, but his boast is more of an idle threat than a statement of fact. All he needs is someone who cares, and Lion's attachment to him begins to smooth down his anti-social rough edges.

Lion is a man who will go to any lengths to avoid unpleasantness and enjoy a quiet, trouble-free life. He likens himself to a scarecrow, arguing that crows don't fly off because they are frightened by the scarecrows but because they are amused by them. Anything harmful can be avoided by not acknowledging that it exists, making light of a situation or simply running away. Max warns him that his inability to deal with reality may have dangerous consequences, and even Lion grows to accept that taking responsibility for his actions is an essential element of living in the real world.

As the drama unfolds, Max offers Lion a full partnership in his business plan. Still careful to moderate this uncharacteristic display of generosity, Max threatens, 'We're gonna have a fair car-wash business or I'm gonna break your neck.'

Travelling by truck, railway wagon and under their own steam, the foot-sore and road-weary duo arrive in Denver and visit Max's sister Coley. Together with Coley's friend Frenchy, the quartet hit the town for a reunion celebration, and dreams are dreamt and voiced of what a wonderful future lies in store. The drunken celebration turns sour when Max starts a fight and both he and Lion are arrested and sentenced to thirty days on the county work farm. Lion blames Max for their predicament and the two erstwhile friends lapse into surly silence and hostility once they are behind bars.

In jail, Lion is befriended by another inmate, Jack Riley, who obtains an easy job for him and ensures that the less amicable Max is banished to the pig farm. One night Riley takes Lion aside and tries to make sexual advances to him, beating him senseless when he is rejected. Riley is consequently sent to the pig farm, where Max brutally avenges the assault on his friend.

Released from prison, the two men head for Detroit, where Lion phones his wife Annie. Annie viciously resents his intrusion into her life and lies to him that their child was stillborn. Lion manages to conceal his grief and tells Max that he is the father of a boy and that Annie was remarried. However, the combined effects of his prison experiences and his wife's vitriol take their toll and Lion later breaks down and goes into a catatonic trance. He is rushed to hospital, where Max is informed that it will take a lot of time and attention to bring Lion back to normality. Max decides to temporarily forego the car-wash business and use his savings to help Lion. He further determines to investigate the truth of Annie's claim, and still promises Lion that someday they will be business partners.

Scarecrow is ultimately a rather uneven film, filled with outstanding isolated moments but also hampered by a directorial hand that tends towards the overemphatic. Vilmos Zsigmond's photography conjures up some strikingly scenic images of an often unfamiliar American landscape, and the characters do engage the viewer's sympathies via their pathetic optimism and the changes they go through, the curmudgeonly Max realizing that he cannot live without some form of companionship and Lion being forced to face reality head-on.

However, the film is saddled with an underlying artificiality as it evokes the dramatic antecedents of *Midnight Cowboy* and *Of Mice and Men* that Hackman had previously cited. This self-conscious derivativeness is less of an obstacle than it might have been, thanks to the calibre of the two central performances and, in particular, Hackman's interpretation of Max. A dog-eared, down-at-heel, growling bear with the proverbial heart of gold, Max represents Hackman at his most dedicated and craftsmanlike; it is a case where the actor has immersed himself so completely in the fine detail and attitudes of his character that the two become one.

An example of Hackman's excellence and the film's periodic deployment of an insightful shorthand comes when the two men have left prison and reaffirmed their friendship.

Max's life has been lived as a solitary struggle against the world, and his habit of dressing himself in several layers of clothing is symbolic of his defensiveness and lack of involvement. Now, undoubtedly for the first time, he has thrown off his defences and committed himself to someone. As an equally symbolic gesture of this abandonment of defences, the two men enter a crowded bar, Lion puts 'The Stripper' on the jukebox and Max begins a striptease as a glorious and hilarious means of expressing his joy in a newfound freedom. Here is one instance where the additional component of humour makes the film's constant use of symbolism and metaphor easier to stomach.

In reviewing *Scarecrow*, Jay Cocks of *Time* voiced his dissatisfaction with the film's inconsistency:

'Scruffy and bespectacled, Hackman has a good time hunkering down into his characterization of the snarling Max. But he gets in so far that no other actor can reach him. Pacino's characterization of Lion therefore remains unresolved. Hackman remains too self-absorbed. The tension between the two actors is tangible and arresting, at least initially, but it eventually hobbles what small humanity the movie might have had.'

Scarecrow never totally wins over an audience because there is just a lingering suspicion of phoniness – that we are witnessing a deliberately staged acting exercise that lacks the ease and spontaneity to overcome its drawbacks. When Schatzberg eschews the portentous and the slightly pretentious we are presented with a visually arresting, well-acted parable about friendship and the thin dividing line between sanity and insanity, as well as an oblique commentary on aspects of contemporary America which is no small achievement in itself. Hackman was pleased with the final result and had actually enjoyed the filming. Years later he told interviewer Susan Royal, 'It was fun. You know, the film itself was fun to work on because we shot it in absolute continuity, which is rare. We started in Bakersfield outside in that opening scene and went to Reno, Reno to Denver and then Detroit. But we had absolute continuity. And it just worked so well. A lot of people come up to me still and say it was one of their favourite films.'

An added bonus for Hackman in this instance was that *Scarecrow* employed his brother Richard as his stand-in and the younger Hackman also appeared in the role of a corrupt prison guard. All told, *Scarecrow* proved one of the most enjoyable and fruitful working experiences of his 'star' years.

As with Schatzberg's earlier work, *Scarecrow* was welcomed with greater enthusiasm in Europe than in America. When it was shown at the 1973 Cannes Film Festival it was awarded the prestigious Palme d'Or as the best film, a distinction shared with Alan Bridges' *The Hireling*. As a mark of the quality of his work at this time, Hackman was seen again at the 1974 Cannes Film Festival in *The Conversation* and that too received the Palme d'Or, making a unique double achievement.

The Conversation was the brainchild of writer-director Francis Ford Coppola, who began working on the script in 1966 after the release of his film *You're a Big Boy Now*. After filming *Finian's Rainbow* he had resolved only to make films derived from his own original stories, and by 1969 he had completed *The Rain People* and the first draft of *The Conversation*. The central figure in the film is a coolly detached surveillance expert who gradually develops a conscience about the consequences of his work.

In publicity material for the finished film Coppola recollected, 'I don't remember how I first became interested in the subject matter, but right from the beginning I wanted to make a film about *privacy*; using the motif of eavesdropping and wiretapping, and centring on the personal and psychological life of the eavesdropper rather than his victims. It was to be a modern horror film, with a construction based on repetition rather than exposition, like a piece of music. And it would expose a tacky, subterranean world of wiretappers: their vanities and ethics; the conventions that they attend; the magazines they read; and the women they value. Ultimately, I wanted the film to come to a moral and humanistic conclusion. As I think about it now it's done, I realize that I wasn't making a film about *privacy*, as I had set out to do, but rather, once again, a film about *responsibility*, as was *The Rain People*.'

Interviewed during the production of *The Conversation*, one of his finest films, Coppola commented on his choice of Hackman and offered more specific details of his plot, telling *Sight and Sound*, 'He's ideal because he's so ordinary, so unexceptional in appearance. The man he plays is in his forties, and has been doing this strange job for years. We begin the picture with an apparently harmless conversation between a young couple in a San Francisco Park. The Hackman character records them, without really knowing why. Gradually, he begins to realize that the couple will be murdered. Their imminent death is due to him, and yet he takes orders from the head of an impersonal corporation, a man of enormous power. During the picture we see the conversation over and over again, assuming different meanings in Hackman's memory. At first it seems a scene of sunny blandness, and then you begin to see that even though the couple are talking about nothing but shopping *they're* very frightened.'

In *The Conversation*, Hackman is Harry Caul, 'the best "bugger" on the West coast'. As a character he shares some interesting traits with 'Popeye' Doyle. Both men are obsessively dedicated to their work to the exclusion of any kind of private life, but whilst Doyle's neuroses are delineated through his brutal manner and violent methods, Caul is all fastidious outward calm concealing inner turmoil.

Coppola utilizes Hackman's 'ordinariness' to devastating effect and Caul is a spectacularly unmemorable face in the crowd, a colourless, bespectacled nonentity shambling around the periphery of life in a drab gray raincoat. It is Hackman's skill that draws us into the man's world and makes us care about the fate of a very anti-heroic 'victim'.

The film is both a complex thriller and a painstakingly detailed close-up of Caul. At the beginning, Caul and his team are at work, unobtrusively gathering the words and sounds that will be re-constructed into a lunchtime conversation that is taking place between a young couple, Mark (Frederic Forrest) and Ann (Cindy Williams).

When Caul returns to his spartanly furnished apartment a neighbour wishes him a happy birthday. Caul is 44, lives alone and zealously protects his own privacy whilst indiscriminately hiring out his services to invade other people's. Yet something about this conversation between the young man and woman penetrates his defences and chips away at the sense of detachment that is crucial to his peace of mind. As the multiple layers of the conversation are played together to give a clearer enunciation to the words, layers of

[101]

Caul's personality are stripped off to expose his soul. We learn that he trusts no one, unable even to confide in his mistress, who knows only that he is a freelance musician, that prying questions are unwelcome and that she could bet her life on the rent being paid regularly on the same date each month.

Caul is under contract to deliver his recording to the director of a large corporation from whom he will receive his fee of $15,000. The arrangement is for a personal delivery, so when he is met by an assistant, Martin Strett (Harrison Ford), he refuses to hand over the tapes. Whilst in the building he sees the young couple in a lift and grows more curious about the affair. Endlessly running and re-running the tapes, he latches onto tantalizing hints of something amiss, some kind of conspiracy being planned, and can clearly hear Mark say, 'He'd kill us if he got the chance.'

Able only to express his fears through the most impersonal of contacts, Caul goes to confession for the first time in three months. He confides that two young people might be hurt because of his work, although he still cannot accept responsibility for what happens after his task is completed.

At a surveillance convention we learn that Caul is a highly respected man with a spotless reputation among his peers. More importantly, we discover Caul's involvement in a previous scandal when three people were murdered. 'I just turned in the tapes,' is his gruff comment, but he is clearly shaken by the parallels with his current job and is outraged to discover that his ebullient rival Bernie Moran (Allen Garfield) has used a give-away pen to record his conversation.

Caul has now teased out certain information from the tapes regarding a crucial appointment on a specific date in Room 773 of the Jack Tar Hotel. The stirrings of conscience begin to pervade his once rigid objectivity and his immediate instinct is to destroy the tapes. To prevent this eventuality Strett has the tapes stolen, although Caul is still to be paid and is offered a personal meeting with the company director (an unbilled Robert Duvall).

Caul is paid off and ostensibly his work is finished, but he remains haunted by certain sections of dialogue on the tapes. He continues to torment himself by booking into a room at the Jack Tar Hotel adjacent to 773. He overhears a violent argument and a struggle and sees a bloody figure through the frosted glass of a terrace window. His worst nightmare has become reality and he attempts to blot out the moment by closing the curtains, switching on the television, covering his eyes and lapsing into unconsciousness. Later, he summons up the courage to investigate what has happened. He breaks into the room, where peace reigns supreme; there is no sign of a struggle, everything is in place. Then he flushes the toilet and the bowl fills and overflows with blood.

Desperately trying to intervene in what he concludes has transpired, Caul seeks out the director. At the company offices he is met by an unexpected scene: Mark and Ann in a crush of reporters questioning her about the sudden and tragic death of her father – the director. Later, Strett telephones Caul and tells him not to get involved and threatens that they will be closely observing his actions. Caul has now become the victim of his own profession and frenziedly demolishes his apartment down to the plaster and floorboards, vainly searching for the devices that were his stock in trade. Confused, guilty and betrayed, he sits in his gutted apartment, plaintively playing a saxophone solo.

The Conversation was Coppola's first film after the massively popular, Oscar-winning *The Godfather*, and as such would have been guaranteed an eager reception from the critics. However, the film gained an even more immediate fascination and timely relevance when it was released as the full extent of the Watergate scandal was haemorrhaging out across America. Coppola felt, though, that the coincidental revelations about the break-in and cover-up may actually have deflected attention from what he considered to be the theme of responsibility central to his film.

'I had been terrified by the whole Orwellian dimension of electronic spying and the invasion of privacy when I started *The Conversation*,' he told *Sight and Sound*. 'I realized that a bugging expert was a special breed of man, not just a private eye playing with gadgets, and I thought it would be fascinating to get inside the mind and experience of such a man. It's just a curious, not a prescient, coincidence that the picture should finally surface, so to speak, at the same time as the Watergate affair.'

The Watergate element neither enhances nor diminishes

The Conversation's position as one of the key films of the 1970s. What it does do is underline the validity of Coppola's concerns over personal responsibility, individual guilt and contemporary alienation. Aside from Hackman, Harrison Ford and Robert Duvall the excellent cast also includes John Cazale as Caul's one-time assistant and Teri Garr as his mistress. However, it is Hackman's angst-torn loner who carries the film. A cautious, self-protective, blank-faced figure torturously unravelling at the edges and seeking salvation, his confusion, guilt, betrayal and final paranoia are skilfully conveyed by Hackman in a performance that moves with superb control from clinical detachment to passionate turmoil. It is one of the most powerful and haunting performances in the American cinema of the 1970s and arguably Hackman's finest hour.

On its release, *The Conversation* received the kind of critical plaudits that it deserved, with *Newsweek* welcoming it as being 'brilliantly original in its basic style and mood and prophetically American in its vision of a monitored society.' The *Hollywood Reporter* spoke of 'a film of triumphant style and overwhelming passion, white hot with American anguish', and *Time* commented, 'For Hackman, Caul presents a substantial challenge. It is a largely interiorized role in contrast to the action parts in which he has recently built his career. He responds with the most substantial screen performance he has done.'

Aside from its Cannes prize, *The Conversation* received two British Academy Awards, three Oscar nominations, including one for Best Picture, and was honoured three times by the National Board of Review, who chose it as their Best Film of 1974, naming Coppola as Best Director and Hackman as Best Actor. Surprisingly, Hackman did not receive an Oscar nomination, a glaring oversight on the part of the Academy. However, he could probably afford to be philosophical about the slight; there are few performers whose careers have progressed so satisfactorily after winning an Oscar. The expected pattern is one of anti-climax. With the immense box-office success of *The Poseidon Adventure* and a brace of distinguished performances in *Scarecrow* and *The Conversation* it appeared that Hackman could only go from strength to strength.

Chapter Eight

Between 1973 and 1976, Hackman was one of the world's most prolific stars; an acting workhorse who rarely seemed to pause for breath between assignments and who apparently thrived on the self-inflicted pressures of a crowded schedule. People persisted in making him offers that were too good to refuse; either the script was well written or his character presented a specific challenge or the director was a man with whom actors were queuing up to work. Yet, by late 1974, even Hackman began to see the drawbacks of his non-stop routine.

He told Bart Mills of *The Guardian*, 'I've been doing too many films. I'm trying to think who I'd go and see at the pictures four or five times a year. I can't think of one. Maybe I'm a special case – I don't know. I don't think so. I need six months rest. You start drying up after a while. It all seems like the same movie. You can't bring something new to each character – at least I can't. You find yourself slipping through things, and you're lulled into a false sense of security. It takes a lot of discipline to overcome that.'

In interviews, Hackman complained that he enjoyed precious few moments with his family and rarely found the time to stop and take stock of his career or even enjoy the fruits of his prodigious labours. The remedy was surely in his own hands; he could choose to be more discriminating and work less, yet he stayed on the treadmill. 'I worry that one morning the whole bubble will simply disappear,' he candidly confessed. ' "Gene who?" Yes, I'm a worrier. Introspective? I tend to be introspective to the point where it's disturbing. Mind you, I wouldn't use the word introspective. Morose or withdrawn is how I would have put it. Introspective sounds as though I'm intellectualizing it.'

Any career worries about 'overexposure' were, for the

moment, unfounded; the tempting scripts and generous paycheques just kept dutifully rolling in and Hackman was able to work with some of the most highly regarded contemporary directors. After Francis Ford Coppola and *The Conversation* it was the Swedish director Jan Troell and *Zandy's Bride*.

Troell was best known in America for his work on *The Emigrants* (1971) and its sequel *The New Land*. With a combined running time of over five hours, the two films covered the life of peasant farmer Max Von Sydow and his wife Liv Ullmann as they decide to leave 19th century Sweden, emigrate to America and settle in Minnesota. *The Emigrants* achieved the rare feat for a foreign-language production of being nominated for the Best Picture Oscar, and Troell also received nominations for his direction and co-writing of the script. Although Troell did not win in any of the categories, Hollywood's acclaim for his work brought him to the attention of producer Harvey Matofsky, who considered him an appropriate choice to direct *Zandy's Bride*, the story of a reclusive pioneering man and his mail-order bride, set in California during the 1870s.

Zandy's Bride was based on a novel, *The Stranger*, by Lillian Bos Ross, that had first been published in 1942. The film rights became the property of a literary agent who later bequeathed them to Charles Feldman, who in turn bequeathed them to the actress Capucine. Matofsky met Capucine at the home of director Federico Fellini and purchased the property outright: 'That way it gave me complete autonomy to make the film as I had seen fit.'

Filmed within a budget of around $3,500,000 on locations at Big Sur and Carmel in California, *Zandy's Bride* was completed on a three-month schedule during the summer of 1973. Industry insiders had considered the project risky, citing Troell's inexperience with an English-language production and the difficulties of filming a period piece in contemporary California as reasons for their unease. Troell, however, was a thoroughly professional director and he did have the distinct advantage of fellow Swede Liv Ullmann as his leading lady.

Hackman described *Zandy's Bride* as a 'fresh, original love story – a left-handed romance' and told Pete Hammill of *Film Comment* his reasons for accepting the film: 'I thought the relationship was not necessarily unique, but it was something that was unique for *me*, as an actor. I think those characters have been seen before – not in that guise, not in that locale, not in all those circumstances – but they are not *really* that different. What attracted me was that *I* had never played that kind of relationship. I'd played the same kind of one-sided characters before, but never with the added thing of having some romance, and then being able to *turn* at the end. Or at least *change* somewhat, which is always kind of exciting for an actor: to be able to make some changes in the character, or let the audience *see* some change, whether the character knows about it or not.'

Elsewhere, Hackman described his character, Zandy Allan, as 'stubborn, egocentric, a mountain man and a real loner. He sends for a mail-order bride simply because he considers the women in the territory not worthy of his manliness. He has no idea how to relate to a woman, no sense of tenderness, and thinks she has no mind of her own, only a body to give him sons. He falls in love with her when he learns she's more than he bargained for. Actually he's quite taken with her right from the beginning, but he's such a cut-off kind of guy he can't even admit it to himself.'

Zandy's Bride, which was never released in Britain, was not a popular success and critical reaction was, at best, lukewarm. The central situation of a battle of wills between the rugged, brutish Zandy and the proudly independent Hannah Lund (Ullmann) offers the possibility of some combination of a role-reversal *Taming of the Shrew* and a backwoods version of a Spencer Tracy-Katharine Hepburn tussle. Zandy is thoughtless and crude in his initial reaction to Hannah's presence, treating her as little more than a slave and yet expecting her devoted love in return. Eventually she insists that her love has to be won through respect and a little compassion.

However, somewhere along the way the plot runs off the rails, cluttering up a simple story of love against the odds with irrelevant incidents involving cattle thieves, blood poisoning and another woman, before the anticipated climax of a sentimental reunion. The *Hollywood Reporter*'s reviewer praised the first quarter of the film for being 'subtle, humorous and even breathtaking in the way [it] brings frontier America to life. . . . [The couple's] initial battles and subsequent love story are the movie's center, and Troell brings it to the screen in a detailed, quiet style reminiscent of John Ford's loving sense of the interplay between pioneer men and women.' The film was generally lauded for its evocation of the pioneer lifestyle and for the performances, but was otherwise dismissed as rather dull, humourless and overlong.

During the production of *Zandy's Bride* there were uncharacteristic rumours of disharmony and dissent between Hackman and Jan Troell. Hackman's reputation for reliable professionalism is undisputed in the industry, hence the surprise at reports of his irritability and outbursts of temper on the *Zandy's Bride* set. Co-star Eileen Heckart, who played Hackman's mother, told reporters of angry exchanges between the men, saying that Troell had been upset when Hackman killed a snake on location. She also suggested that the actor was bringing his personal problems to work with him. Certainly Hackman was under a number of pressures and was perhaps exercising his 'star muscle' to let off steam. In interviews, although doggedly diplomatic, Hackman was evidently unhappy over his relationship with the director, claiming that there had been difficulties for Troell in his command of English and a lack of understanding regarding the particular idiom of a period picture. 'We finally got to a place where we worked quite well together, where we kind of respected each other,' Hackman has said. 'But I also think, besides the language problem, he is the kind of director who has a *tunnelized* vision of what it is that he wants; and when you are working in someone else's country, it's sometimes hard to communicate that. But most of the great directors, most of the *good* directors, have that kind of singlemindedness, that kind of purposeful attack on things. All in all, I think he's very talented.'

Troell's English-language films, particularly the disastrous remake of *Hurricane* (1979), have fallen way below the standards of his Swedish work. In an interview with *Rolling Stone* he described *Zandy's Bride* as a 'very useful experience', but it must have proved far from satisfactory, sounding merely frustrating from the tales that he had to recount. 'The first problem with me on *Zandy's Bride*', he said, 'was that I wasn't allowed to operate the camera (because of the

[108]

US union rules). That makes a lot of difference to me because I feel very awkward sitting beside the camera. I had thought that working with a big crew would be more of a problem than it was. The crew members are so professional that you don't notice the big organization. Almost *too* professional, because having a good assistant director who prepared every shot sometimes made me too passive at the beginning. I even fell asleep once. It's not in the final movie, but in one scene Gene Hackman had to knock a stunt man off a horse with a pitch fork or something, and the stunt man was tied with wires so that he would fall off when he came to a certain point. I was drowsing, thinking a director can add nothing to such a scene. I came to my senses when I heard someone say, "We're just waiting for your 'Action!' "'

Any disappointment that Hackman may have suffered over the production and final outcome of *Zandy's Bride* was short-lived, as he was quickly back at work, this time on something completely different.

If his appetite for filmmaking was so insatiable that he was afraid of taking a break, he could at least relax by appearing in a production where he did not carry the responsibility of being the above-the-title star. Hence, the offer of a comic cameo in Mel Brooks's *Young Frankenstein* was an ideal restorative.

Having exploded a few cowboy myths in *Blazing Saddles*, Brooks had swiftly set about making an affectionate parody of the classic 1930s series of Universal *Frankenstein* films in which Colin Clive had played the misunderstood doctor and Boris Karloff his creation. In Brooks's version, co-written with Gene Wilder, Wilder plays the original doctor's grandson, who returns to Transylvania to continue the family legacy of trying to re-animate dead tissue.

Hackman appears, with uproarious effect, as a blind hermit called Harold in the film's funniest sequence. Frankenstein's latest experiment, wittily played by Peter Boyle, has broken free from the local castle and, whilst rampaging through the countryside, chances upon Harold's cottage and seeks shelter therein. Harold has just finished praying for a temporary companion to 'help pass a few short hours in my lonely life' and is delighted to find his prayers answered by the arrival of the creature, whom he assumes must be mute.

Warmly welcoming his guest, Harold's joy and hospitality are limited only by the constraints of his blindness; thus he serves hot soup in his guest's lap, destroys a clay drinking-mug with an over exuberant toast and sets alight the creature's finger in the mistaken belief that it is a cigar. Unsurprisingly, the creature takes flight, preferring to chance his fate to the mercy of the bloodthirsty villagers.

Made-up like a latter-day Sterling Hayden, with grey hair and a beard of Biblical proportions, Hackman is a delight in this rare comic role, milking every laugh from the situation, gently underplaying and delivering his lines with impeccable timing. One regrets his all-too-brief screen time and his lack of opportunities to essay a fully-fledged comic character.

Young Frankenstein is an engaging rib-tickler, lavishing some delicious black-and-white photography and evocative set designs on the usual Brooks mixture of adolescent humour, hysteria and flashes of inspired lunacy. Hackman's scenes fall within the latter category, as does the performance of 'Puttin' on the Ritz' by Wilder and Boyle. The film was an enormous popular success worldwide and earned around $35 million in America alone. Hackman said, 'I think my work in *Young Frankenstein* is what acting should be about. You do big roles, then you do two days with Mel Brooks. I enjoy doing large roles *and* supporting roles, otherwise you become too precious – you take yourself too seriously.'

Young Frankenstein had been a perfect opportunity for Hackman to show that he possessed a sense of humour; it gave him a chance to let off steam in a positive manner and make the refreshing admission by a 'star' name that there was fun to be had in acting for pleasure without worrying over status. The success of his participation in *Young Frankenstein* may well have persuaded the likes of Burt Reynolds, Paul Newman and James Caan to accept guest roles in Brooks's next extravaganza, *Silent Movie* (1976).

Hackman worked on remorselessly, attracted to his next film by the prospect of a leading role for *Bonnie and Clyde* director Arthur Penn. The project, originally known as *The Dark Tower* but later retitled *Night Moves*, proved a worthy reason for their professional reunion.

Night Moves began life as a script by the Scottish-born

writer Alan Sharp entitled *An End of Wishing*. From the outset it was an ambitious and audacious attempt to create a quintessential detective yarn and then subvert the traditions of that genre by focusing on a case and a world where there are no easy solutions, and where the problems lie inwards and not in some external mystery that can be readily resolved by revealing 'whodunnit' in the final reel.

In the film Hackman plays Harry Moseby, an ex-football player turned private detective, who is hired by former Hollywood starlet Arlene Iverson (Janet Ward) to find her runaway daughter Delly (Melanie Griffith). As Moseby embarks on the case he discovers that his wife Ellen is sleeping with another man; he follows her as he would any adulterous wife and later confronts her lover with his knowledge.

Moseby travels to the Florida Keys, where he finds Delly living with her former stepfather Tom Iverson (John Crawford) and his mistress Paula (Jennifer Warren), who warns Moseby that 'if we all get liberated like Delly there'll be fighting in the streets'. The promiscuous teenager is reluctant to return to Los Angeles, claiming that her mother only misses the cash income that the girl's custody entails and has no other motive for wanting her back.

The idyll in Florida momentarily diverts Moseby from his other worries; the climate is appealing, the case has been surprisingly straightforward and he finds himself strongly attracted to Paula – a woman whom he can talk to, a woman who seems to understand his moods. On a boat trip with Moseby and Paula, Delly discovers the crashed remains of a light plane and the skeleton of the dead pilot. She is shaken and terrified and vows that she will now willingly return home with Moseby. The position of the wreck is marked for the coastguard. Before Moseby leaves for Los Angeles he and Paula make love.

Back home, Moseby begins a process of reconciliation with his wife. However, his interest in Delly is rekindled when he hears a radio report of the girl's death in a film stunt that has gone badly wrong. He visits one of her former lovers, Quentin (James Woods), who informs him that the dead pilot in the Florida waters had been another of her lovers, stuntman Marv Ellman (Anthony Costello). Moseby subsequently concludes that the jealous Quentin had murdered Ellman and then arranged Delly's death after she had discovered the body.

Moseby follows Quentin to Florida, only to find that he has been murdered by Tom Iverson. It transpires that Iverson had been smuggling archaeological finds worth $500,000 out of Yucatan. The plane crash had never been reported to the Coast Guard and Moseby's night of passion with Paula was a distraction to prevent his further snooping. Paula sails with Moseby to the spot where the artefacts are hidden. Whilst Paula is diving they are attacked from the air; Moseby is shot and Paula is mown down by the plane, which then crashes into the sea. Moseby recognizes the pilot as film director Joey Ziegler (Edward Binns), the man who had been driving the car in which Delly died. As Ziegler drowns, the injured Moseby attempts to pilot the boat but he only succeeds in sailing around in circles.

The final moments of *Night Moves*, with Hackman's Moseby disillusioned, hurt and only able to travel in concentric circles, going nowhere, is an apt metaphor for Penn and Sharp's view of America in the mid-Seventies: confused and battered in the wake of Vietnam and Watergate, uncertain over its role in the world and receiving no sense of direction or leadership from those in power. In a retrospective review of the film, Sharp called it 'essentially an allegory about what I perceive to be the American consciousness, both its strengths and its blind spots, and Moseby was the guy representing that. It was a time for a certain kind of consciousness, which I'm calling American: a recognition that the world is more complex than what it was believed to be and that there are things that just cannot be solved.' Penn too was alert to the notion of twisting the detective genre, where the urge is towards a final explanation that ties up the loose ends, so that the actual mechanics of Moseby's investigation are an irrelevance to what is going on in his life. He is seeking specific answers to external mysteries like why Delly has died or whatever, whilst ignoring his own problems of relations with his wife having, perhaps irrevocably, broken down; of his never having known or loved his father; and of why he keeps doing the same job when it affords little satisfaction or self-respect.

Penn and Sharp worked in close harmony on the substance and development of *Night Moves*, sharing a similar viewpoint on the state of the nation but parting company over some of the fine detail of the script. Sharp had wanted Moseby and Paula to take off with the treasure, grasping a fleeting chance for a love that will flounder at some future date. Penn insisted that there be some glimmer of a chance that Moseby and his wife could be reunited. Sharp felt that if there was a possibility of Moseby returning to Ellen (Susan Clark), then he should be seen to die at the film's conclusion. The two men compromised, avoiding a conventional ending but refusing to overplay a sense of pessimism, settling instead for ambiguity.

Some years afterwards, Sharp still seemed to resent Penn's inability to stamp his total authority on the project, commenting, 'There were some problems with the movie when it was made which, I think, stemmed from Arthur's uncertainty about the kind of film he was going to make. We exhausted quite a number of conversations during which I expected Arthur, at some time, to step in and say, "OK, here's my hero; this is my Moseby", which I felt was not only his right, but his duty as an *auteur* director. That never really came out. But we had very amiable relations throughout.'

The amiable relations between director and writer extended to the rare allowance of ten days of rehearsals during which portions of the script were reworked and the actors were able to run through their lines, suggest changes and improvise new scenes. For an actor like Hackman, with his background in improvisational theatre, the preproduction period on *Night Moves* was a stimulating bonus to the usual grind of film work.

However much they may have differed on other aspects of *Night Moves*, Penn and Sharp were in perfect agreement over the choice of Hackman as their Harry Moseby. Penn has described Hackman as 'a very visceral person and a very visceral actor. He has a first-rate mind, but he doesn't work intellectually without working intuitively as well.' Asked how he preferred to work with actors, Penn told *Sight and Sound*, 'I get to know about their personal lives, and I ask them to draw on that every once in a while; a lot of it is confidential. But I try to find parallels in their own lives to the sort of situations they're experiencing in the film, and to give them a point of recognition.'

[113]

Hackman's portrayal of Moseby could be viewed as a mixture of his own introspective mood at the time and his unobtrusive observations of Alan Sharp, who invested the character with many of his own worries and personal preoccupations. If Moseby can't see the woods for the trees, is determined to neatly conclude his investigation but blind to the problems that impair his personal life, then Hackman was similarly, if more consciously, torn between the demands of his career and other pressing concerns that he was neglecting – his wife, his children and the really important matters in life.

The particular strengths of Hackman's performance in *Night Moves* lie in the quality of his observation and the level of concentration he deploys, not content to relax whilst others hold centre stage but keenly reacting to their presence, words and deeds; actively listening, purposefully challenging their space. He is particularly adept at the small physical gestures that either add a patina of naturalism to his work or express Moseby's frustration and confusion; thus he wipes his eyes, clicks his fingers or impatiently shakes his leg in a very positive use of body language. He also adds just the right touch of weary melancholy to the way he intones lines like, 'Nobody's winning. One side is losing slower than the other.'

Alan Sharp was immensely impressed by the actor's contribution to the film and gave this unsolicited testimonial to *Literature/Film Quarterly:*

'He's an exceptionally professional and skillful actor. He'll do anything up to six takes and just go on adjusting each take. He won't change it so you get a different reading or interpretation, but he'll give you four or five variations just to give you choices. He's a wonderfully skilled actor who seems able to make very complex perceptions without having to verbalize or intellectualize them. He was marvellous for that. Lines that had been written just to get you from one line to the next line came alive with him. In his scene with Delly, when she cries out and he goes over and sits with her, he says, "It's bad when you're sixteen but when you're forty, it's no better." This was stuff that was much better than what was written on the page. When I saw that rendition I was so astonished; there was that personal content which I found worked successfully.'

The critics tended to agree with Sharp's assessment, with *Time*'s reviewer noting, 'Hackman, the archetype of contemporary ordinariness, is as usual superb in the central role. Perplexed, dogged, distracted from the main issues in the case by everything from the economy to the mysteries of feminine psychology, he is an enormously appealing everyman under pressure.'

Despite critical goodwill, and a real sense in which the makers achieved what they had set out to do, *Night Moves* was not a commercial success. The warning signs were evident when Warner Brothers delayed the release of the film, uncertain of how to handle it or how it would be received. Sharp believed that at a cost of $4 million the film had been overpriced in relation to the level of box-office response that they could realistically count on; had it been made for $2 million there would have been a greater chance of profitability. In explaining its financial failure he also seemed to blame Penn for refusing to stamp his imprimatur firmly on the production, choosing instead to shoot a lavish amount of film that still left him with many options during the editing process.

Penn seemed to blame the film's failure on the stated intent of cheating an audience's expectations of what a detective story should deliver and hence alienating their interest. If an audience is conditioned to accept the appearance of certain elements and is then presented with a film that pushes out from these limits, asking it to think and look beyond the obvious, then it may well not make the effort. Penn has said, 'I think we were trying to counter that impulse towards solutions in this genre of film. Now, whether you can do that with a genre film is a fundamental question. If you're doing a detective story, can you say, "Yeah, but we're not going to solve it"? I don't know that you can, any more than I know if you can have the good cowboy meet the bad cowboy in the last reel on the street of Laredo and the good cowboy gets shot down. There are certain obligations of the genre.'

Sharp has suggested one final and very pertinent possible reason why the film flopped: 'It's hard for me to imagine who'd be better than Gene Hackman, although he was, in the end, one of the liabilities in the film. You see, people don't go to see Gene Hackman movies, although sometimes they go to see movies that Gene Hackman is in. His gift is that he's not a star.'

Hackman has always stated his preference to be known as a movie actor rather than a movie star, but this distinction means that his name alone cannot carry a film to financial success. There is generally enough of an audience to make a sensibly budgeted Clint Eastwood film a guaranteed hit, regardless of the individual merits of the film. There is not that devotion to Hackman; esteem for his gifts as an actor, but not blind loyalty to whatever he may turn out. In 1973 he was listed at the eleventh position among the year's top box-office attractions, yet *Scarecrow* was not a financial hit, much to his chagrin. By 1974 he was still in the magical top twenty-five, admittedly having slipped to sixteenth, and yet neither *Zandy's Bride* nor, more astonishingly, *The Conversation* was a hit. Indeed, in the years following the double triumph of *The French Connection* and *The Poseidon Adventure*, despite a body of work that is virtually unrivalled among his contemporaries, only *Young Frankenstein* was a solid box-office smash and his contribution to that was modest. In 1975 he would bounce back into the top-ten, at number ten. However, 1975 was the year in which the *French Connection* sequel was released. The only conclusion to be drawn is that as 'Popeye' Doyle, Hackman is a major box-office star, but in anything else he is merely a damned fine actor.

The coldshouldering of *The Conversation* was a severe and disheartening disappointment to both Hackman and director Francis Coppola. Perhaps, as in the case of *Marooned*, potential audiences were more fascinated by the reality of news headlines than they were by their dramatic interpretation on film. *Marooned* had suffered in comparison with the moon landings, whilst *The Conversation* was overshadowed by Watergate and its reverberations. Whatever the reason, it did not lessen Hackman's sense of injustice – his feeling that work of integrity had not received its due reward. 'It was a major disappointment to me that more people didn't see the movie. Not for my performance or my having been in it, but I thought it was a valuable film in terms of content and what films can be.'

Coppola cryptically alluded to why the film may not have done as well as it deserved when he observed, 'It was not a film that I set out to earn a great fortune on. I do think that a very awkward distribution made the difference between a picture that might have made a profit and a picture that had a loss.'

Hackman's yardstick for measuring the success of any film is the profit and loss accounting. Personal satisfaction is a factor, but glowing critical notices are largely immaterial and thus the ultimate reckoning is in how many people buy tickets. On that criteria some of his finest work in *Scarecrow, The Conversation* and *Night Moves* is judged by him to have failed; an overwhelmingly disheartening discovery that would profoundly affect his career in the latter half of the 1970s.

'In the final analysis you have to trust the box-office grosses,' he has said. 'If people like a film and go see it then that means it works. I don't necessarily trust a critic's view of what a film is, and there are only a few film critics who I think really know what they're talking about. It's one person's opinion of what a film can be or should have been. I think many times people's whole careers are changed by what someone says about them or about their performance and that's why I choose not to read reviews.'

The *French Connection* sequel could probably be guaranteed a wide and welcoming audience and would do no harm to Hackman's career, even though the prospect of working on the film did not fill him with great anticipation. His philosophy as an actor is always to seek fresh ground and new challenges. Thus, the prospect of reprising a character, particularly one as influential as 'Popeye', was something to be avoided at all costs. Unfortunately, he had unthinkingly signed away any protection against that eventuality.

'I contracted to do it as soon as I had finished the first film, but in the two years that the sequel took to set up, all sorts of interesting things were offered to me. In the long run I began to dread going back and doing that character again. I didn't want to go to France and I knew enough about myself to realize that I wasn't going to be very docile about it.'

French Connection II was unavoidable, although that didn't mean that Hackman was obliged to be co-operative or gracious towards those entrusted with its production. The long-awaited event was postponed even further when

Hackman was generously allowed to delay his participation in the film to permit the filming of another script that had attracted his eye: *Bite the Bullet*.

Hackman has often said that his choice of material is a direct reaction against the last film that he has made. Thus, after the soul-searching introspection of *Night Moves* and *The Conversation*, he was quite amenable to a rugged outdoor story that tested his physical mettle. *Bite the Bullet* perfectly suited his requirements.

A grand and sporadically glorious multi-star, high-adventure yarn, *Bite the Bullet* was the brainchild of veteran writer, producer and director Richard Brooks and centres on a 700–mile endurance horse race across the southwest of America in 1908. For Hackman it would linger in his memory as 'the toughest [film] I ever worked on'. The sixty-eight days of location shooting in Nevada, New Mexico and Colorado brought every possible variation in weather from snow to pouring rain, from bitter cold to the scorching heat of the desert. The cast worked in all climates and in some desolate spots from the desert flats to altitudes of up to 11,000 feet. Hackman, at least, had the advantages of stardom and the resulting financial security to indulge in a few rich man's toys. During *Bite the Bullet* he was free to pilot his private plane home for weekends.

Hackman's *Bite the Bullet* character is cowboy Sam Clayton, a former Rough Rider with Teddy Roosevelt and a sensitive man whose concern for the welfare of the horses takes precedence over almost any other consideration in the marathon race. His competitors include his long-time friend and rival Luke Matthews (James Coburn); Carbo (Jan-Michael Vincent), a young hothead seeking fame and fortune; Norfolk (Ian Bannen), a titled Englishman in search of fresh adventures; the grizzled veteran 'Mister' (Ben Johnson); the only female rider, Miss Jones (Candice Bergen), who desperately needs the prize-money for her convict husband; and a Mexican who wants the cash for his people. The prize is $2,000 and the rule is that the winner takes all.

Clayton is an impossibly noble, self-sacrificing figure as he becomes nursemaid and saviour to any two or four-legged creature in distress during the eventful 700 miles. Along the way, he performs some emergency dentistry on

[118]

the Mexican, tends to the dying 'Mister', persuades Carbo to bury his horse (which has died of exhaustion and maltreatment), tries to assist Miss Jones in rescuing her husband and then insists that Matthews join him as they cross the finishing line together in a democratic draw. The latter action is consistent with the character, who seems continually sceptical of the competitive ethos and more disposed towards the brotherhood of man than the survival of the fittest.

Bite the Bullet is an enjoyable, sweeping epic entertainment of the outdoors in which the level of characterization is necessarily sketchy and the comparisons with Brooks's earlier film *The Professionals* (1966) are both inevitable and invidious. The plot is overly schematic and Hackman is saddled with a character who is just too good to be true. Despite the beautiful scenery and a marvellous cast, time had somehow diminished the lusty vigour and spring-coiled tension that so distinguished *The Professionals*.

Having delayed the inevitable as long as possible, Hackman moved straight on from *Bite the Bullet* to France and the location shooting of *French Connection II*, a film he readily reminded interviewers that he 'would prefer not to be making'. He had negotiated the contract whilst *The Poseidon Adventure* was in production, and 'as they say, it seemed like a good idea at the time.' He had been offered director or cast approval on the film and opted for the former. John Frankenhemier was an acceptable choice for director and although he did not have the contractual right of script approval, Hackman was consulted over the various ideas that had been suggested for the continuance of the 'Popeye' Doyle story.

Hackman later described the filming of *French Connection II* as 'appalling' and he was not afraid to let anyone around him know that he would prefer to be elsewhere. Growling through the production like a bear with a sore head, Hackman must have been able to make use of his disgruntlement to illuminate Popeye's sense of frustration and unease at being a stranger in a strange land. Nevertheless, he was still an intimidating presence to work with and an anonymous member of the *French Connection II* production team was quoted as saying, 'Hackman? He was a nice guy but

[119]

he's developed into a four-star, homogenized, all-American pain in the posterior.'

In his comments to the press Hackman strained to be more even-handed and philosophical about his dilemma, telling *The Guardian*, 'I don't mean to do a poor-mouth job on the sequel. Three years ago, after the original *French Connection* was completed, I talked to Billy Friedkin, the director, about what kind of film we'd made. Either it was a masterful art film or it was an adventure film. Yet somehow it was both. This one may very well be as good as the first one. Even if it's better, there will inevitably be comparisons, since the first one was so fresh. Since then there have been any number of police films, and some were good ones.'

Hackman's unhappiness and concern were unfounded; many people found *French Connection II* not only the equal but even the superior of its predecessor.

Followers of the *French Connection* saga will remember that at the end of the first film the drug-ring masterminded Alain Charnier (Fernando Rey) eluded capture and presumably returned to his safe haven of respectability in Marseilles. The second film has Doyle dispatched to Marseilles as a sort of hands-across-the-sea gesture of cooperation between the American and French narcotics squads. Doyle is the only one who can recognize Charnier as 'Frog One', but he has been unwittingly sent as bait to tempt Charnier into the open. It is assumed that Doyle's renowned lack of subtlety will inevitably smoke out Charnier.

The years have neither mellowed Doyle nor cooled his blistering ardour. Arriving in Marseilles he is an archetypal 'ugly American' abroad, dressed in the most garish of shirts, unable to communicate with the locals and as conspicuous as a giant in Lilliput. He introduces himself to his French colleague Barthelemy (Bernard Fresson) but is met by open hostility; his reputation precedes him, even in Marseilles.

He is allowed to accompany Barthelemy on a drugs raid but only on the strict understanding that he must not carry a gun, he must not interfere and he must honour his status as an observer. Doyle instantly disregards these ground rules when he witnesses an assumed suspect running away. He relentlessly chases the man through the cobbled streets but has to let him go when the French inform him that the man is one of their undercover operatives. His 'cover' blown, the man is subsequently stabbed to death.

Doyle's unthinking action and its consequences make him *persona non grata* amongst his French hosts and he spends his time lost and lonely, trying to find an English-speaker to share a drink with him in a roadside café. One evening he is knocked unconscious and abducted by members of Charnier's gang. Charnier wishes to know the purpose of his secondment to Marseilles and has him injected with heroin until he acquires the truthful response that Doyle knows nothing of Charnier's operation but can identify him. Now a heroin addict, Doyle is given a massive dose of the drug and unceremoniously deposited at the steps to police headquarters.

Barthelemy and the medical experts manage to save Doyle's life and he then endures the painful withdrawal symptoms of coming off the drug 'cold turkey'. Over a period of weeks Doyle recovers his sanity and recuperates before returning to the streets more determined than ever to exact revenge and nail his man.

He discovers the Hotel Colonnades, where he had been held captive, and then proceeds to set it on fire. He later attacks a suspect to extract some information that will implicate Charnier. Through various surveillance measures the authorities learn of a large drugs shipment waiting to leave port in a foreign ship. As police surround the vessel, Doyle spots Charnier overseeing the operation. The subsequent shoot-out proves disastrous, with another policeman killed, Barthelemy injured and Charnier still at large. Barthelemy's superiors decide that enough is enough and Doyle is asked to leave the country. Barthelemy, however, buys him some time.

The two men keep watch on the ship's captain, whom Doyle insists will have to be paid before the vessel sails. On the day of departure the captain finally leaves his ship for a rendezvous on board a pleasure boat to receive his payment. The courier is followed and leads Doyle and Barthelemy's forces to Charnier's warehouse. During the final shoot-out Charnier discreetly leaves the building with Doyle in grim pursuit. Even when Charnier boards a bus, Doyle chases after him on foot. Facing exhaustion, Doyle loses his quarry in the crowds and is distressed to witness

[121]

Charnier slip aboard a yacht and sail off. Summoning up his remaining energy, Doyle staggers along the shore, following the yacht until it comes back into plain view. He then takes careful aim and shoots Charnier twice through the heart.

French Connection II is a suspenseful and satisfying sequel that probes the character of Hackman's cop more deeply and critically than the first film, questioning his theory that the end justifies the means and depicting the distaste with which he is viewed by friend and foe alike. His sense of isolation in France gives the man moments of pathos as he hits the bottle in maudlin loneliness, and the scenes of his enforced drug addiction are harrowing and powerfully performed. There is also pleasure in watching the final chase in which the heart and lungs of a determined man are pitted against car, boat and the eternally elusive 'Frog One'.

With Doyle seen largely as a victim of both his bosses' duplicity and Charnier's deviousness, the film ultimately reveals the character's vulnerability and his tentative acknowledgement of his own limitations.

Hackman here gives another awesomely impressive display of commitment, not only in terms of the crippling physical requirements of his tough-guy role but in his unstinting depiction of heroin addiction and withdrawal. Ragged, crawling up the wall with paroxysms of craving, babbling on about sports heroes in a desperate bid to maintain a grip on sanity, he gives a gripping and touching portrait of a man being torn apart by something over which he has no power. Hackman's overwhelming ability to make a situation credible and affecting has never been more severely taxed and he has rarely been found so equal to the challenge.

French Connection II was the expected success and Hackman's critical notices, whilst admittedly of no great concern to him, were universally approving. *Time Out* noted, 'Hackman takes the enlarged role by the scruff of the neck and delivers yet another fine performance of doubt and the gradual dawning awareness of his own weakness,' whilst *The Listener*'s critic added, 'I haven't enjoyed an American thriller as much since *The Conversation* – which also starred Gene Hackman. The man will soon be a walking guarantee.' The finished film even earned the endorsement of its reluctant star, who commented, 'Although the whole experience was appalling to me, I was pleasantly surprised by the way it turned out.'

Chapter Nine

Upon completion of *French Connection II*, Hackman paused from his usually hectic schedule to step back and take an objective look at the state of his career. His ruminations brought some depressing conclusions. Firstly, it seemed that no one wanted to see the kind of films that he wanted to make; secondly, however much he felt mature enough and prepared enough for the event he was unable to satisfactorily resolve all the pressures and conflicting demands that stardom entailed; finally, he had been disappointed to a degree in the lack of variety in the offers he had received after his Oscar. Where were the good comedies, the light romances or even the musicals to balance his diet of cops and cowboys? Why was it that he still never walked into the sunset with a leading lady on his arm?

In a mood of discontent, Hackman vowed that if the public didn't want to see films of the calibre of *Night Moves* or *The Conversation*, then it was his duty to make the type of films that they did want to see. In future, he would play safe, he would just take his fee and make whatever was popular and well-liked. The only trouble with such a cynical attitude is that the actor will eventually sicken himself with self-loathing by working at such a variance from his natural instincts. Furthermore, it is impossible to second-guess public taste. If it were possible to accurately predict the elements that will automatically guarantee a box-office hit then no major Hollywood studio would ever have lost money.

As Hackman would later admit, he was selling out, lulled into a calculating course of self-destruction by fits of depression and the temptations that Hollywood could offer to ease his qualms. In 1982 he told Robert Ward of *American Film*, 'I had gotten very depressed after *Scarecrow* and *Conver-*

sation failed to make money, and I was drinking. Not that I was an alcoholic, but I was at the point where I was having two vodka and tonics to start the night just to quench my thirst. Then a couple more later. And I started to say, "Hell, I'll do movies that will definitely make money and then I'll have plenty of dough." It was real establishment thinking and of course it didn't work. It doesn't work for anybody, really. Not any more. So, I took pictures to play it safe, and they turned out to be very dangerous pictures for me to make.'

Thus, Hackman embarked upon what he would later term his 'felony period', when he made a succession of films for all the wrong reasons. He was only fooling himself if he thought such a policy would bring long-term satisfaction. 'When you're on top, you get a sense of immortality,' he explained. 'You feel you can do no wrong, that it will always be good no matter what the role. Well, in truth, that feeling is death. You must be honest with yourself.' Blithely proceeding in a haze of self-deception, Hackman learnt the truth of that last statement by painful experience.

Early in 1975 he was being sought to complete a star triumvirate in a pre-packaged, guaranteed surefire hit that should have immediately appealed to his now less discriminating tastes. The project, entitled *Lucky Lady*, concerned the adventures of three rum-runners during Prohibition who also enjoyed a jolly ménage-à-trois. It had been written by the husband-and-wife team of Willard Huyck and Gloria Katz, who had received an Oscar nomination for *American Graffiti* (1973). For a reported fee of $400,000 they had concocted a lavish, lighthearted old-style entertainment deliberately designed to evoke Hollywood's golden age with three personable star roles, good guys versus bad guys, chases, songs, fights and merry badinage.

Stanley Donen, once a member of the M-G-M creative family responsible for *On the Town* and *Singin' in the Rain*, had been chosen by Twentieth Century Fox President Alan Ladd Jr. as the project's director in 1973. At the time he was involved in post-production on *The Little Prince*, but considered the new material and was eager to proceed. Asked why, he replied, 'It was the script. I found it funny, touching, romantic, different. I'm always intrigued when a motion-picture script has a truly strong leading lady's part.'

Together with producer Michael Gruskoff, who was then engaged in filming *Young Frankenstein*, Donen began work on the film with a definite idea that Liza Minelli would be his lucky lady. 'She was the first person I sent it to. She liked it, and of course I was delighted. Two years ago she said to me, "Let's find a movie to do together" and I had agreed, so when this script came up I wrote saying, "Dear Liza, I think you'll like this", and she read it that day and said, "I'll do it. You're absolutely right." '

Minelli signed on for what would be her first film role after her triumph as Sally Bowles in *Cabaret*. Finding two male co-stars of comparable stature was the opening headache in what would become an increasingly strife-ridden production. 'The first stumbling block was casting,' Donen subsequently told reporters. 'It may have been that the woman's role is strong and that Liza was picked first. Men may have felt their roles were less important. Whatever the reason, people were either unavailable, or didn't like the billing. In all, it took eighteen months to cast the film.'

Eventually, Burt Reynolds and George Segal were enlisted as Liza's co-stars and in February of 1975 the cast and crew assembled in Guaymas, Mexico for the beginning of what had been scheduled as twelve weeks of location filming. Unfortunately, Segal did not appear, suffering from an unspecified malady. If was uncertain whether he would recover in time to allow production to commence. In the end he resigned, leaving Donen in the unenviable position of finding a replacement in a hurry. 'Once Fox hired all these high-powered stars, bought the script and brought me in, they couldn't get out of it,' he explained.

A telephone call was placed to Sue Mengers, one of the most powerful of Hollywood agents. Would her client Steve McQueen be prepared to fill the breach at short notice in return for a certain financial consideration? The answer was no. Warren Beatty was next on the shopping list and the response was equally negative. Then, thoughts turned to Hackman, also represented by Sue Mengers. Michael Gruskoff had employed him on *Young Frankenstein*, and when Frank Sinatra had dropped out of *The Little Prince*, Donen had considered Hackman as a possible replacement along with Richard Burton, Jim Dale, Robert Goulet, Richard Harris and Nicol Williamson.

Initially, Hackman joined the list of those who rejected *Lucky Lady's* desperate entreaties. His decision was surprising, given that the role in question needed a 'personality' performance, something rarely demanded of him. Here was his chance to be romantic and charming and charismatic in the tradition of Cary Grant or Errol Flynn that he so admired yet felt himself so ill-equipped to continue. The film required not his acting prowess but his presence, in every sense of the word.

Twentieth Century-Fox needed someone fast and refused to take Hackman's 'no' as his final answer. The more he demurred, the more they raised the ante until it became almost churlish to persist in his stubbornness. Finally, he accepted in a lucrative deal that was said to include a salary of $1,250,000 plus the hire of his King Air twin-engine plane by the studio as a shuttle service between Los Angeles and Guaymas. 'I was seduced' was Hackman's comment on the negotiations. At least if he was selling out he was doing it in style and amongst good company. Incidentally, his fellow stars were practically poverty-stricken in comparison; Reynolds received $500,000 and Minnelli a paltry $350,000.

Now that a cast was gathered in Mexico, Donen could begin production on a rollicking, rumbustious yarn reminiscent of the days of Clark Gable, Spencer Tracy and Jean Harlow and the type of pure entertainment that they just didn't seem to make anymore. Unfortunately, *Lucky Lady* was a victim of Murphy's Law; everything that could go wrong, did go wrong.

A fair proportion of *Lucky Lady* was filmed at sea, which presented numerous practical difficulties for Donen. 'When what you want in the picture keeps moving around you have an impossible task,' he told *Photoplay* reporter John Austin. 'On the water you can't make a camera or boats or actors stay still. Therefore, when you shoot the picture, most often there is nothing in view. Boats are nowhere to be seen. They are impossible to anchor, even if they swing two degrees it's too much. When you have an armada of sixty-five boats it is an almost inhuman problem. Unpredictable problems and accidents such as an actor losing his hat can cause hours of delay.'

During the spring and early summer of 1975, as Donen and his crew worked off the Mexican coast, the seas were rough and the weather unpredictable. Few escaped the debilitating combination of seasickness, Montezuma's Revenge and an outbreak of dysentery. Minelli was particularly disabled by illness and lost weight rapidly, leading to the inevitable inconsistencies in her physical appearance on screen. One boat crashed into a Mexican Coast Guard cutter, a camera slipped its moorings and plunged into the Sea of Cortez, taking film of a completed scene to a watery grave, Michael Gruskoff left the film after an altercation and, inexorably, *Lucky Lady* was going over budget and behind schedule. Twelve weeks of star-laden fun stretched into nineteen weeks of a living nightmare. A finishing date of June was postponed until August, with the film still slated to open for Christmas 1975.

Whilst everyone gamely and grimly insisted on seeing *Lucky Lady* through to its bitter conclusion, it had proved an experience that few would willingly repeat, million-dollar salary or not. In interviews, those involved reacted with differing degrees of calm when questioned as to how things were proceeding.

Reynolds reported, 'It's very important to me that *Lucky Lady* be a success since my last three films have gone down the tubes. I am not considered a member of the Golden Group, but I am a top box-office draw, in spite of my reviews, and I desperately want to stay there.'

Hackman was clearly less tolerant of the situation, claiming that the success or failure of the film was immaterial to him. Near the film's completion he said, 'I can hardly stand it another day. The work is not satisfying. It's not acting, it's trying to remember what went on before. I'm going bananas. The major effort of each day is just getting to the location.'

Donen was even more bleakly succinct: 'There are times that I feel like committing suicide.'

Everything must come to an end sometime, even *Lucky Lady*, and everyone called it a day in the late summer. At least, that's what they thought. . . .

During the closing months of the year, when the film was being prepared for its first public showings, a dispute arose over the ending. In the original script, Reynolds and Hackman are killed by Federal agents. After careful consideration, Donen decided that the film's mood of jollity and escapism didn't really go with such a downbeat conclusion and felt that his heroes should survive to enjoy a long and happy retirement. The three stars were recalled to shoot an alternative ending, aged beyond their years, caked in make-up and sharing a bed. Fortunately, this too was abandoned and the film ends, as it started, in the 1930s with the trio leading a fleet of small-time smugglers in a successful rout of the local Mr Big.

At a fractious and shambolic press-conference, Donen and the duo of Minnelli and Reynolds publicly defended the merits of their chosen endings with the director insisting on his right to make the final selection and Minnelli voicing the strange view that 'the changes made in the film mark the difference between a work of art and a commercial movie.' Hackman kept quiet on the subject, content, for the moment, to take his money and run, reverting to a previous philosophy that moviemaking was akin to some form of legitimate theft.

Lucky Lady is set in Tijuana in 1930 and features Minnelli as Claire, a tough but vulnerable, ill-educated but resourceful floozie with social aspirations. Her former lover had special-ized in smuggling liquor and Mexican labourers across the American border. when he dies she joins forces with his partner Walker (Reynolds) and plans to continue business as usual. However, on one run Walker is ambushed by a US Border Patrol and then badly beaten by the Mexicans, who suspect that they have been duped. To make matters worse his $600 profit is stolen by Kibby (Hackman) whose initiative is rewarded by an offer to join Walker and Claire in partnership.

Hiring a young crewman, Billy (Robby Benson), the trio purchase a consignment of liquor from Captain Rockwell (Michael Hordern) and set sail aboard the 'Lucky Lady'. Rockwell has generously sold them some of the supplies intended for local operator Christy McTeague (John Hill-erman), hence they must evade capture by McTeague's men as well as the ever-vigilant Coast Guard patrols. They manage to reach San Diego, complete their transactions and celebrate in style at a luxury hotel.

Happily ensconced in a *ménage-à-trois*, the two men are reluctant to immediately join Claire on another dangerous run. She leaves with a wealthy friend, returning later to embark afresh on their adventures in a lavish new mansion that she has purchased. Walker, Kibby and Billy head for Mexico where they find Captain Rockwell dead. Later, they are ambushed by McTeague's men; Billy is killed whilst Walker and Kibby are seriously wounded. Claire joins them and nurses them back to full health in Tijuana. Then the trio round up a small fleet of equally aggrieved small-scale smugglers and launch an assault on McTeague, who is ultimately defeated. In the great tradition of screen heroes, Walker, Kibby and Claire are assumed to have lived happily ever after.

When the film was made available for critical review the comments were harsh and brutal, with many writers focusing on the troubled production history of the project and the escalating budget, which had seemed to grow daily from an initial ten million to some twenty-two million dollars. The main criticisms surrounded the lifelessness of the calculatingly commercial mix that had been served up. Jonathan Rosenbaum complained in the *Monthly Film Bulletin* that 'the presence of Stanley Donen seems to count for little in a project that might more logically have been entrusted to a computer. All it has to express, quite simply, are its deliberations: to combine as many saleable features as can be packed on a screen within the space of two hours.'

By trying to be all things to all men, *Lucky Lady* had apparently wound up a big, charmless nothing. Nevertheless, other, more sympathetic, reviewers did detect some virtues in the star trio, in Geoffrey Unsworth's photography, in the songs by *Cabaret* team Fred Ebb and John Kander, in the insouciant *joie de vivre* that intermittently shone through and in the determination to entertain at all costs.

On a certain level many people, including this writer, enjoyed *Lucky Lady* as unpretentious fun. In *Films Illustrated* Susan D'Arcy hailed an 'accomplished trio of performers' and said, 'The combination of Reynolds, Minnelli and Hackman works perfectly: Reynolds's likeable fall-guy is all charm and confusion; Minnelli's easy showgirl wants to be respectable; the multi-talented Hackman is the one with the know-how. . . . Only the churlish could dislike such a winning confection.' In *Focus on Film*, Tom Vallance singled out Hackman for specific praise and perceptively noted that 'the film was perhaps luckiest in the last-minute casting switch involving the replacement of George Segal by Gene Hackman. Segal's extrovert, jokey comedy style would have provided little of the superb contrast that sparks the Reynolds-Hackman partnership. Hackman has probably received more critical accolades during his film career than any actor since Marlon Brando, and though *Lucky Lady* will never be mentioned among his greatest performances or films, it is important because it provides him with the final test of the true *film* actor. Far from being the sort of tour-de-force showcase role in which he tends to be cast, it is a part calling instead for *star* charisma, that mysterious blend of presence, personality and instinctive skill that separates the great movie actors from the merely accomplished. Hackman passes the test with flying colours.'

For his first trip on the money-go-round, *Lucky Lady* proved a rather good value at $1,250,000 for Hackman and even distinguished itself on the one criteria that he acknowledged as important – the box-office. Contrary to popular expectation, *Lucky Lady* was not a total financial disaster, earning an impressive $12,655,000 in American alone during its first year of release, which placed it within the top ten hits of 1976. In a way, that partial success served to validate Hackman's decision to be led in future by money; $12 million was probably more than the combined revenues of *Scarecrow*, *The Conversation* and *Night Moves*.

In 1976, the three *Lucky Lady* performers all appeared on the list of the year's top twenty-five box-office stars. Reynolds was sixth, Minnelli was fifteenth and Hackman was twenty-fourth. It was to be Hackman's final reckoning in the box-office listings. *Lucky Lady* was to be the one exception to the rule that films made solely for the financial inducement are not worth it.

Hackman's play-it-safe formula of this period resulted in his refusal of some potentially interesting but risky ventures. He is alleged to have rejected both *One Flew Over the Cuckoo's Nest* and *Network*. In partnership with Irwin Allen, who had produced *The Poseidon Adventure*, he purchased the rights to *Walter*, a 'mystery melodrama' by Richard Neely that was never heard of again. His only genuinely adventurous aspiration at the time was a reiteration of his future intent to direct.

[131]

'I have no idea if I have the credentials to be a director. But I want to try,' he confided to *Photoplay*. 'As an actor I really get weary of waiting to be called for a scene. As an adult, I ask myself why I am sitting my life out on the sidelines. All an actor is concerned with is himself and his performance. He isn't really involved with the rest of the picture. That's why I'm attracted to directing. The director knows what's going on in every aspect of the film. While the actors are idle on the set he is busy setting up scenes, checking the camera, interpreting the script – everything.'

Directing remained a long-term pipe dream whilst Hackman continued to sell his services to the highest bidder. His standard fee around this time was a reputed $700,000, and he next chose to film *The Domino Principle* for British entrepreneur Lew Grade.

The Domino Principle, a conspiracy thriller with Hackman as a Lee Harvey Oswald type of dupe, was not without promise; director Stanley Kramer had been responsible for some notable and popular films, like *Judgement at Nuremberg* and *Guess Who's Coming to Dinner*, and his able cast on this occasion included Candice Bergen, Mickey Rooney, Richard Widmark and Eli Wallach.

The film was described by Kramer as 'a human document of a man trying to survive in the jungle.' Adam Kennedy, a former actor turned bestselling novelist, adapted his own work for the screen, and following two weeks of rehearsals, filming started on 12 April 1976 at San Quentin with prisoners used as paid extras.

Hackman was no stranger to filming in prisons after his experience on *Riot!*, but even he must have found the tense atmosphere on *Domino* overly oppressive; after a knifing incident on the first day the company were understandably on edge. However, the week of filming was completed without anything else untoward happening, and the unit then decamped to north Hollywood and Puerta Vallarta, which was used as the fictitious Central American city of Puntarenas.

Kramer later admitted, 'Puerta Vallarta was the roughest location I have ever been on. I scouted locations all over Mexico and Central America and I would have preferred to shoot the Puntarenas scenes in El Salvador, but we couldn't find a town with a town square or house we could use. So, we had to settle on Puerta Vallarta.

'Unfortunately, we had to be there during the hottest time of the year. It was hot and humid and everyone in the company came down with the 'touristas' on the second and third day. And the insects! Well, you could have put saddles on them and ridden them out of the room.'

In publicity material for the film, Hackman described *The Domino Principle* as 'an interesting film' with 'a very interesting director and cast'. His own role of Roy Tucker was 'interesting' and 'an exciting character to play'. However, on the set Hackman and Kramer were often in dispute about the clarity of the material, the credibility of the plot and the conviction of Hackman's 'interesting' character, and the director later told how unduly argumentative he had found his star.

For Hackman there was, at least, a delight to be derived from working with such a fine range of actors, and he told the film's publicist, 'We have great fun working with both Richard Widmark and Eli Wallach. I had never worked with either one of them. And they are really old professionals. They are professionals – I shouldn't say old. But they are both exciting guys to work with because I had known their work for years and years and such a backlog of wonderful material that they have both done, and that's been great fun – a great experience. Mickey Rooney is also in the film and that's been great fun. We started with Mickey in rehearsal and he was flying in and out doing the Cavett show and going back to Chicago doing whatever it is he does in Chicago, and then we started working in San Quentin. And it was a mile a minute with him. He has more energy than anyone I have ever worked with and it's all – just a giant machine – he's five feet tall and he seems like he's nine feet.'

Candice Bergen was making her third screen appearance with Hackman. Their time together on-screen in *The Hunting Party* and *Bite the Bullet* had been limited, but in *The Domino Principle* they shared many scenes and Bergen spoke in glowing admiration of her co-star:

'He has such a love of acting that he has really been able to communicate it to me and has taught me a lot and it's been really exciting as a process. He's really taught me about a love for a trade. He always puts himself in jeopardy. He always takes the risk of failing. I don't know many actors who are willing to do that. For me it is Gene Hackman, Marlon Brando and Jack Nicholson – the three who really put themselves in jeopardy – and I have great respect for it.'

In the film, Hackman plays Vietnam veteran Roy Tucker, who has 15 years to serve of a sentence for the murder of his wife's first husband. In jail he is visited by Marvin Tagge (Widmark) and Ross Pine (Edward Albert), representatives of an unspecified organization. In return for a task that he will be asked to perform, they arrange a fresh identity, provide a bank account containing $200,000 and engineer his release.

Tucker is flown to Puntarenas for a reunion with his wife Ellie (Bergen) and then returns to Los Angeles in preparation for his assignment. When he learns that he is to assassinate the United States President he wants no part of the arrangement, but Ellie is held captive to guarantee his co-operation. A helicopter flies him to within firing range of his target and the President is shot dead. Afterwards, as Ellie and Tucker board their flight to Puntarenas he tells Tagge that none of his shots hit the President and Tagge admits that two other marksmen were on the ground. As their plane lifts off, they see Tagge killed when his car explodes.

In Puntarenas, Tucker finds that he no longer has a false passport and his bank account has been emptied. Ellie is slain by a hit-and-run truck. When Pine and his former cellmate Spiventa (Rooney) pay a visit, Tucker kills them both. The film closes with Tucker walking along a deserted beach within the sights of a mystery marksman.

When *The Domino Principle* was released in America during the spring of 1977 it quickly sank without trace. A dreary, portentous and muddled thriller that never caught fire, it lacked pace, excitement or clarity. Events that were necessarily cloaked in secrecy appeared deliberately confusing and uninvolving. In Britain the film's release was delayed whilst a certain amount of re-editing took place, but its belated arrival in the summer of 1978 was largely ignored. Re-edited and retitled *The Domino Killings*, it failed to elicit any greater interest. It appeared that nothing could help it gain audience appeal.

*

Despite the failure of *The Domino Principle*, Lew Grade appeared to like the idea of having an Oscar-winner like Hackman on his team and enthusiastically plied the actor with books and scripts that he envisaged as feasible joint projects. When the two next worked together it was on a film entitled *March or Die*.

The French Foreign Legion was founded in 1831 and helped the French to conquer Algeria and exploit the mineral wealth of a vast territory. On the long, arduous marches that were an everyday element of Legion life, the men were under orders not to aid any of their comrades who fell by the wayside, hence the Legionnaires tattoed their feet with the phrase 'March or Die' and provided writer-director Dick Richards with the title for his epic film.

Richards had first envisaged making a Foreign Legion story in 1973 and even at that early stage wanted Hackman as his leading star. Richards had mapped out a career plan whereby he would make just one film from each classic genre that he cherished. In 1972 he made his western, *The Culpepper Cattle Company*, and followed that with his detective story *Farewell My Lovely* (1975). *March or Die* would be his adventure yarn, combining the romanticism of *Gunga Din* with the greater sense of realism that a contemporary audience demanded. The story would be based on actual incidents from Legion history and the film would be shot on genuine desert locations where the daily temperatures often brushed the 125 degree mark.

After several uncomfortable months in Mexico for *Lucky Lady* and several uncomfortable weeks in Puerta Vallarta for *The Domino Principle*, Hackman would probably have been profoundly grateful to have been offered a two-character farce to be made entirely in a studio within commuting distance of his front door. The last thing he wanted to do was sweat out another physically demanding tough-guy role in the Sahara desert. Quite logically, he rejected the offer. However, as with *Lucky Lady*, his rejection was merely taken as a signal that he wanted more money. As Hackman has said, Lew Grade can be extremely persuasive and thus he wound up making *March or Die*.

Hackman's character, Major William Sherman Foster, was in the venerable tradition of military martinets and was described by the star as 'a complex character to play,

[135]

although he's a born leader. Major Foster is an American West Pointer who has risen to high rank in the French Foreign Legion. He has spent most of his military life in the Legion fighting in the desert, and for the last four years he has been leading men in the trenches, which has burned madness into him. I'm walking the thin line of dealing with a neurotic or psychotic, although he would not have been called that in those days. You were either sane or batty.'

Although the film was a period piece, dealing with a renowned institution, Hackman didn't feel it incumbent upon him to undertake any detailed research for his role. The acting options were, as always, contained within the script. 'I read a couple of technical pieces on the Foreign Legion – where they operated and what they did – but it's an area that doesn't need a great deal of research because it's a matter of personal choice as to how you want to do the character. It wasn't as if there was anything in him I didn't know about, and we had some Legionnaires on the set to act as advisers.' It is not inconceivable that Hackman dredged up the distant memories of his years in the Marines to essay the unmerciful discipline and dedication of his Legion commander.

Having secured Hackman, Richards completed his cast with an international directory of name players, from Italy's Terence Hill and Sweden's Max Von Sydow to France's Catherine Deneuve and Britain's Ian Holm. Production began in Madrid and continued in Almeria on the southern coast of Spain, and then in Agadir, Morocco on the border of the Sahara desert. Richards's search for authentic period detail was exhaustive and expensive; ex-Legionnaires were hired as technical experts, 800 period rifles were purchased and scenes aboard a troop ship were filmed on a coal-burning steamship built in Scotland in 1912. 'For the first time the Legion will be shown on the screen as it really was,' Richards declared, and although there can be no doubting the sincerity of his conviction, it is just a shame that such steadfast attention wasn't paid to the calibre of the script.

The film begins in 1918. After the recent World War, Major Foster is assigned to protect an archaeological expedition in Morocco led by François Marneau (Max Von Sydow) from the Louvre. The group are seeking the tomb of the Angel

[136]

of the Desert and the priceless treasures rumoured to be contained therein. Prior to the war, Foster had promised the Arab chieftain El Krim (Ian Holm) that the excavation would be permanently halted but now the treasure is desperately sought to cover the cost of France's involvement in the war.

At the legion post in Bousaada, Foster begins the rigorous training of the new recruits and is particularly irked by Marco Segrain (Terence Hill) a former cat burglar with no respect for authority. Segrain casually romances the widowed Simone Picard (Catherine Deneuve), whose father had worked on the site, and even assists a fellow Legionnaire who has been abandoned during a desert march.

Whilst Foster and his men depart for the site at Erfoud, Simone arranges a passage home for Marco by sleeping with the unsavoury businessman Léon (Marne Maitland).

When the Angel's coffin is unearthed Foster gives it to El Krim as a gesture of appeasement. However, it suits the ambitions of the chieftain to protest against the desecration of the tomb and he leads his men in a massed attack on Erfoud. Only Marneau and a handful of Legionnaires survive, as El Krim does not relent until Foster is dead. He halts the fighting and sends Segrain back to Bousaada to tell of his great victory. At the camp, Segrain is now imbued with the spirit of the Legion and his dead comrades. He refuses Simone's offer of a passage home and then assumes Foster's role as he begins the training of a new group of recruits.

The promise of *March or Die* and one's faith in Dick Richards's vision of the film he aimed to make are quickly dispelled. Within the opening minutes, as the war-weary Legionnaires disembark from a troop ship, a young widow with a child in her arms starts singing a tremulous emotional version of La Marseillaise and we are off and galloping head first into the sands of cliché. Hackman's battle-hardened veteran is lumbered with lines like, 'There are no heroes in war – only survivors', and he can add nothing to a character that has already been embalmed in movie history.

March or Die was a further costly flop and the second consecutive failure for the Hackman-Lew Grade team. Reviewing the production, the *Monthly Film Bulletin* observed, '*March or Die*, yet another of Lord Grade's wholesome moneyspinners (sic) is an overheated mixture of stock characters and antique situations: its evocation of the soldier's life is pure "Luck of the Legion", while its treatment of the final massacre (hundreds of corpses, hardly a drop of blood) is deliberately but unsuccessfully intended to conjure memories of days when it was still possible to fill an auditorium with a ripping yarn set in foreign parts and featuring the demise of a sizable number of non-Europeans.' In America one Hollywood wag quickly redubbed the film 'Watch and Die'.

Apparently unscathed by the experience, Hackman changed uniforms, exchanged World Wars and enlisted in the truly all-star cast of Richard Attenborough's epic recreation of the Arnhem landings, *A Bridge Too Far*.

Cornelius Ryan's book *A Bridge Too Far* gave a comprehensive account of the 'Operation Market Garden' manoeuvre which had been designed to end the war by Christmas 1944 but ended, instead, in ignominious failure. The plan in September 1944 was to drop 35,000 Allied troops behind German lines to capture a group of bridges along the Belgian-Dutch border as a prelude to the occupation of the Ruhr and outright victory for the Allies. In its execution the plan was a disaster, resulting in thousands of casualties. The German forces were not caught unprepared: one Allied battalion was cut off without radio contact, weather conditions delayed the arrival of the Polish Parachute Brigade, who were slaughtered during a night attack on Elst, lines of supply were hopelessly overstretched, one bridge was destroyed, and troops who made it across the Rhine were held in check waiting for reinforcements. All told, it was heroic blunder that cost dearly. After nine days of fighting the men retreated, with Lieutenant-General Browning blaming the failure on their decision to capture Arnhem: one bridge too many.

Producer Joseph Levine acquired the screen rights to Ryan's book in 1975 and began the complex procedure of assembling the necessary finance and talent to undertake his film. Attenborough accepted the role of director when his plans to make *Gandhi* were once again temporarily abandoned. A budget of $25 million was set and the date of the world premiere was announced before one foot of film had passed through the camera.

The film features fourteen roles of varying length and

significance and it was decided at an early stage that each one should be filled by a star. Attenborough justified the spot-the-star casting by saying, 'The people we were dealing with, people like Horrocks, Cook, Urquhart, Frost, were stars in their own right. Tens of thousands of men followed them into battle unhesitatingly. Their persona was enormous. Within thirty seconds of them arriving on the screen that presence has to be felt in the audience. The only way to get that effect is use stars, the biggest we could get. And that is what we did.'

Of the names approached only Steve McQueen refused Attenborough's blandishments and Levine's apparently bottomless cheque book. McQueen had been absent from the screen for a couple of years and wanted to return in something where he was *the* star and not just another face in the crowd. Peter Finch and Robert De Niro were among those considered for roles, and Audrey Hepburn was definitely offered the only significant female role. When her salary demand was revealed as $750,000, Levine chose Liv Ullmann, who only requested $150,000. However, Attenborough nearly enough gathered together the troupe that he wanted. Robert Redford, at $2 million for five weeks work, headed the salary bill and the American contingent included Ryan O'Neal and James Caan, while Sean Connery, Michael Caine and Dirk Bogarde were amongst the British and Maximilian Schell led the Germans. Add to this Laurence Olivier as a Dutch doctor and you have, in Attenborough's words, 'a cast list rarely, if ever, equalled in any other film'.

The stars, other than Redford, were reckoned to be receiving around one million dollars each. Hackman played the Polish Major-General Stanislaw Sosabowski and confessed, 'I did it for the money. But it was all good company and it was a worthwhile role and a worthwhile film. I've been offered that much money and more to do things that I wouldn't do because I didn't particularly like them. I wouldn't do anything solely for the money if I didn't like the role.'

At a press conference where he discussed *A Bridge Too Far*, Hackman seemes almost defensive about his casual acceptance of Joseph Levine's money. 'People are always disturbed or curious about why an actor is paid a fortune for only ten days' work. The fact is that when they paid me

[139]

that money they weren't really buying me for any length of time. There were a lot of actors who could have done that role as well as, if not better than I, who are well versed in Polish accents and the rest. But what they were using was my name for whatever that's worth, just like they used Robert Redford, James Caan and the others. You don't get paid for the number of days you work on a film, you get paid because they need you.

'It's nice for me. It wasn't anything I was ashamed of doing and there's a point where it's attractive to be able to go off to Holland for a few weeks and work with people you enjoy being with.'

Filming began in Holland on 26 April 1976 and was completed six months later, under budget and twelve hours ahead of schedule. Attenborough worked an eighteen-hour day and ran his production like a military operation dependent on human resources, supplies and fine timing.

'The schedule was for twenty-three weeks and in the middle of that schedule I had a frightening six-week period when some of the stars were finishing their roles, others were in the middle of theirs and others were just about to start. Some, like Sean Connery, Dirk Bogarde, Ryan O'Neal, Gene Hackman, all *had* to meet on one particular day.

'If we'd have lost that day for whatever reason it would have been absolute chaos. God knows what would have happened to the schedule. What would have happened to the cost would have been unthinkable.'

A Bridge Too Far was completed in time for its scheduled opening during the summer of 1977. A massive, three-hour statement on the folly of war, it suffered from a degree of overstatement; a point is made, then bludgeoned by overemphasis and reiteration. However, the initial level of business was strong until a curious backlash started whereby the film was taken to task for presenting a tragic moment from the war as a slab of all-star summer entertainment. The *New Yorker* wrote, 'One finds oneself angered and harrowed by a film that can make something like "A Night of a Thousand Stars" at the London Palladium of such an unforgettable military tragedy.'

In America, the film earned an impressive $21 million and went on to earn enough around the world to ensure profitability. In Britain the film won Academy Awards for its soundtrack, John Addison's stirring music, Geoffrey Unsworth's cinematography and for Edward Fox as Best Supporting Actor. In general, the British actors fared best on screen, with Fox's hearty Brian Horrocks and Sean Connery's gritty Roy Urquhart impressing the most.

Hackman's role as Sosabowski is a thankless one. Perpetually frustrated by the inclement weather, and put on hold, he is required to watch and wait, offering only a gruff stoicism, a dour personality and an 'interesting' accent. The *Monthly Film Bulletin* noted, 'Gene Hackman plays Sosabowski with one-note dolefulness tempered by an extraordinary Polish accent.'

It was now apparent that Hackman was in slow retreat from the big screen. After the commanding heights of powerful, dominating charaterizations like Harry Caul (*The Conversation*) and Harry Moseby (*Night Moves*) he had gradually slackened his grip and lowered his standards, first by agreeing to play mere ciphers like Roy Tucker in *The Domino Principle* and then by losing himself amidst all-star casts where there was less effort required, less importance attached to his individual work and less of an impact made. It was as if he were regressing to the state of a dependable character actor, only now he demanded and won immense financial remunerations for his modest appearances. The hapless condition of his career was not improved by his next choice: a lucrative supporting role in the all-star film *Superman*.

Chapter Ten

The father-and-son team of Alexander and Ilya Salkind were riding high on the critical and commercial success of *The Three Musketeers* when they decided to make a film of the cherished comic-book hero Superman. Their plans were hatched during a celebratory meal at the Café de la Paix in Paris during May of 1974. Also present that evening was their business partner Pierre Spengler. As the conversation ranged over current triumphs and future plans, Alexander innocently enquired what they might contemplate for their next major project. It was Ilya who suggested Superman, and his eager enthusiasm quickly convinced the other two that they need look no further.

Once the initial decision had been taken, the first item on the agenda was to acquire the screen rights from D. C. Comics. The character of Superman had been created in 1933 by Jerry Segal and Joe Shuster and had first appeared on the book-stalls in 1938. D. C. Comics were understandably protective of the half-century legacy of their heroic idol, and among the points crucial to the negotiations were guarantees that the film would not be a satire or spoof nor would it be pornographic. The latter contract clause would avoid the possibility of something like *Flesh Gordon*, while the former would prevent the high 'camp' extremes of *Modesty Blaise*.

Once D. C. Comics were satisfied that their property would be treated with due respect, Ilya Salkind began to dream about the type of film that they would make. He envisaged not just one Superman film but a whole series. They had secured the rights for the next 25 years and he started to describe Superman as the natural successor to James Bond as the screen's premiere adventure hero. It was decided, in the wake of The Three and The Four *Musketeers*, that the filming of *Superman* would also entail a large proportion of the filming of *Superman II* so that a sequel could be 80 per cent completed by the time the first film was ready for release. On this occasion, the actors were forewarned that they would be making two films at once.

If the Salkinds' plan was to work, *Superman 1* needed to stun and stagger an audience into wanting more. The essential ingredients for that to transpire were a good script, lavish special effects and the right actor to play the Man of Steel. A tentative figure of $25,000,000 was mentioned for the budget and whilst Alexander Salkind wanted the biggest star that money could buy for the title role, Ilya favoured the selection of a total unknown. Meanwhile, they set about finding an appropriate scriptwriter; William Goldman wasn't interested but Mario Puzo, of *The Godfather* fame, joined the team for a reputed fee of $350,000 plus five per cent of the film's gross.

Having made steady, satisfactory progress with their package, the Salkinds publicly announced the film at the 1975 Cannes Film Festival: a plane circled the area every hour flying the banner headline 'Superman, Salkind, Puzo'. At the 1976 Festival the banner read, 'Superman, Salkind, Hamilton', for Guy Hamilton, director of some of the best James Bond films, including *Goldfinger* (1964) and *Diamonds Are Forever* (1971), had been signed as the director of *Superman*.

Hamilton found that Puzo's script lacked the proper reverence for its subject, and thus the triumvirate of David and Leslie Newman and Robert Benton were hired to work on the document. Benton and David Newman had written the Broadway musical *It's a Bird, It's a Plane, It's Superman* whilst waiting to make their entry into the film world with the script of *Bonnie and Clyde*. As they polished Puzo's storyline, work proceeded on preliminary set building at the Cinecitta studios in Rome. The one crucial element still lacking was a cast.

Salkind senior seems to have felt that the best means of retaining the faith of his investors was to secure the services of a major star. He would happily consider anyone whose name alone could guarantee a certain level of audience interest. The most popular choice was probably Robert Redford, but he was reluctant to commit himself without

[143]

seeing a final version of the script, and negotiations over his salary also proved a stumbling block. Paul Newman was then approached and he too declined. The roster of stars in the reckoning at various stages of the film's development included Charles Bronson, Clint Eastwood, Kris Kristofferson, Steve McQueen, Nick Nolte, Ryan O'Neal, Burt Reynolds, David Soul, Sylvester Stallone, Robert Wagner and Jan-Michael Vincent.

As frustration mounted it became increasingly evident that the best policy would be to cast a total unknown as Superman. An audience could never be expected to integrate an established star with the role and accept, say, Charles Bronson in red cape and tights flying through the air. The prospect of being laughed off the screen was a more alarming one than that of an anonymous actor's lack of drawing power at the box-office. The odd star name was essential to placate the moneymen, but some of the other roles could be easily adapted to the demands of a star. The two roles most likely to attract the luminaries were considered to be Superman's father Jor-El and his archenemy Lex Luthor.

Fate finally smiled on the Salkinds when a telephone call alterted them to the possibility of purchasing the services of Marlon Brando to play Jor-El. Within hours his demands had been met and the first member of the cast secured.

Brando's salary was judged to be the largest ever paid in the history of the cinema, with estimates varying between $2 and $4 million dollars plus 11.3 per cent of the final profits, all for twelve days work. 'Some put his price too high, some too low,' said Ilya Salkind. 'The higher ones tend to be the nearest.' Unperturbed by the expense, the Salkinds claimed that he was worth every cent in publicity value alone, never mind his thespian gifts. Unfortunately, Brando had one other request to make of them: because of legal complications over a number of obscenity charges brought against *Last Tango in Paris* he would not be willing to work in Rome. The Salkinds agreed to move the filming to England, but Guy Hamilton felt that he was unable to work there because of his own problems in Britain. Hamilton bade them farewell, and now the film possessed a major star but no director.

The Salkinds now returned to Paul Newman and asked if

he would play the flamboyant villain Lex Luthor. Newman declined their invitation, and they next approached Gene Hackman. Hackman had been a comic-book fan as a child, although with no specific affection for Superman: 'We didn't take them at all seriously, of course. Whoever would have thought that one day I'd be starring in a mammoth film based on them? I'd just buy one, then trade it for a Tarzan or a Captain Marvel.' Hackman read the *Superman* script and was sufficiently intrigued by the Lex Luthor character to consider the film.

'I felt I could do something with the character. It's been a long, long time since I have been offered a part in such a broad, comedic vein. I'm not normally one for make-up and hair and that's what Luthor is all about. He's a snappy dresser, wears a series of wigs – the whole works.'

Apart from the stimulus of trying a fresh characterization, there was also the prospect of another healthy pay packet; Hackman was reported to be earning $2 million for two months' work. 'I actually read the part before any money was discussed. And I liked it,' he told Roderick Mann. 'But the money was a big inducement. I won't deny that. I probably wouldn't have done the film at all if Brando hadn't been involved. But I thought: If he is doing it, why not?' Hackman would receive second billing, above the title and behind Brando, the man who had been part of his early inspiration to become an actor. Despite their closeness on the credits, the two men share no scenes in the film and their shooting schedules did not coincide.

With Brando and Hackman now on the team, the pressure diminished to have a 'name' as Superman and the Salkinds decided to opt for an unknown. Just for insurance, however, they signed up a stellar supporting cast from Harry Andrews to Susannah York via Glenn Ford, Trevor Howard and Terence Stamp. Peter Boyle was announced as Hackman's bumbling sidekick Otis, a rather inspired notion after their memorable brief encounter in *Young Frankenstein*. However, and for whatever reasons, Boyle was replaced by Ned Beatty.

The need to find just the right actress to play Superman's love interest, *Daily Planet* reporter Lois Lane, involved almost as wide-ranging a search as the hunt for Superman. Amongst the candidates for the job were Jill Clayburgh,

[145]

Carrie Fisher, Jessica Lange, Shirley MacLaine, Liza Minnelli and Natalie Wood before Canadian actress Margot Kidder won the coveted role.

As all the pieces of this most complex of movie jigsaws slotted into place, the Salkinds also found their director in Richard Donner. A television director of high repute and vast experience, Donner's cinema reputation was negligible, resting precariously on three features, *X–15* (1961), the Sammy Davis Jr-Peter Lawford caper *Salt and Pepper* (1968) and the dim older man-younger woman drama *Twinky* (1969) (US title *Lola*). He could hardly have appeared the ideal man to direct a multimillion dollar spectacular until the 1976 release of *The Omen* and a worldwide box-office gross of $100 million. Ilya Salkind called him and offered him the job.

The selection of Donner was one of the Salkinds' shrewdest pieces of casting; from the outset he insisted upon treating the film with the seriousness that it merited. 'I was brought up on Superman, and I believe this myth,' he insisted. 'There is a little bit of God Bless America in it. There is a purity and fantasy in it that is right for our times.' Donner expressed his dislike of the existing script and was given the right to have it extensively rewritten. Mario Puzo's version had allegedly included an excessive amount of groan-inducing puns, juvenile humour and even a comic encounter with Telly Savalas's Kojak. Tom Mankiewicz was hired to produce a final draft of the script and to act as the film's creative consultant.

The only outstanding member of the cast still to be chosen was Superman himself. 'I always knew it would be hard casting Superman,' Ilya Salkind said, with decided under-statement. 'We saw lots of people, and as the weeks went by I got very depressed. Then one day Skye (his wife) came home and said, "My dentist looks after Ryan O'Neal and Ryan says that if you're looking for an unknown, he'd be ideal." I groaned. I mean, Skye's dentist? But finally we agreed to see him, and when this guy (Don Voyne) walked in we went crazy. After the guys we'd seen who were hope-less, he looked terrific. So, we tested him. And he wasn't bad. The only trouble was he was a bit old for the part. And, of course, he had no acting experience.'

When Voyne was ruled out as a possibility, Salkind

became even more depressed; almost 200 people had been considered for the role, ten of them had undergone screen tests and yet they were no nearer finding their man.

With grim resolution, Salkind sifted through photographs of some of the actors who had already been interviewed and came across one of Christopher Reeve, marked with an X. When he had been interviewed in New York, Richard Donner had considered him too young and too handsome. Now, Salkind wasn't so sure that Reeve was that far from meeting their requirements. A screen test was arranged and the results removed all doubts: 'When we showed that test to Warners they stood and applauded. And we knew then that everything was going to be all right. . . .'

Reeve had played opposite Katharine Hepburn on Broadway in *A Matter of Gravity* and made a modest appearance in the Charlton Heston nuclear submarine drama *Gray Lady Down* (1977). A naturally blonde, six-foot-four figure, Reeve dyed his hair black and embarked upon a gruelling programme of physical exercise under the supervision of Dave Prowse, the body of Darth Vader in the *Star Wars* series. Reeve's daily schedule included two hours of weight-lifting and ninety minutes on a trampoline. All told, he added between twenty and thirty pounds of muscle to his already considerable frame.

As well as his duty to capture the physical presence of Superman, Reeve also felt a strong sense of his responsibility to accurately embody the qualities that make the character so beloved of the American populace:

'The Superman I wanted to play – the only one I *could* play – was a low-key one. Very warm, very friendly, very accessible and not at all impressed with himself.

'Any time that you try to play someone who is not only the ultimate hero but also an American ideal, you can be setting yourself up for an amazing and painful pratfall. It's a trapeze act without a safety net. The whole film is, but particularly so for me. I can't single-handedly make it good, but I sure as hell can go a long way towards ruining it.'

Reeve sought advice from Sean Connery about the problems of becoming too closely associated with one character and the perils of giving his producers a commitment to a long-term series. Connery advised, 'You had better be good in the first *Superman* or you won't have to worry about the second and the third.' Reeve was paid a considerate $250,000 in an attempt to secure his initial good will and prevent his taking legal action over underpayment, as Connery had done.

Superman was to be filmed on locations in New York, Canada and Mexico, with the interior work undertaken at Pinewood Studios. The first day of filming was pencilled in for 28 March 1977. It was apparent to Donner that the production would be unlike any other that he, or perhaps any director, had ever worked on. He later told *Time Out*, 'Apart from the locations, we constructed the Golden Gate Bridge, the Hoover Dam, the *Daily Planet* building, a heliport, Air Force One and an ice fortress, all at Pinewood. The Salkinds kept coming up with the money but they would not show me a budget, which was great but it was also kind of frightening. And the same applies to the schedule. They never really scheduled anything until the final script, and even then they would say something like "Superman flies from here to there and saves the Golden Gate Bridge – three days?" Well, I mean, what kind of schedule is that? It could have taken six months to shoot that sequence alone. So we really did it without a budget or a schedule.'

The scenes with Marlon Brando were the first to be finished. He arrived on the set suffering from jet lag and an irritating cold, refused a rehearsal of his first scene, a tricky, ten-minute monologue, and completed it in one perfect take. He was encased in a heavy costume and wig and running a high temperature, his interest in the film was minimal as it was merely a means to an end (earning money to help the American Indians), but his professionalism was intact and still awe-inspiring. Richard Donner, in an interview for the *Telegraph Sunday Magazine*, recalled, 'Two days into the role he came to me late in the afternoon and said he had a cold and was still a bit jet-lagged. Would I mind if he finished early that day? That floored me. Knowing how little time we had with him, I'd even been figuring out what it cost us every time he went to the lavatory. Now this. But I said the only thing I could say: "You're Marlon Brando. How can I stop you?"

'Then he said, "Tell you what, I'll give you an extra day. How about that?" Well, at his salary that extra day was worth a fortune. And it meant that we could get everything we needed. So, I sent him home happily.'

Brando departed in April, after his thirteen working days, and Hackman arrived to film his scenes during May and June. His principal co-stars included the aforementioned Ned Beatty as Otis, Valerie Perrine as Miss Teschmacher and Christopher Reeve. Later, Hackman admitted, 'I did Superman because they offered a lot of money and I liked the director. I thought it would be a lark, but it turned out to be a bit boring because it was a big production and a long schedule.'

Playing Lex Luthor should have been a chance to relax and just have some fun with his character, secure in the knowledge that Reeve and the special effects team faced the real challenges. However, Hackman owned up to a rather perverse reaction to this lack of pressure. 'That sort of movie is a terrific holiday for most actors, but it has the reverse effect on me. The more technical a film becomes the more inhibited I am. Therefore the harder I have to work at it.'

Explaining the differences between something physically exhausting like *March or Die* and something mentally draining like *Superman*, Hackman noted, 'You get a little lost in the equipment and the technical necessities. Sometimes it takes an hour or two to get a character in *Superman* to fly from one wall to another and to have him fly in the proper way, making sure that whoever's holding him up doesn't show! And that's difficult. So as an actor your energy and your attention level becomes somewhat dissipated by the amount of energy going into that and when it comes time to do your section, it gets a little soft.'

On July 3rd, Donner and his crew moved to New York to film in the city and then move on to Niagara Falls. The rough, seven-month shooting schedule finished at the end of October but many of the technical problems had still to be surmounted. The film's proud boast had been that an audience would believe that a man could fly. The details of how this could be achieved were to consume months of work and innovation and ensure that the film would not open in time for its planned spring premiere, nor for a summer release. Instead, *Superman* would be performing minor miracles to be ready for Christmas 1978.

The Salkinds chose to expend whatever sum of money

[149]

and time was necessary to make Superman fly; if such a feat was worth doing it was worth doing properly. It is perhaps impossible to put a final figure on the budget; as two films were being made side-by-side some costs were shared, others could justifiably be accounted for as belonging to one film or the other. However, a sum of between $40 and $65 million is said to have covered all the costs.

Superman was able to fly via a mixture of wires, the use of miniatures, complicated matte effects, Christopher Reeve swinging fifty feet from a crane and, finally, Donner's determination that he would. 'When he flew I wanted to see all sides of him. And how the hell do you roll somebody in flight when they're on wires? So one of the reasons it took so long was that we had to invent, literally *invent*, new special effects techniques as we went along.'

In America *Superman* was premiered before President Jimmy Carter; in Britain the Queen attended a similar function. Long-delayed and eagerly-anticipated, the film did not disappoint the faithful. Donner and his vast team had created the best-ever screen adaptation of a comic-book legend, mixing sincerity and special effects with a sense of wonderment and sprinkling it all with the undefinable quality of movie magic.

The film begins on the planet Krypton with Marlon Brando adding the necessary conviction to his scenes as Superman's father Jor-El. Although he successfully oversees the trial and banishment of three traitors led by General Zod (Terence Stamp), no one will listen to him when he warns of the danger of their planet falling into its own sun. Before their destruction, Jor-El and his wife Laura (Susannah York) launch their son towards the relative security of a primitive planet known as Earth.

After his discovery by Jonathan and Martha Kent (Glenn Ford and Phyllis Thaxter), the film follows the development of Superman and his alter ago Clark Kent as he displays superhuman strength and is taught all his father's accumulated wisdom. Then, he emerges as the shy, gauche, bespectacled *Daily Planet* reporter who dons his distinctive red and blue costume to fight for 'Truth, Justice and the American way'.

Eventually he is called upon to combat the evil designs of megalomaniac Lex Luthor, who has purchased vast expanses of arid land to the east of California and now plans to detonate a nuclear missile along the San Andreas Fault, thus precipitating a massive earthquake that will leave an entirely new West Coast of America in its wake. Needless to say, Superman saves the day and turns over the defeated Luthor to the proper authorities.

Much to the relief of the Salkinds, *Superman* was a soaraway success straight across the globe. The American takings amounted to $81 million, comfortably placing *Superman* on *Variety*'s top-ten list of the most popular films ever made. It was also, at that time, the most profitable release in the history of Warner Brothers. The film was nominated in three Academy Award categories for sound, editing and John Williams' musical score. The one Oscar that it actually received was a non-competitive 'Special Achievement Award' for visual effects.

After applauding the special effects, Donner's efforts, Brando's sonorous presence and Reeve's skilful dual characterization, it must be said that the least satisfactory element of *Superman* is Hackman's drab villainy. His scenes with Beatty's hopelessly inept assistant and Perrine's voluptuous, not-so-dumb associate reduce the film to the more mundane level of the *Batman* television series.

As the self-styled 'greatest criminal mind of our time', Hackman is given the characteristics of a sarcastic sense of humour and a garish wardrobe. He scarcely seems capable of masterminding the 'crime of the century' nor of living up to Superman's description of him as a 'diseased maniac'. Hackman offers a genial stroll through some mild buffoonery and thus upsets the balance of the film. Can Superman be truly super when there is no sense of genuine threat or menace in the man who is his sworn enemy? Perhaps the film would have been somewhat more effective if the function of the villain had been as respectfully considered as the attributes of the hero. Hackman was perhaps even a poor choice for the role. If one is convinced that his finest quality is his ordinariness and ability to document the minutiae of recognizably human characters, then it seems inappropriate to expect him to be at his best as a larger-than-life comic-book villain with absolutely no foothold in reality. The result is an inevitable letdown.

Regardless of one's reservations over his performance

Hackman could still reflect on what is undoubtedly the most popular film of his career. Later he would admit, 'I was disappointed when I saw the film.'

The inevitable return of 'Popeye' Doyle, this time on location in Marseilles, in *French Connection II* (1975). *(Kobal)*

In a rare comic role as the blind hermit in Mel Brooks's *Young Frankenstein*, Hackman serves hot soup in his guest's lap. Peter Boyle plays the Monster. *(20th Century-Fox/Kobal)*

'I was seduced', was Hackman's comment on the offer he was made for *Lucky Lady*, a film he hated making but which became a box-office success as well as earning him $1¼ million. His co-stars were Liza Minnelli and Burt Reynolds. *(Kobal)*

Made for Sir Lew Grade's Associated General Films, *March or Die* saw Hackman cast as a battle-hardened Legionnaire in what turned out to be a costly flop. *(Kobal)*

With cell-mate Mickey Rooney in the political thriller *The Domino Principle* (1976). *(Kobal)*

The first of the *Superman* movies, and the birth of a billion-dollar money-spinner: Hackman as Lex Luthor, Superman's arch-enemy, with his assistant, Otis (Ned Beatty). *(Kobal)*

Hackman's return to movie acting after a short-lived retirement was in the modestly-budgeted *All Night Long* with Barbra Streisand. *(Kobal)*

Joining up with Warren Beatty again in 1981, Hackman had a cameo role as a newspaper editor in *Reds,* the epic story of John Reed and Louise Bryant. *(Paramount Pictures/David Appleby/Kobal)*

In *Eureka* (1982) Hackman plays the role of Jack McCann, whose discovery of a gold mine brings him 'one moment of rapture followed by decades of despair'. *(Kobal)*

One of the first films to explore the theme of Vietnam veterans still held as POWs was *Uncommon Valor* (1983). *(Paramount Pictures/Kobal)*

With Matt Dillon as his son, Hackman plays a retired CIA agent in search of his kidnapped wife in *Target*. *(CBS/Kobal)*

Ann-Margret and Gene Hackman taking a second chance at happiness in *Twice in a Lifetime*. *(Kobal)*

Chapter Eleven

In the summer of 1977, with his work on *Superman* and *Superman II* completed, Hackman quietly embarked upon the process of retirement. There was no official announcement of his intentions; he simply returned home to California and instructed his agent to let it be known that he was no longer available for work. He wasn't willing to read any new scripts. He didn't want any producer to circumvent his agent and approach him directly. He had merely decided to have nothing more to do with the film business.

As news of Hackman's retirement spread around the film community, his resolve was considered rash and ill-judged. After all, he was a major star near the peak of his career. He had struggled many years to attain his current preeminence and it just didn't make sense for him to turn his back on all the rich rewards of stardom. However, perhaps he was carrying on a tradition, that stretched from Mary Pickford through Greta Garbo to Cary Grant, of quitting whilst he was ahead, and if that was his decision, then so be it.

Hackman's choice of retirement was certainly not prompted by a lack of work. He had only recently been approached by his *Conversation* director Francis Coppola about appearing in his new production, *Apocalypse Now*, which was scheduled for filming in 1977. Hackman was allegedly offered the part of Lieutenant-Colonel Kilgore, a role ultimately played by Robert Duvall. Coppola wanted him to work for a percentage of the hoped-for profits without the guarantee of any upfront sum. Hackman was unwilling to countenance such an arrangement and parted company with Coppola on amicable terms: 'Francis has a way of asking you to work on the come, which I didn't think I should do. But I have all the respect in the world for him. I think maybe he's the best director there is.'

Hackman's reasons for retirement were far more deep-rooted than a transitory sense of regret over a lost opportunity. In many ways the decision was the only logical conclusion of his slow retreat from the big screen. If you select progressively less significant roles, in increasingly unworthy projects, then inevitably you are moving towards not accepting any roles at all. He was profoundly disillusioned at the state of a career where he could earn vast fortunes for work that neither interested nor stimulated him. He could fool himself and journalists that every role presented its own challenges, but you can't fool all the people all of the time and there is a limit to the number of occasions on which you can spout baloney about another 'interesting' script and 'interesting' director. Hackman at 47 plunged into the mid-life crisis, and the first step towards recovering his self-esteem was to step off the money-go-round.

In a sense, Hackman was the victim of his own success and had fallen for the oldest cliché in the book: the one about being seduced by the system and believing in his own immortality.

'I don't know that I was terribly well prepared for success, although I thought I was. I just got swept along – it was like a fantasy come true for me. I hadn't thought the fantasy out, but I've concluded now that it's very fleeting. The reality is that you have to continue to do the work that got you there. You can't live a myth.'

Hackman had been living the myth of being a movie star whilst neglecting his true instinct for being a movie actor. He had made all the copybook mistakes of an ordinary fellow catapulted into an extraordinary position. Firstly, he hadn't ceased working because he could never convince himself that the fantasy would endure. Then he had eagerly embraced the kind of grand lifestyle that he had never really coveted in the first place, but which was the way movie stars were *supposed* to live.

'It's funny that having been poor, you do all the classic poor things,' he later reflected. 'You get nine of everything. I've had all the airplanes, all the cars, all the houses, and now I've worked my way up to a house on a twenty-two acre estate with three floors, twenty rooms, an elevator, and nine bathrooms – its's a palace. And now I just want to get out. I just want a little Spanish-style house and a pick-up truck or something.'

Retrospectively analyzing where he went wrong, Hackman described the period between his Oscar win and his retirement as 'a long nightmarish blank when I couldn't have told you from one day to the next what I was doing or what I was going to do. I just knew there was a lot of money to be made and I didn't have to think too much about it. For ten years I've done nothing but work because I could never believe that an ugly schmuck like me could stay so lucky.'

Some were sympathetic to his plight, and Arthur Penn wisely observed, 'It's a tough life being an American movie actor. An actor doesn't have control over the quality of a film he's working on. You may take a picture because you like the director or you like some of the other actors you'll be working with, but so many people are involved in the finished product that it's hard to tell how a film will turn out when you agree to appear.'

In a mood of painfully honest self-examination, Hackman was willing to shoulder sole responsibility for his predicament. 'I made four bad pictures in a row – *Lucky Lady, The Domino Principle, A Bridge Too Far, March or Die*. I should have stopped after *Lucky Lady* and gone back to being straight, to taking parts for what they were and not what they paid. But I didn't, and I found my bad decisions were coming back to haunt me. I was making *March or Die* and not enjoying it. Things suddenly seemed very simple. I decided to stop acting before I was forced to stop. Actors are judged by the films they choose to make. And that's right. If you're a "name", you're blamed for a bad film, and what you're being blamed for is your choice of material.'

Now that he was removed from the film business he need no longer hold himself in check out of consideration for his colleagues' feelings, and he began to talk realistically about some of the mistakes that had been made. 'When you make a bad picture, people in the street are the first to tell you. "That was a rotten picture," they'll say. They said it a lot about *The Domino Principle*. Most people didn't seem to understand that film. I'm not surprised. I didn't understand

[155]

it either. I had lots of arguments with the director, Stanley Kramer. Some time later I read an article in a magazine where he talked about my behaviour on the film. Apparently he had kept a diary. It was embarrassing to read it, but I have to say it was accurate. The truth was I knew we were in trouble on that film, and I got scared.'

Hackman had become so miserable over the recent films he had made that he had even grown to dislike watching himself on screen. 'What I was seeing was an old man, an uncle figure of around fifty. I still believed I was a young guy in his twenties!'

Fretful about how to grow old gracefully on screen, unhappy with his career and the compromises he had made, Hackman needed time, time to re-think his priorities, learn from the lessons of his past and rekindle his enthusiasms. Making a complete break from what had been his life and work was a severe solution to his problems, but there was also his family to consider.

Trying to reconcile the demands of family and career is one of the hardest tasks facing any successful star. Hollywood is the film capital of the world in name only. In reality film is the most internationl medium and an actor can be called upon to perform in virtually any location around the globe. Hackman's home may have been in California but he rarely, if ever, hung his hat there. He had worked in France (*French Connection II*), Mexico (*Lucky Lady*), Morocco (*March or Die*), Holland (*A Bridge Too Far*) and Britain (*Superman*). There were times when he could pilot his own plane home for the weekends, but inevitably he missed out on a great deal of 'normal' family life. He couldn't give enough attention to the children, their education or their welfare, and there were bound to be moments that found him on the other side of the world when he was most needed at home.

Over the twenty years of his marriage to Faye the couple had separated, argued, fought and made up. Now, however, he could be the father and husband that he wanted to be: present instead of absent, interested instead of preoccupied and, above all, available. By Hackman's own reckoning he had almost left it too late.

'I wasn't easy to live with anymore and my home and family life were in a turmoil as a result. If I had stayed acting, there would have been a real personal disaster for me. My wife Faye is not an actress, so she could see what was happening to me. She didn't want the effects to rub off on her.' The pressures of his work had begun to intrude too forcibly into the personal domain, and he observed, 'I found my personality was changing. I was becoming mean and arrogant. I didn't slap my wife or three children at home as I did people on the screen, but they noticed the difference in me.'

Taking all these factors into account, Hackman gathered his family at their weekend home in Monterey and prepared to ease into the good life. He was a wealthy man and there were plenty of pursuits to occupy his bountiful free time. Now he could catch up on all those books he had been meaning to read. He could travel at leisure with his family. He took up tennis and began to chip away at some large stones in an attempt at sculpture. Soon he felt relaxed enough to contemplate sketching and painting again. If he didn't want to do anything he could sit around being lazy. If he still hankered after adventure he could, and did, compete in some of the more prestigious car races at Sebring and Riverside. For total contentment he could fly one of the three planes he owned. 'I'd take my Pitts biplane solo above the clouds; up there is perfect peace and relaxation,' he claimed.

It all sounded idyllic – the perfect happy ending. However, it wasn't enough. The warning bells started to sound after eighteen months when he began to consider starting his own theatre group to recapture some of the pure enjoyment that he had once derived from acting. Simply put, it was a classic diagnosis of once an actor, always an actor.

In interviews he confessed, 'It's all been such a disappointment. I thought I'd enjoy myself so much. But all I've done is miss acting. Isn't that ridiculous? All those things that kept me busy during retirement I thought I was going to enjoy because I'd never had time for them before. I didn't really accomplish anything during those years. There were things I thought I wanted to do, but I was a mess. I wound up lying around. I finally had to admit to myself that I could do none of those things anywhere nearly as well as I can act. And I don't mean that in any egotistical sense.'

What Hackman did accomplish during his lengthy

sabbatical was to learn that he had lost none of his love for the actual craft of acting. What had depressed and soured him was all the clutter of money and image that he had allowed to obscure his judgement. 'I lost enthusiasm for the business, not for acting. The business is ugly. There's so much money involved. It's corrupt. As an artist, you want to open up. As a businessman you have to keep your guard up.'

If he was to be tempted back to the screen, then it must be on his own terms. Money could never be completely ignored because it is a reflection of status and respect within his industry, but he didn't need to work solely for the money. He needed to work because he enjoyed it and because it was what he did best. If he was also well-paid, then that should be considered a bonus, something that he would neither crave nor disparage.

Turning the tables on his perceptions made the possibility of filming again both tempting and attractive. He needed no further inducement than the prospect of a good role and he would be back in front of the cameras. His retirement may even have been beneficial as it gave him the thinking space to resolve so many of his problems and find peace of mind. 'I'd thought that after twenty years of acting I'd be glad of a rest. But sailing off to Tahiti isn't the answer, obviously. Perhaps there is no answer.

'I have come to accept that the rest of my working life will be devoted to acting,' he concluded. 'I've tried other things, but this is what I do best; it's what I look forward to most of all when I wake in the morning.'

Chapter Twelve

Hackman had not worked in front of a camera since 1977. His pause for reflection had refreshed him and recharged his creative batteries. However, now that he was more than willing to work again there was nobody clamouring for his services. Absence had not made the heart grow fonder, merely forgetful.

His retirement cannot have made much of an impression upon the cinema-going masses. He may have been able to walk away from the *Superman* set in 1977, but his colleagues had toiled on, preparing for the film's world premieres during Christmas of 1978. Thus, whilst he had been deep in retreat and contemplation, his absence was only just entering public consciousness when the film's wide, general release came in the opening months of 1979. During that year *Superman II* went into production, Hackman's contribution having been filed away for future reference two years previously. The complete film surfaced in Britain in 1980 and the following year in America. This apparent continued flow of work from Hackman ironically served to conceal the fact that he was unemployed.

Amidst some controversy, Richard Donner was asked to relinquish the direction of *Superman II* in favour of Richard Lester. Lester had directed The Three and Four *Musketeers* for the Salkinds and was hired as a consultant and unofficial second-unit director on *Superman*. Donner had regarded it as his unspoken right to direct the sequel and was understandably hurt by his exclusion: 'I am heartbroken. I gave two years of my life to the production and I cracked the technical difficulties of getting Superman to fly.'

Pierre Spengler reported, 'As for Richard Donner we decided we did not require his talents to complete *Superman II*.

Most of what remains to be done requires technical rather than creative ability.'

Allegedly some 80 per cent of the sequel had been filmed in tandem with the original, yet *Superman II* still manages to bear the recognizable signature of Richard Lester, who indulges his penchant for slapstick and satire. His film is a sly, witty comic-book entertainment that lacks only the sense of awe and wonderment that Donner had managed to conjure up.

Hackman's Lex Luthor is overshadowed on this occasion by the arrival of the rebel General Zod (Terence Stamp) and his cohorts. They escape their interstellar banishment and wreak havoc on Earth, forcing even the American President to acknowledge their supremacy. Meanwhile, Lois Lane has finally twigged that Superman and Clark Kent are one and the same. Deeply in love, Superman chooses to surrender his extraordinary powers so that he may marry Lois and live as a human. When the President calls upon him in his hour of need, Superman is powerless to respond.

Eventually, a shard of Kryptonite revives Superman's strength and he is able to overcome Zod and the threat he poses to mankind. The President resumes office in the White House and Superman vows that he will always be vigilant in future.

Lex Luthor's involvement in this scenario is necessarily limited. His villainy is not a major challenge to Superman and his presence is expected rather than justified. Along the way he opportunistically offers his services to Zod and later tries to curry favour with Superman when the tables are turned. His function is almost as comic relief from the real struggle at the centre of the film and this tends to relegate him to the sidelines of the main drama. He does not appear at all in *Superman III*.

Despite his appearance in *Superman II*, the success or failure of the series was a remote concern for Hackman as he began to pick up the pieces of a career on which he seemed to have pressed the self-destruct button. Older and wiser, he chose to proceed with caution.

If Hackman had learnt one lesson from his lay-off, it was the virtue of patience and the value of not rushing into the first well-paid film offer that came along. Favouring prodigality over selectivity had been his undoing in the first place, so now he would focus on quality instead of quantity.

'The only good thing about this break is that it's got me off the take-the-money-and-run bandwagon,' he told Roderick Mann. 'I'm certainly going to stop making three pictures a year. For a start, there aren't three good films to make. I've done a lot of things that I wasn't proud of in my time. It seems to me that now they're making fewer movies, but bigger and better ones. So my way of life doesn't make sense.'

As his enforced idleness continued, Hackman grew steadily more bored and restless. He watched his son race motorcycles and drew some solace from painting. 'I work in oils and find it enormously soothing. Nothing about it is competitive. It's a very private thing with me. I would never put myself in a situation where my paintings could be judged: they'd immediately become the paintings of "Gene Hackman, the actor" and I wouldn't get an honest reaction.'

Nothing, however, could actually substitute for the exhausting satisfaction to be derived from making a decent film. 'Retirement is a kind of death, isn't it? And no fun at all. One tends to forget the pain of moviemaking. I guess it's like pregnancy – something compels you to go through it all over again.'

He nearly went back to work later in the year when Robert Redford contacted him about appearing in his first film as a director, *Ordinary People*. Hackman is wary about discussing the 'ones that got away' and it is uncertain whether the role in question was that of the father, played by Donald Sutherland, or the psychiatrist played by Judd Hirsch. Nevertheless, it proved to be another instance of the businessman smothering the artist. He told the tenacious Robert Ward of *American Film*, 'We just couldn't make a deal. I would have loved to have done that film, but I wanted some points, and they were willing to give me points but not enough to make the picture feasible. It was just one of those deals that fell apart.'

His agent, Sue Mengers, was instrumental in prompting his return in a project that was something of a family affair. Her husband, Jean-Claude Tramont, was about to make his English-language directorial bow with a film called *All Night Long*. It was a romantic comedy about a middle-aged businessman dropping out of the rat race to grasp perhaps his last chance for happiness. The character even managed to walk into the happy-ever-after with the woman he loved. It was the type of role Hackman had always spoken of playing, it involved no gruelling foreign locations and it sounded perfect. *All Night Long* would be his 'come-back' film.

Before beginning *All Night Long*, Hackman tested the waters of his second-time-around career with a cameo role as a newspaper editor in *Reds*, Warren Beatty's epic story of John Reed and Louise Bryant and the Russian Revolution. Hackman remained happy to acknowledge his debt of gratitude to Beatty for casting him in *Bonnie and Clyde* and readily responded to Beatty's offer of a very minor character in his long-planned directorial venture.

All Night Long appealed to Hackman because 'almost all my previous pictures were packed with action and heavy, heavy drama. This movie is set in mid-America and gives me a chance to play a light role for the first time.' Working on *Superman* had almost been like an impersonal, industrial process with Hackman little more than a small cog in the machinery. Facing the cameras three years later, he was striving and stretching to produce his best work as a character of substance and feelings.

Initially, his co-star in *All Night Long* was Lisa Eichhorn, who had previously been seen in *Yanks* (1979) and *Why Would I Lie?* (1980). However, once filming had begun she abruptly departed, citing 'artistic differences with the director'. Her undeniably surprising replacement was Barbra Streisand, who coincidentally also happened to be a client of Sue Mengers. Hackman wasn't disturbed by the swap but wanted to make sure that audiences would not be led astray by the prominent display of Streisand's name on theatre marquees. 'It's mostly my film,' he told a reporter. 'She has five or six good scenes and that's it. It would be unfair to audiences to suggest this is Barbra's movie. It's about *my* character, not hers.'

When *All Night Long* was released in 1981 it made little impact on the public despite the supposed drawing power of Hackman and Streisand in partnership. It will probably never be rated amongst the Hackman greats, yet it is a modest, engaging production that never overstays its welcome and contains one of his most relaxed and attractive performances.

Having been repeatedly passed over for promotion, Hackman's George Dupler confronts his superior and throws a chair through the man's office window as a mark of his frustration. In response, he is transferred to the position of night manager at one of his company's all-night stores.

As he attempts to cope with the indignities of his new position, George's life is beset by domestic problems. At a family funeral he notices that his teenage son Freddie (Dennis Quaid) is overly familiar with the flighty Cheryl (Streisand) who is married to his cousin Bobby (Kevin Dobson). He correctly surmises that they are having an affair, and tells Freddie that the liaison must end.

Cheryl's insensitive husband is a fireman. She is bored and unhappy, with time on her hands. Very early one morning, whilst Bobby is on shift work, she arrives at George's store to discuss Freddie. They have a meal together during his twilight-zone lunch break and George discovers a sympathetic audience for his many woes. They meet again when he has to return her cigarette lighter and he tries to resist falling in love with her.

George dines at Cheryl's during his night-time break and is discovered there by Freddie, who returns home and informs his mother Helen (Diane Ladd), 'He's cheating on you with my girl.' George leaves home and moves into a hotel, falling deeper in love with Cheryl, who counsels, 'everything always works out in the end.' Helen files for divorce and embarks on an affair with her lawyer. George quits his job, rents a warehouse apartment and plans to become an inventor, meanwhile supplementing his income as a singing waiter.

George is totally re-invigorated by his second lease on life and wants Cheryl to escape her loveless marriage and join him. Cheryl is frightened of taking such a great leap into the unknown but does move in with him. However, she soon reconsiders, leaving a taped message explaining that she lacks the courage of his convictions. When she seeks a reconciliation with Bobby, his faults are made glaringly obvious to her and she finally commits herself to a future of happiness with George. Freddie even accepts their compatibility and helps Cheryl to move in with his dad.

[163]

All Night Long may be insubstantial and predictably schematic, but it does possess an engaging charm and off-beat appeal. Streisand's uncharacteristically subdued performance as the delicate suburban housewife provides an endearing foil to Hackman's genial, middle-aged dreamer. The parallels between George's mid-life crisis and Hackman's own state cannot have been lost on the actor and he responds with a wry performance of good-humoured, casual ease tempered with just the right accompaniment of wistful world-weariness. His work is subtle and satisfying, supplying the necessary warmth and personal charisma to make George akin to an audience's well-loved friend.

Despite the personal satisfactions of *All Night Long*, the fact remained that it was not a hit. The critics welcomed the maturity of Hackman's work but audiences were indifferent to a film that was perhaps too mild-mannered and old-fashioned for its own good. Nevertheless, it did serve as public notice that he was alive, well and back in the marketplace.

Hackman's three-year break had repercussions beyond the running of his career. He wanted to divest himself of all the unnecessary trappings that had somehow accumulated around the once simple and straightforward pursuit of a happy life. In 1982, the Hackman home was put on the market. His 'palace' was reported to include a full-size croquet court, a thirty-foot playroom, a pantry with a soda fountain and a special room reserved for the cutting and arranging of flowers. Hackman now described it as 'too big for one man and his family'. The selling price was said to be a cool eight million pounds.

The time he had devoted to his family was insufficient to rescue his marriage to Faye, and in 1982 they were separated once again. This time there was to be no easy reconciliation as a union of twenty-six years floundered on irreconcilable differences. He had taken care to reassess the balance of his life, making his family ever more one of his top priorities, but he had to admit, 'It's very difficult to have a personal life in this business. I've been away so often on location. Pictures aren't shot in Hollywood any more; I've only done two there in all the films I've done. That affects your wife and it affects your children. I think a celebrity's kids have a hell of a tough life.'

This period found Hackman at a low ebb, with his marriage disintegrating, his career slow to pick up and then the suicide of his lawyer Norman Garey, who was also a close friend. He needed work as an escape valve to avoid the opportunities for gloomy introspection that idleness presented. 'It wouldn't be good for me to lie about for the next year or so,' he said. 'For a number of reasons I'm going to have to work hard. It's something I know how to do, and it's something I can rely on.'

However, it was difficult to shake off a mood of melancholy. He told Mike Bygrave, 'I'm not really content. I feel my career kind of slipping away from me because I really don't care enough about it to give it one hundred percent every day of my life. It means a great deal to me to be well thought of as an actor, but it doesn't mean enough to me to do a hell of a lot about it.'

Hackman's enthusiasm was finally aroused by an offer to work on a film to be directed by Nicolas Roeg, a former cinematographer whose work included *Don't Look Now* (1973) and *The Man Who Fell to Earth* (1976). A gifted 'jigsaw' man of the British cinema, Roeg has a virtually unparalleled ability for making complex dramas of often obscure and intimate significance that dazzle with their intelligence, ingenious intertwining of labyrinthine narratives and audacious direction. Each film is a personal statement by a filmmaker of world-class distinction. The opportunity for Hackman to appear in his latest project, *Eureka*, was the actor's best offer since the days of *The Conversation* and *Night Moves*.

During the production of *Eureka*, Roeg discussed what he considered to be the essence of the film. 'I wanted to make a film about ecstasy and what happens afterwards. What happens after one has achieved one's greatest ambition. How is the rest of one's life affected? It's a story of obsession, I suppose. And it's about what happens to the people around this man who also had this obsession. He's a maypole figure around which the other characters dance. It's a classic dramatic structure, where the characters reveal themselves to each other through one man, and through him you understand more of them.'

[165]

The inspiration for the film had stemmed from the real-life murder of Sir Harry Oakes in Nassau in July 1943. Years before, Oakes had been among the many young men hoping to strike it rich as a gold prospector in the Yukon. Oakes had refused to relinquish his goal, and an almost superhuman persistence was rewarded when he discovered the second largest gold mine in the western hemisphere in northern Ontario. Oakes was instantly transformed from an impecunious prospector into one of the world's richest men.

Oakes's murder in the wartime Caribbean remained a puzzling mystery. His playboy son-in-law, Alfred de Marigny, was accused of the crime, tried and acquitted. The case continued to intrigue many observers as the decades passed. Amongst those linked with the incident was the Duke of Windsor, who was then Governor of the Bahamas and had been involved in a financial partnership with Oakes and a local businessman. There were stories too of a Mafia boss trying to wrestle control of the island to build a casino and rumours of death threats to the Duke of Windsor if he did not comply with their plans.

In the 1960s, the American lawyer Marshall Houts wrote an account of Oakes's story, and later James Leasor covered the trial of the son-in-law in his book *Who Killed Sir Harry Oakes?* Roeg had known about the case for almost a quarter of a century. 'It was one of those miscellaneous pieces of information that fascinate you. And it had cropped up at odd times with different people, just in conversation. Like a curious omen, it had come up. On my honeymoon I'd met a woman in a bar who had talked about this. It was as though it was standing by for me.'

Roeg finished work on *Bad Timing* in 1979 and then happened to read James Leasor's book. Initially, reading the book was only a form of relaxation after his prodigious labours. Then, he began to discern the elements of a subject that could be a new film. His interest was not in providing a solution to the question of who did kill Harry Oakes but in exploring the reasons for his violent death at that time and in that place.

'Something touched a chord,' he told *The Times* in 1983. 'I found that the incident and the position of the character reflected some kind of truth in my head. I would hope that anyone who sees the film would feel something of Jack

McCann's predicament. It is about a man who experiences the ecstasy of finding what he is searching for. But ecstasy is a dangerous emotion to reach. Where do you go after that? What can you reach for after ecstasy? A more ecstatic ecstasy? In a way his story is over, but his life is not. He has to live on to wonder what his life means.'

David Begelman, who had known Roeg for many years, was now in charge of production at M-G-M and approached him to discover whether there was any project that they might work on together. Roeg suggested the Oakes book and was given some finance to develop a script. Roeg sat down to ponder the reasons for his fascination with the Oakes story and then contacted Paul Mayersberg, who had written the script for *The Man Who Fell to Earth*. The two men enjoyed a rare collaboration, able to freely exchange ideas and notions that were seamlessly woven into a cohesive overview of the material.

With a working title of *Murder Mystery*, the duo set to work on a vast and comprehensive documentation of what the film would be about. Their efforts ran to 1800 pages and only Begelman exhibited the kind of faith in the work that permitted the project to progress beyond a first draft. To begin with they planned to use the names of the real people concerned, although the aim was never to produce a dramatized biography. M-G-M insisted on the wisdom of using fictitious names as several of those most closely involved, including De Marigny and the Duchess of Windsor, were still very much alive.

Over the course of two years, the script for the film was revised and redrafted, embellished and refined until it was distinctively a product of the joint sensibilities of Roeg and Mayersberg and the host of unforetold external influences operating on them. At one stage the girlfriend of the film's producer, Jeremy Thomas, noted a kinship between their script and Edgar Allan Poe's *Eureka* and this became the title of the film. Others noted similarities with Citizen Kane, and the island fortress of 'Eureka' bore a 'no trespassing' sign similar to the one at the portals of Orson Welles's Xanadu. A typist, working on the script, noted that the idea of a destiny stone was contained within the Book of Revelations.

'It's quite odd if you remain open to all kinds of influences,' Roeg told the *Monthly Film Bulletin*. 'Then you see all the classical analogies. Everything comes tumbling in: the link with the gold cities, every damn gold city was called Eureka, and base metal – how much base metal in the gold, etc. It's all too shocking to refuse.'

Mayersberg neatly encapsulated the prime concern of *Eureka* when he noted, 'Most of the classic stories, like *Greed* or *Treasure of the Sierra Madre*, end with the loss of the gold, blown away as dust. *Eureka* wonders what happens to a man who keeps the gold, yet is still blown away as dust.'

Harry Oakes now evolved into the character of Jack McCann, giving Roeg a definite point of reference to open his discussions with Hackman about playing the role. Always someone who responds to the challenge of a strong director, Hackman was keen to work with Roeg: 'I like him as a filmmaker. I saw *Don't Look Now* and *Bad Timing* and I felt that he has complete knowledge of what the camera can do. And I like that. I like the total visual concept. Roeg is the sort of director who can exploit an actor for the best advantage of the script. He's somebody I'm on the same wavelength with.'

Hackman read *Eureka* and thought, 'It was one of the most unusual scripts I'd read in quite some time. It's not your normal adventure story, although it has all those elements; it's not a mystery, although it has mystery involved in it; it's not just a drama about a family, and yet it has that too. All those elements plus some really exciting locations.' As for Jack McCann, 'What attracted me basically was the change in the character from a real adventurer, a driven kind of man, to twenty years later when he has become this patriarch and great landowner, one of the richest men in the world. And that's what really attracted me to the role: that difference – the difference between that man then and now . . . how he grew . . . or did he grow? . . . Or is he still holding on to the past?'

Very much at the personal insistence of David Begelman, *Eureka* went into production on a generous budget of eleven million dollars. The locations shifted from the extremes of winter in northern British Columbia to late spring in Jamaica, and the film's five-month schedule also included spells in Miami and at Twickenham Studios in Britain. The filming in the Canadian Rockies, some four hundred miles north of Vancouver, was undertaken in treacherous conditions involving temperatures of forty degrees below zero and ten-foot drifts of snow. It was just the physical and emotional contest that Hackman needed to exhaust his energies and smother any inclination towards gloomy self-analysis.

In both the chilly Canadian winter and the balmier climes of Jamaica, Hackman was a remote and aloof-seeming figure. On *Eureka*, at least, he did have the companionship of his son Chris, who was working on the crew, but generally he prefers not to socialize with his fellow actors. 'I don't like to talk to other actors off the set,' he explained. 'It isn't snobbery. When actors get together, they tend to talk about their roles. My training is in improvisation so I like the idea of turning up for work in the morning a little bit frightened, not knowing the script that well, coming in with no preconceptions about what I'm going to do.'

Hackman did relent a little, however, and joined in a cast versus crew darts match and a beach volleyball match.

After twenty-five years as an actor he now began to realize that very few situations could surprise him or upset his rhythm and he needed to constantly seek new sources of inspiration to maintain his interest and freshness.

'I'm looking at things in a different way from the way I used to. It used to be easy for me to slough things off. Now, I'm trying to find other areas of film-making that interest me – art direction, cinematography. I've always been involved with the technical side, much to my detriment at times. It's just more interesting to me at this point to watch the director and the crew instead of committing myself to what I'm supposed to be doing, because much of that is easy for me now. I don't have to spend every minute of the day thinking about my performance, so to keep myself from going tremendously crazy, I observe a lot.'

Eureka begins amidst the snowy wastes of Canada during the 1920s. Jack McCann has been prospecting for many years, and only grim persistence and unyielding stubbornness provide the fuel for him to continue his quest. Spurning the need for a partner, McCann travels alone, claiming, 'I never earned a nickel from another man's sweat.' He struggles against the Arctic conditions and the hungry wolves, looking to the stars and a prophecy of his destiny to sustain him in his darkest hour.

At a brothel for miners, Frieda (Helena Kallianiotes) foretells his future and he proceeds to discover gold in a quantity beyond his wildest imaginings. As he strikes it rich, life itself ebbs out of Frieda, who tells him that this supreme moment, the realization of his life's ambition, is both an end and a beginning.

Twenty years later, McCann lives in splendid isolation on his own island in the Caribbean surrounded by his immediate family. He is extremely possessive towards his daughter Tracy (Theresa Russell), his pride and joy, who had been his constant companion before her marriage to the feckless Continental playboy Claude Maillot Van Horn (Rutger Hauer). Van Horn is bitterly resented by McCann, who considers him unworthy of her.

McCann's wealth appears to have brought him neither pleasure nor contentment, only two decades of aimless leisure. Now, he begins to feel the oppression of everyone's desire to know the secret of his success. Destiny is closing in on him. His business associate Charlie Perkins (Ed Lauter) nervously attempts to secure his co-operation in a property development scheme for the island. However, Perkins is merely a go-between for Mafia boss Mayakofsky (Joe Pesci) and lawyer Aurelio D'Amato (Mickey Rourke), who plan to build a casino and refuse to believe that McCann cannot be bought. 'Who is he? Find out what he desires,' Mayakofsky instructs D'Amato.

At a dinner, Van Horn angers McCann with expressions of contempt for his wealth and expounds a belief that McCann had raped nature to gain his gold. Later, McCann attacks him with an axe. To avoid the pain of further conflict, Tracy joins her alcoholic mother Helen (Jane Lapotaire) on a visit to her brothers in Rhode Island. McCann, meanwhile, has declared war on Van Horn and is ready to stare death in the face. 'Once I had it all,' he muses, 'now I just have everything.'

On a rainy, windswept evening McCann dismisses his servants and heads for a confrontation with Van Horn, who is absent, attending a voodoo orgy with two married women. That evening, McCann is met by D'Amato and three gangsters who make him a final offer that he promptly refuses. Returning to his mansion where Van Horn, Perkins, D'Amato and and his men are all present, McCann is savagely slain; clubbed over the head, decapitated and set alight with the flame from a blow torch.

Van Horn is arrested and tried for the murder. He conducts his own defence and calls Tracy as his only witness. In her emotional, tear-stained testimony Tracy publicly declares her devotion to Van Horn and claims that his one crime is innocence. She explains that her father's physical death is irrelevant because the discovery of his gold twenty years before had embodied the culmination of everything he considered worth living for. She claims that he truly died in 1925. 'How could he ever recapture that moment of triumph?' she asks. 'One moment of rapture, followed by decades of despair.'

The jury find Van Horn not guilty, although he is to be deported as undesirable. These events coincide with the end of hostilities in the Second World War. Afterwards, Tracy and Van Horn talk of a fresh start together. However, Tracy's experiences throughout the trial have been her equivalent of her father's discovery of gold. Her love for Van Horn was her gold, its public declaration her moment of ecstasy. Uncomfortably aware of how the events surrounding McCann's death have tarnished their relationship, the couple have nothing left to offer each other. Van Horn sails away on his own and Tracy is left alone, perhaps to face her own 'decades of despair'.

Eureka is a staggeringly accomplished, densely scripted epic that repays repeated viewings and probably deserves a book of its own to fully analyze the intricacies and patterns of its mosaic-like structure. It explores the occult and the mystical, destiny and providence, cross-referencing events and juxtaposing images to underline the parallels and repetitions that map out the awkward shape of human existence. For Mayersberg, 'the film is about a personal kind of astro-chemistry. We are trying to look at characters and relationships in a way that reduces them to their elements.'

The film abounds in potent visual imagery, presented to the eye by opulently brilliant camerawork, and the script could well have been carved in stone, such is the precision and exactitude of Mayersberg's phrasing, his uncanny ability to coin a sentence that is the perfect expression of a thought or a mood. The acting serves the mastery of the script; Hackman is powerfully and calmly resolute as McCann,

Hauer elegantly preening as Van Horn and Russell torn and passionate as Tracy.

Because *Eureka* is a work of individuality and not some easily consumed and forgotten assembly-line package, the film produces highly personal reactions from each viewer. To some it appears pure gold, to others base metal. Reviewers have praised it and damned it in almost equal measure, one calling it a masterpiece, one dismissing it as a 'portentous conundrum'. Roeg makes teasing, elliptical dramas that can appear deliberately obscure, but to those who grasp his meaning this ambiguity is merely a door through which they will experience a set of emotions open to their own interpretation.

Roeg has said, 'I don't believe my films are inaccessible. If they were I would be inaccessible myself. What I am trying to do, as anyone who works in any form of art or communication is trying to do, is to express emotion. The film audience is so curiously demanding in conservatism. You don't find that in any other form of expression, such as dance or theatre. People never say of dance, "I don't understand what is happening!" Yet film is the newest and should be the freest art of all.'

The individualism of Roeg's work does not make his films easy products to market to a mass audience. *Eureka* opened in London in some out of the way venues and then disappeared. Its distributor refused further screenings and botched an American release. Claims were made that no audience existed for this 'difficult' film, but few people were given the chance to judge this for themselves. David Begelman had fallen from grace at M-G-M and there was speculation that the attempts to bury the film resulted from the natural vindictiveness of his successors in the executive suite. With such a sparse and inadequate release, *Eureka* sits on the ledger books as a costly flop. It now has a cult following, but it remains one of the great little-known gems of Hackman's post-retirement career.

Chapter Thirteen

After *Eureka*, Hackman made three films within the space of a year. There were two main reasons for this sudden burst of activity: firstly, it consumed his energies and diverted his thoughts from personal problems, and secondly, he was making up for lost time, appreciating afresh the opportunities to practise his skills on a trio of interesting and diverse characters.

'As an actor, I feel fortunate I've been given a chance to start the process again,' he admitted. 'Now I have a better view of what I want from acting: personal satisfaction from being proud of the work, and the realization that if I do something not up to my standards, it will come back and haunt me. I'm selfish about what I do. I try to hold out for a really good story and script. If I can't have that, I have to have a lot of money and good locations.'

Now that Hackman was back in harness he wanted to play a different kind of character. He hoped to be cast in more refined and polished roles, avoiding, if possible, the brutality of 'Popeye' Doyle or the violence that seemed to go hand-in-hand with his screen image prior to his retirement. He was in his fifties and wanted his mellower moods to be reflected on screen. 'Most of all in going back to work, I have this feeling: I don't want to be ugly any more.'

Within weeks of completing *Eureka* he was in Mexico playing a seasoned war correspondent in *Under Fire*, a superb thriller that managed to combine political comment and a triangular romantic entanglement with the events of the late 1970s in Nicaragua.

Canadian-born Roger Spottiswoode, a former editor turned director, had read a script by Clayton Frohman set mainly in Vietnam and New York that was ostensibly a dramatized biography of war photographer Tim Page. The script itself did not particularly appeal to him, but what did was the notion of incorporating the lives of war correspondents within some dramatic structure. When he read a further piece about a photographer, a virtual 'war junkie' who had relinquished his camera and walked away from all the carnage, he discussed a potential film with Frohman and another writer, Ron Shelton, and they pieced together a script for *Under Fire*.

Within the corporate mentality of the Hollywood studios, politics on film spells box-office poison. Apart from *All the President's Men*, very few dramatic pictures with even a modicum of political content have been solid financial successes. Spottiswoode was therefore pleasantly surprised to discover that the finance for *Under Fire* fell rather easily into place.

'By every law of nature we should have had trouble, but we didn't,' he explained to the *Monthly Film Bulletin*. 'We've been turned down on a couple of scripts that in theory were infinitely more financible. It was luck, a good script, and getting the actors first – both Gene Hackman and Nick Nolte actually read the script when it was given to them, which is remarkable, it usually takes months. Within ten days we had three actors, all at less than their [usual] price, and the first studio we went to said yes over the weekend. Had we gone to the agents first, we'd never have had it. Because the agents would automatically say that the last thing they'd want is their client in a movie about Central America. We had to orchestrate the whole thing very carefully.'

Although Hackman's role in *Under Fire* is a supporting one if measured in terms of screen time, his presence is crucial to every aspect of the plot and its development. He read and accepted the script so quickly because, perhaps like *The Conversation*, it was a 'valuable film in terms of content and what films can be.' Later, he detailed more specific reasons for his acceptance:

'It made a number of points. But the thing that most appealed to me was the idea of the interplay between the three characters. It began with me being in love with Joanna Cassidy and then had Nick Nolte coming in and stealing her. And within that content we were also covering the war. So it was a fascinating attempt to make a triangle work within the context of a real war.'

The character of Alex Grazier was one that suited the mood of the mature Hackman; he is romantic, charming, self-deprecatory, able to deploy the wisdom of his years, reflective but still vital. As well as the chance to immerse himself in the characteristics of the man, Hackman also welcomed the further technical demands placed upon him by Alex's love of music. Spottiswoode and Shelton had assumed from Hackman's soulful saxophone playing in *The Conversation* that he was a man with an affinity for music. One scene in *Under Fire* calls upon him to sing 'Spring Can Really Hang You Up the Most' whilst accompanying himself on the piano at the front of a three-piece band.

Of course, Hackman had learned to play the saxophone specifically for *The Conversation*, and now he rented himself a piano, chose a music teacher and diligently practised for *Under Fire*. The scene on film is a tricky one, requiring the co-ordination of numerous fine details; Hackman has to sing, play piano, act, direct his performance towards Nolte and Cassidy, and then conclude in harmony on a final chorus with a singer portrayed by Ella Laboriel. He brought off the moment with aplomb and his work caused Spottiswoode to call him, 'A writer and director's delight, an actor who works intensively with the text in preparation. He finds all the options, explores all the possibilities and then comes up with surprises on every take. His performance is always on many levels. He paints with many colours, always preserving the freshness and spontaneity of a moment, with the effortlessness of a man who knows his craft.'

One of the problems facing Hackman now was his exhaustive and comprehensive knowledge of his craft. Filmmaking is un unavoidably time-consuming business and he couldn't escape the tedium of endless waiting to make his contribution and the frustrations of wanting to do more, to share more of the responsibility. Ultimately, the only solution was to direct a film of his own but in the summer of 1982 in Oaxaca, Mexico he still voiced his discomfort to a visiting journalist:

'You have to wait forever in this business. I'm in jail at this point. If I had to be here for eight weeks, I'd probably be tearing up the walls by now. You know, you can divert yourself by having a lot of people around, or you can just do it the way I do – kind of agonize through it.'

Whatever the agonies he experienced in the making of *Under Fire*, they are justified by the final result of what was seen on cinema screens in 1983. The film is a tense and potent combination of narrative drive and intimate drama, with an overall perspective of examining the moral ambiguities and ironies of beliefs, actions and their consequences.

Nick Nolte is photojournalist Russell Price, who covers the front lines for the front pages of the world's leading periodicals. A professional with a professional's sense of objectivity, he claims, 'I don't take sides, I take pictures.'

In 1979, after covering events in Chad, he leaves for Nicaragua. *Time* correspondent Alex Grazier (Hackman), who gave Price his first job, is already there with his lover, radio journalist Claire Stryder (Joanna Cassidy). Grazier has accepted a job as a television anchorman in New York and fails to persuade Claire that they should burn their suitcases and settle into a comfortable life together on Long Island.

At the Viking Club, Grazier plays sentimental songs whilst Claire promises Price, 'You're going to love this war; good guys, bad guys and lots of cheap shrimp.' Their evening is interrupted when the Sandinistas bomb the club in a failed assassination attempt on the life of Marcel Jazy (Jean-Louis Trintignant), who is widely assumed to be working for the CIA.

Price's interest in the local issues grows when he learns that the rebel leader Rafael has never been photographed. When Price is arrested and then apparently released by Jazy, he visits the Frenchman with Claire. Jazy is a suave, roguish figure who implicitly confirms his status as a spy and suggests they they try the provincial capital of Leon for a glimpse of Rafael.

In Leon, Price and Claire become involved in a skirmish and later make love together. Back in Managua, Grazier senses their love and leaves for New York, joking that he will soon be a household name.

Later, as Claire interviews Somoza, the President receives word that Rafael is dead. If substantiated, this rumour should turn the tide in Somoza's favour and guarantee further arms from the American government.

Price believes that Rafael is alive and goes in search of him with Claire. A Sandinista woman leads them to a rebel outpost where Rafael lies dead. The rebels beg Price to fake a picture of Rafael to convince the world that their leader still lives and allow them precious time to win their struggle. Price is sympathetic to their cause, and although it goes against all his professional ethics, he takes the picture.

Grazier then returns to Managua, seeking Price's assistance to scoop an exclusive interview with Rafael. Neither Price nor Claire feel able to reveal their deception and Grazier is led on a wild goose chase. At one checkpoint, Grazier and Price encounter a government firing squad where Oates (Ed Harris), an American mercenary, is using Price's photos of the rebel camp to identify and kill Rafael's supporters. Price later discovers that Jazy had stolen his photographs and passed them on to the government.

Price and Claire later tell Grazier that Rafael is dead. He is upset by the irresponsibility of their actions, claiming to understand their feelings but resent their lies. The next day, Price and Grazier lose their way in the war-torn capital, and when Grazier approaches an army unit to seek directions he is casually shot dead. Price captures the murder on film and runs for his life.

Somoza claims that Grazier's death was the work of the Sandinistas, and as the entire press corps pulls out of the city, Claire goes in search of Price, who is now the subject of a massive manhunt. Jazy is shot by the rebels whilst Claire manages to find Price and smuggle his film back to her hotel. The next day a photomontage of the killing is broadcast on television. Somoza leaves for Florida and the rebel forces are victorious. 'Maybe we should have killed an American journalist fifty years ago,' someone remarks. Claire and Price are re-united to join in the street celebrations where they once again encounter Oates, who has been in Chad and promises they'll meet again in Thailand.

As a work of commitment and complexity, *Under Fire* stood out from the bulk of 1983 cinema releases. Nolte's flawed, blundering photojournalist is far removed from the conventionally romantic mould. His actions, dictated by the heart rather than the head, have lethal consequences for those nearest to him. Yet, despite all the false moves and fatalities, the end result is the one he would have wished. *Under Fire* very intelligently deals in convincing moral dilemmas and fallible human beings about whom one genuinely cares. The script is incisive, the pace tense and gripping, and the performances exceptional. Joanna Cassidy is allowed to create a compelling portrait of an independent professional woman, coping with the stress of her working environment and the demands of a daughter in Los Angeles. She is a credible, realistic character and not merely a redundant love interest tacked on with one eye on the box-office. Nolte gives what is probably the best performance of his career to date, and Hackman captures the afterglow of a once passionate, energetic man graciously handing over to the next generation and positively approaching the onset of a more settled, deskbound life with dignity.

Under Fire had been a film worth making; a rare instance where everyone concerned could take pleasure in producing something in which they believed. Unlike many films, past and present, it was not just another job of work. One assumes that this was the reason for both Hackman and Nolte's speedy acceptance of the script. Its box-office impact was modest and it received a solitary Oscar nomination for Jerry Goldsmith's pulsating musical score. However, nothing can detract from the excellence and integrity embodied in every frame of the film.

As a mark of the degree to which Hackman was back in circulation, intent on keeping busy, he appeared as a presenter at the Oscar ceremony during which Jerry Goldsmith lost to Bill Conti's score for *The Right Stuff*. Together with Dyan Cannon, he presented Linda Hunt with the Best Supporting Actress award for *The Year of Living Dangerously* and was spotted in company with Jack Nicholson offering congratulations to Best Actress winner Shirley MacLaine.

Continuing his globetrotting, travelling player existence, Hackman next journeyed on to Tunisia and a reunion with Jerry Schatzberg, the director of *Scarecrow*.

Based on a 19th century novel by Florence Montgomery, *Misunderstood* had previously been filmed under the title *Incompreso* by Luigi Comencini in Italy during 1966. Comencini's film had starred Anthony Quayle as a British consul stationed in Rome. Sixteen years later, the novel had been turned into a script relocated in New Zealand, but the setting was switched to Tunisia by producer Tarak Ben Ammar with the intention of stimulating production in his home

[178]

industry. Filming, on a budget of $8.5 million, began on 11 October 1982.

Schatzberg described the film as a 'sentimental melodrama film certainly, although the approach of my film will be rather different to the first version. But I cried when I saw it, and I also cried when I read the script, so I thought it must have something going for it.'

The lead character, Ned Rawley, is a recently bereaved, wealthy businessman who becomes so self-absorbed in his sorrow that he fails to recognize his son's need for love at this most crucial time. 'I had thought of a number of people to play Rawley,' Schatzberg said, 'and Gene Hackman was among them, although for some reason he wasn't the first choice. But the more I thought about it the more I realized that he was right.'

In guiding his career, Hackman now had a stated preference for interspersing action pictures with sensitive pictures. *Misunderstood* offered him a film that underlines the power of love and the need for communication within the family. In a personal drama dealing with powerful emotions, he would be playing a father and businessman with fine suits and an opulent mansion; the role offered just the type of refinement for which he had been searching.

At the beginning of the film Lily Rawley (Susan Anspach) has succumbed to some mysterious ailment. Her grief-stricken husband retreats into the demands of his business, trying to spare his two sons the hurt of the loss but intensifying it instead. When he is needed most he becomes a stranger to them. It is left to the oldest son, Andrew (Henry Thomas), to explain his mother's death to his supposedly delicate brother Miles (Huckleberry Fox).

Rawley promises to spend some time with his boys but other demands on him continually disrupt their plans and he assumes from Andrew's sturdy demeanour that he has come to terms with the loss. Rawley's brother-in-law Will (Rip Torn) accuses him of neglect: 'You treat that kid as if he has a cold you don't want to catch.'

As father and son move towards a reconciliation and an opening-up of their feelings, Andrew falls from an overhanging tree branch onto a cliff. Facing certain paralysis and perhaps even death, he berates his father for only loving Miles. Rawley breaks down in tears and admits he was 'so blinded by my own sorrow I didn't realize you were suffering too.'

Misunderstood is a low-key, insubstantial melodrama that doesn't amount to very much. In the original film Andrew dies, and Schatzberg was reportedly unhappy with some re-editing that resulted in the current ambiguous conclusion.

Andrew, dead or alive, would add little lustre to the film. The potential for a tearjerking, sentimental wallow does exist but is largely contained until the closing moments; instead the film drifts along going nowhere in particular and offering little by way of profound or novel variation on its dramatic situation. The scenery is nice, Rip Torn has a few lively scenes, the children are sly scene-stealers and only Hackman is unsatisfactorily cast. His character is written as rather dour, preoccupied and distant, and, unsurprisingly, Hackman responds with a doleful, uncommunicative reading of the man. He is lumbered with an uninspired character and does little to enhance it. Nevertheless, he had enjoyed the filming:

'It was the first time I'd worked with children and it was really fun and interesting. I loved doing it because I found you have to take a whole different attitude with child actors. It was amazing to me how they could be playing a game at one moment, then jump back and do the scene and then resume the games they were playing. I wish I could do that as an actor! It takes real concentration. I know W. C. Fields once said the worst things to work with are animals and children because they steal the scenes. I didn't feel like that. I really enjoyed it.'

Although filming was completed in 1982, *Misunderstood* went unreleased in America until the spring of 1984, and in Britain, by-passed cinema distribution to appear only on cassette and television. The critics were politely under-whelmed. The *Hollywood Reporter* offered some helpful advice, noting, 'Hackman's character forces him into some-thing of a strait jacket, and the suspicion persists that the father doesn't feel nearly as deeply for his sons as he evidently did for his wife. A few glimpses of genuine care or warmth might have helped.' Their reviewer concluded, 'Together with narrative shortcomings, the film's enigmatic title, better suited to a perfume than a motion picture, is not likely to assist the box-office.' However, Janet Maslin observed in the *New York Times*, 'Without Gene Hackman and two appealing young actors to hold the audience's attention, there wouldn't be a movie here at all.'

After his 'sensitive' picture, the pendulum swung back to action and Hackman searched around for a suitable project to complete his year-long trio of films. He found something satisfactory in a script originally known as *The Last River to Cross* but later retitled *Uncommon Valor*.

The film touches upon the sensitive topic of Vietnam veterans listed as Missing in Action who may still be incarcerated in enemy work camps. Hackman's character is a military man who believes that his missing son may still be alive and decides to lead his own rescue mission into Vietnam. 'It's not just an adventure story,' he explained. 'This has something to say about the war, and about the unresponsiveness of the US Government towards people who have been affected by the Vietnam war ten years down the line.'

The film began as an idea in the mind of actor Wings Hauser, who took his concept to a young writer who developed it into a script. Paramount secured the rights, assigning John Milius and Buzz Feitshans as producers and hiring Ted Kotcheff to direct. Kotcheff had just completed *First Blood* with Sylvester Stallone and was becoming something of an expert on the psychology of the Vietnam veteran. 'I've always been interested in outsiders,' he claimed. 'Those who have been rejected by society have always intrigued me. The veterans in this film are truly forgotten men. Their journey back to Southeast Asia resolves the unanswered questions that have filled their lives ever since the war.'

Kotcheff thoroughly researched the subject to satisfy his own curiosity as to whether American soldiers could still be alive in the Mekong jungles and whether private citizens could actually stage their own raid. He was convinced of both possibilities.

'The Vietnamese have a long history of holding people. French prisoners captured as Dien Bien Phu only emerged 19 years later. I think the MIA relatives suspect that they wouldn't have survived the experience of prison, but it was heartbreaking visiting families who have not seen a son for 14 years and keep hoping he may one day come back, always

[181]

buying him a present each birthday and Christmas, in case. . . . However, I have a very good friend high up in the Democratic Party and when I asked him what he thought, he said, "Of course there are Americans there." So I said, "What are we going to do about it?" And he said, "What do you want us to do? Go to war?" '

If further proof were required of the dramatic validity of *Uncommon Valor*, then it was provided by real life events in the spring of 1983 when retired Marine colonel Bo Gritz made a return visit to Vietnam in search of POW camps. His trip was apparently financed by Clint Eastwood and William Shatner, among others.

With a budget of $14.5 million and locations in California, Hawaii and Thailand, *Uncommon Valor* began filming in Los Angeles on 6 June 1983. Prior to that date the actors underwent a week of intensive military training, and Hackman certainly looks lean and fit on screen.

The cast and crew moved to Hawaii for six weeks on July 12th, with Kotcheff explaining how the locations had been chosen: 'We wanted a jungle look, and the flora and fauna in Hawaii are very similar to Vietnam and Laos, and certainly Thailand, where I've been. The choice was between Mexico, the Philippines and Thailand. We couldn't shoot all of it in Thailand – both the Philippines and Thailand were in the monsoon season – and in Mexico they didn't feel that the sets could be built in time. So it was by process of elimination that we arrived in Hawaii.'

Numerous sets were constructed on the remote island of Kauai, including a ten-acre reconstruction of a Vietcong POW camp. American helicopters were painted over to look like Vietnamese helicopters and later restored to their original colours; the film's helicopter budget alone was over one million dollars. The film was in production six days a week but on the Sunday everyone rested; Kotcheff went snorkelling with his son Aaron, Patrick Swayze went water-skiing, diving and hiking whilst Hackman chose less energetic forms of relaxation, painting and sculpting. A final week in Thailand completed their chores on the film before September and the onset of autumn.

Kotcheff had cast Hackman as Colonel Jason Rhodes 'because he has a credible quality, not gung-ho – any one of us might act his way in such a situation.' It is the solid conviction of his performance and those of the other cast members that prevents the film from being just another action-packed rerun of *The Dirty Dozen* and a score of other 'mission impossible' style scenarios.

Ten years after the official end of the hostilities, Rhodes believes that his son Frank may still be alive and held captive in South-East Asia. His own government are unwilling to take action on the matter. Wealthy industrialist Hugh MacGregor (Robert Stack), whose own son is also MIA, is willing to finance a rescue raid into a reputed POW labour camp that has been spotted from the air in Laos. Hackman assembles his son's former Marine colleagues and drills them for action.

Despite pressure on MacGregor to abandon the mission, Rhodes's team proceed to Bangkok where they are intercepted by the local authorities and a sympathetic CIA agent. Their weapons are confiscated, but the men re-arm on the black market and are led into Laos by a drugs dealer and his two daughters. In a dangerous and costly raid on the camp, several of Rhodes's men are killed but four Americans are rescued. They fly home via helicopter. One of the Americans is MacGregor's son, who tells Rhodes that Frank had saved his life but died of illness whilst in captivity. In America, the prisoners are met by jubilant relatives and an army of cameramen and reporters.

Uncommon Valor was a surprise box-office success in America, grossing some $30 million over the peak Christmas season of 1983–4. A competent action film, its theme struck a responsive chord with audiences, and has been capitalized on in later years by films like Chuck Norris's *Missing in Action* (1984) and Sylvester Stallone's *Rambo* (1985). Kotcheff seemed as surprised as anyone by its popularity.

'Paramount said as most audiences are under 25 I should put something in for the under 15s. I said, "I don't *like* 15-year-olds, let alone know what they want!" But the film has been a hit with young women dragging their men to see it, for apparently they respond to male bonding and identify all the characters as their father/boyfriend/brother or whatever! Thank God American TV stays as bad as it does and drives people into the movies.'

Critical reaction to *Uncommon Valor* was diverse; it was reviled in some quarters as a right-wing fantasy, viewed elsewhere as a crypto-Western in the manner of John Ford's *The Searchers* and casually dismissed as a big-screen version of *The A-Team* by the *Monthly Film Bulletin*. It is certainly a film that poses more questions than it answers, but Hackman's rugged authority adds a semblance of integrity to the action-man heroics.

Hackman's trio of films had produced a satisfactory tally of one brilliant drama, one inconsequential weepie and a popular, mass-audience hit. With a batting average like that he had underscored his renewed bankability as a leading man and speedily reasserted his pre-eminence as an actor. After a three-year absence and four films in two years he was unarguably back on form.

Chapter Fourteen

On 16 July 1984, Hackman began filming *Twice in a Lifetime*. The script, by Oscar-winner Colin Welland, had already served as the basis of a British television play, *Kisses at Fifty*. Americanized and relocated to Seattle, it now presented Hackman with the most personally involving and emotionally draining of all his recent assignments.

Twice in a Lifetime tells of a middle-aged steelworker who abandons his wife of many years in favour of the attractive widow who is serving behind his local bar. He knows that his marriage has lapsed into unenthralling routine and eagerly pursues a second chance for happiness. The film charts the pain and anguish that ensue as his nearest and dearest react to his decision with varying degrees of incomprehension and hostility.

Hackman's marriage to Faye had lasted twenty-eight years and was now officially no more as they embarked upon divorce proceedings. In the less serious newspapers his name was linked with that of Hawaiian-born pianist Betsy Arakawa, who was just a year or two older than his eldest child Christopher. It can only have been the masochist in Hackman that persuaded him to undertake *Twice in a Lifetime*, whose art uncomfortably imitates his life. It must have inevitably provoked guilty introspection over the demise of his own marriage and his part in its dissolution. A couple of years later he admitted, 'It was a little painful for me to play that role, and although I thought I could use some of what I was going through at the time, it didn't really work out that way.'

The film's director, Bud Yorkin, was also going through a divorce at the time and the film was almost a form of mutual therapy for both men's menopausal marital difficulties. Yorkin had been so impressed by Welland's material that he encouraged him in the development of an American version of a script first set in Manchester, and agreed to direct what was to be his first film in over a decade. Originally transferred to the steel mills of Pennsylvania, the setting later became Seattle because, according to Yorkin, 'I liked the city so much. Architecturally it's beautiful, and I like the weather because cinematically you have cumulus clouds and a density – a reflectiveness – that you get in England. It's that wonderful look you get from enough dampness and rain which gives you a texture difficult to get elsewhere.'

Hackman was Yorkin's first choice for the central role of Harry Mackenzie, and the actor was ready for a 'sensitive' picture in the wake of *Uncommon Valor*. '*Twice in a Lifetime* attracted me because of the subject matter,' he explained. 'I liked the challenge of trying to make a film work for a general audience where the leading character is not necessarily sympathetic in his actions. One of the points of the movie is to show that over–45s are still sexual beings.'

Even though his period of retirement had instilled a renewed sense of responsibility towards his career, it was still impossible for Hackman to feel deeply committed to every single film that he chose to make. *Twice in a Lifetime*, however, engaged both his heart and mind.

'This one moved me more than anything I'd read in a couple of years,' he told *Films and Filming*. 'Colin had lived outside of Pittsburgh for some six months, researching this. He hung out at some of the pubs and got the know some of the people. There's a scene in the film where the daughter comes in with the mother and confronts the father with the fact that he's living with this other woman. That's something Colin actually saw happen! That was one of those very uncomfortable scenes, and tremendously embarrassing. Being uncomfortable and selfconscious is one of the things that we all dread, because we are then vulnerable in some way or another. When we went to shoot it, everyone wanted to reduce their lines and some tried to wriggle out of doing the scene in some peculiar way.'

Yorkin decided to film *Twice in a Lifetime* as an independent production, raising the $8 million finance through his own company and casting many of the secondary roles from within the thriving theatrical community of Seattle. For the leading roles, 'I got who I thought were the best in the business – it's a real acting piece.'

Prior to filming the company were assembled for a fortnight's rehearsals, one week in Los Angeles and one week on the actual locations to be used in Seattle. Although still a lover of the spontaneous and unplanned, Hackman has grown to value any time allowed for rehearsal and regarding *Twice in a Lifetime* he felt, 'I don't think that film would have worked on any level without rehearsal because there was just too much to find. It was just too difficult.'

The personal identification between Hackman and his character extends beyond their shared marital crises. One suspects that Harry Mackenzie is similar to the vaguely dissatisfed blue-collar worker that Hackman might have become had he chosen to remain in Danville. As a youngster he had spent a summer in a steel mill and has always suggested that he would never have branched into the arts if he had not left Illinois.

At the beginning of *Twice in a Lifetime*, Mackenzie appears a straightforward character, comfortably entrenched in a network of relations that include not only his immediate family but a virtual second family of workmates and social contacts. He celebrates his fiftieth birthday at home with his wife Kate (Ellen Burstyn) and his daughters Sunny (Amy Madigan) and Helen (Ally Sheedy). Afterwards he seems almost relieved to leave them and head out for a night with the boys at the Shamrock Bar. It is there that he meets the new barmaid Audrey (Ann-Margret).

With Harry working nightshift and Kate employed at a beauty parlour during the day, their contact is reduced to a passing greeting in the morning and a snatched meal in the evening. Harry meets Audrey again. He tells her of the staleness in his marriage and his lack of enthusiasm for his job. She talks of her late husband and the opportunities that life may still hold for a woman of her age. Their clandestine meetings become public knowledge when Kate's boss spots them together. Kate is shattered by the news, and when Audrey asks Harry to choose between them he leaves his stunned family and eagerly grasps another chance for happiness. 'It's been a long time since I didn't know for certain what a day had in store for me,' he says.

Kate still loves Harry and blames herself for his decision

[187]

to move out, but Sunny bitterly resents such self-pity and directs her anger towards her father. Audrey experiences the guilt of the pain her relationship with Harry has caused when Sunny blasts into the Shamrock and uncompromisingly berates him for what he has done.

It becomes apparent that there will be no reconciliation. Harry finds an apartment of his own and 'gets a kick out of life again', and even Kate accepts that 'something in our marriage died. I guess I didn't know it but it did.' In time Kate begins to assert herself again, socializing with her daughters, winning at bingo and visiting a disco. Sunny's anger remains constant and she is the one who can neither forgive nor forget.

Ten months later, Helen's forthcoming wedding is the first test of the changes within the family. The eldest son Jerry (Darrel Larson) arrives from California and is sympathetic to his father's need to find a new life. Kate is regretful but seems to feel that it may have been for the best. Only Sunny is totally unforgiving.

On the eve of her wedding, Harry talks with Helen, afraid that she may be marrying too young and rushing into the same mistakes that her parents made, but she promises that her life will be different. Harry is present at the wedding as the father of the bride but saves himself, and Kate, further discomfort by declining an awkward invitation to the reception. Choosing a few flowers from the wedding bouquets for Audrey, he leaves alone.

An acutely-observed and perceptive film, *Twice in a Lifetime* is a qualified success. It offers a thoughtful and well-acted study of the effects of divorce on a typical family. It is a refreshing change from the prevalence of cinematic tales of adolescent angst and does convincingly assert the notion that 'over–45s are still sexual beings'. However, its subject matter and treatment would still seem more ideally suited to the small screen. The issues raised are a little too neatly resolved, with no one truly hurt by Harry's actions; Harry is happy, Audrey is happy, and even Kate seems a more fulfilled and assertive character as a result of their marriage breaking down.

Hackman's character is never viewed in an entirely consistent manner; as he embarks upon the affair with Audrey he seems to lack the foresight or intelligence to contemplate the repercussions of what he is doing. Yet once the affair is public, he can justify it, analyze it and discuss the slow death of his marriage and the hypocrisy of staying together out of familiarity as opposed to enduring love. Despite such inconsistencies, Hackman is in fine form and the detail, naturalism and conviction of his performance call to mind the relaxed, seemingly effortless credibility that an actor like Spencer Tracy could bring to the screen. It represents one of the increasingly rare instances of his 'ordinariness' being employed in a character that is an everyman figure of worker, husband and father. Such is his animation and understanding of the man that he doesn't strike a false chord. David Denby noted in *New York*, 'He's such a powerful yet unemphatic performer, with so intimate, easy and unforced a relation to the reality of whatever situation he's in, that you simply accept what he does as an expression of his entire being.'

The acting throughout *Twice in a Lifetime* is of a high calibre, particularly from Ellen Burstyn and Amy Madigan, who received a Golden Globe nomination as Best Supporting Actress. Released in 1985, the film earned a modest $9 million and generally congratulatory reviews, although there were exceptions, notably that of Pauline Kael, who wrote, 'It is like a sermon on the therapeutic value of adultery, divorce and remarriage, given by a minister who learned all he knows from watching TV.'

Twice in a Lifetime was filmed on a fifty-five day schedule and was barely completed before Hackman was back at work for a man who must rate as one of his favourite directors – Arthur Penn. The film, their third together, was a spy thriller which began life as *On Target* and was later known by its abbreviated title, *Target*.

Sadly, *Target* was the least significant of the collaborations between Hackman and Penn. Each one appears to have accepted the film for the wrong reasons. Penn had been preparing another film that had fallen through when he was offered the *Target* script by producers Richard Zanuck and David Brown. He warmed to the notion of signing on as a hired hand, accepting the film as the melodrama it was and trying to make the most of it.

'I was just hoping for a good yarn,' he said with becoming

modesty. 'I had been missing that in a lot of recent films which are so 'cool', which take such a snide attitude to events. I thought it would be fun to go for the heart of the narrative, to go directly for that kind of excitement the way that Hitchcock did. When you're dealing with a film with that high a degree of plot, it really is like putting a watch together. Then through the acting you can perhaps open up other aspects: with an actor like Hackman you are constantly open to subtle things.'

Hackman was increasingly drawn to the prospect of direction, and he tried to prepare for the task by vigilance and constant observation of the directors he worked with. One of the most obvious ways to learn about the director's art is to watch its best practitioners in action, and Penn is one of the finest directors that Hackman knows. On the set of *Target* in December he told visiting reporter George Perry, 'I don't think I would have done this if it had been any other director. When I first read it, it wasn't anywhere near in the shape it is now.'

Reflecting on what dictates his choice of material after almost three decades of acting, Hackman has said, 'I think the longer you go in a career the more you're attracted to things you haven't done. And I've become more and more attracted to relationships and exploring them. It may not be commercial, but I feel that it's a more interesting attitude to play. More interesting films seem to come out of relationships than the singular one being cast against the system.'

Twice in a Lifetime had explored the relationships within a family under stress, and *Target*, whilst also an action adventure, was similarly concerned with the family – more specifically with the relationship between a father and son portrayed by Hackman and Matt Dillon. 'It's an interesting role for me,' Hackman felt. 'I've been offered so many father-son relationship films lately, but this one is totally different because my character changes so radically, comes out of the shell. What's fascinating are the two sides of the man – the soft and the hard – and how the son seems to have those same qualities. He's sensitive, yet has strength and a rebellious nature.'

Target, in its ideal form, presented Hackman with the chance to combine elements of both his 'action' and 'sensitive' pictures: a physically demanding, location-hopping race against time blended with incidents that reveal a father and son to each other as never before.

'One of the things about this genre of film is that if you can convince the audience that you are respectable, attractive and sympathetic, they believe that and go with you. If they don't believe you, either physically or emotionally, there's no contact and they won't believe anything you do. We hope that they leave a film like this saying, "Hey, that was entertaining. I really enjoyed it." You tug an audience's heart, then you scare the hell out of them. That's the entertainer's job, and I consider myself an entertainer.'

The sixteen weeks of filming began on 8 October 1984 in Paris. The peripatetic schedule called for a move from France to Germany for three weeks on location in Hamburg, and then half a day in Berlin at Check Point Charlie, before returning to Paris and the production headquarters at the Studios de Boulogne. After an eleven-day Christmas break, filming commenced again in America and was completed early in 1985 at the Dallas/Fort Worth Airport.

One aspect of *Target* that had appealed to Penn was the chance to direct in Europe. In 1963 he had worked for around ten days on *The Train* before being replaced by John Frankenheimer at the request of the film's star Burt Lancaster. The experience had left him wary of filming abroad and *Target* was an attempt to overcome that unease.

'*Target* had one of the best crews I've ever worked with,' Hackman said afterwards. 'That film was about an $11 million film, yet the crew was tiny by American standards. It was maybe thirty people and they each loved film. The French who work on films seem to love doing what they're doing. They don't have a big strong union. I don't know what their salary scale is, obviously less than ours, and there is something very nice about that. Because when you go to work it's like you're with fellow workers as opposed to people who are showing up and taking the money and couldn't care less about what's going on. And it's less like a factory.'

On the set of *Target*, time had clearly dimmed none of Hackman's intensity of approach to his craft. He was still unable to unwind between shots, still anxiously involved in every aspect of the production and still very keen to undertake his own stunts. Producer David Brown observed, 'I've never known an actor who spends so little time relaxing in his trailer between takes. Gene wants to know everything that goes on.'

According to Arthur Penn, 'Gene is a consummate actor – and a perfectionist. Every move, he knows exactly what he's doing. But he agonizes over it for hours, even days, before he gets to the camera.'

One scene in the film, involving Hackman's character in a chase across the bridges of Hamburg harbour, ends when he dives into the icy water. Against the advice of his producers, Hackman refused the use of a stunt man and insisted upon performing the scene himself. Dressed in thermal underwear and a frogman's suit under his ordinary clothes, he duly plunged in. 'It's part of the actor's job to do as much as he can,' he argued. 'It's important. I have to signal my son from the water to *run*. It had to be me. So why not get it done and get it over with?'

Other scenes were less personally hazardous, but just as arduous. Filming throughout the night on the chill, windswept streets of Hamburg was enough to curb even Hackman's natural ebullience. Fortified with steaming bowls of goulash soup, the cast and crew plodded on until the early hours of the morning.

'Arthur asks a lot of everyone, but then he asks a lot of himself,' Hackman said. 'At three or four o'clock in the morning you really want to quit. One night in Hamburg it was really miserable but we went on till 5:15. Arthur was still there, punching away.'

In the film, Hackman plays Walter Lloyd, a staid and sensible middle-class, middle-aged businessman. When his wife Donna (Gayle Hunnicutt) departs on a solo European vacation she implores him to spend some time with their son Chris (Matt Dillon) and try to bridge the generation gap that separates them.

Chris has dropped out of college and is now dabbling in stock-car racing. He finds his father's lifestyle and values dull but agrees to go fishing with him so they can spend some time together. However, during their retreat, Walter receives a telephone call from the American Embassy in Paris informing him that Donna has been missing, believed kidnapped, for the past forty-eight hours.

Chris surmises that his mother has run away from a

routine marriage; Walter suspects foul play. The two men rush to Europe, where Walter is forced to reveal his hidden past as a CIA agent living in inconspicuous anonymity all these years. As they chase through Hamburg and Berlin it transpires that Donna has been abducted by an Iron Curtain agent who holds Walter responsible for the death of his family many years previously in a mission that had gone badly wrong. Walter vigorously denies the man's charges and is able to reveal the presence of an American double-agent who really caused the deaths. Donna is rescued and the family is reunited and strengthened by their experiences.

Target is a listless, run-of-the-mill espionage yarn based on an over-elaborate long-distance revenge scheme and replete with the predictable genre stand-bys of double-agents, car chases and foreign intrigue. It's all reminiscent of a flat Hitch-cocktail from a lesser vintage. Hackman is solid enough, but really should have trusted the instincts that informed him at the outset, 'This is really a director's film. Almost all action films are director's films.'

Arthur Penn has subsequently claimed that his film was misunderstood and was never intended to be taken entirely seriously. He had planned to work within a very classic form of narrative and have some fun with the archetypes and stereotypes unavoidably encased in the script. 'It really is a melodramatic narrative, with one thing happening after another, with all the events happening from the outside,' he told the *Monthly Film Bulletin*. 'I thought it would be fun to work in that style, and I did it with quite a lot of brio. It was an old-fashioned melodrama with slightly more sophisticated devices: the mother wired to the explosives in the hangar is like the heroine being tied to the railroad tracks.'

Regardless of Penn's intentions, *Target* is a damp squib of a film, and a particularly acute disappointment when compared with the exuberance and complexity of *Bonnie and Clyde* and *Night Moves*. Public response to the work was decidedly muted, and the American box-office gross of under $10 million signalled that it had failed to recoup its production costs, a rare financial flop for producers Zanuck and Brown, who have been responsible for *The Sting*, *Jaws* and *Cocoon*.

Continuing to work with the finest of American directors,

[193]

Hackman then signed on for the latest Sidney Lumet film, *Special Election*. Ten years previously Hackman was reported to have been offered a role in Lumet's Oscar-winning *Network*. At the time he was far gone on the road to a healthy bank balance and an early retirement. Most actors would have cancelled everything to work with Lumet, but Hackman had declined the invitation. He wasn't about to make the same mistake twice.

Special Election, subsequently retitled *Power*, was written by David Himmelstein, a journalist and former speech writer and press aide. His subject was the all-pervasive power of the media in manipulating and packaging political candidates for easy consumption by a gullible nation of television gogglers. An earth-shattering Orwellian theme for a drama in the 1950s, but something of an antediluvian storm-in-a-teacup by the summer of 1985. Nevertheless, Lumet said, 'The point of the picture is that it doesn't matter if you believe in your client or not. The whole political process has become dehumanized.'

Richard Gere plays Pete St John, a ruthless, cynical, jet-setting public relations consultant widely acknowledged as 'the best there is'. Hackman is Wilfred Buckley, his former mentor and partner who has attempted to remain pure about his profession and only support the issues and candidates in whom he personally believes. One of the few remaining points of contact between the two men is their mutual friendship with St John's ex-wife, British journalist Ellen Freeman (Julie Christie).

The stage is ultimately set for a confrontation between St John and Buckley over the forthcoming election for the Ohio Senate. St John is hired to handle the candidacy of Midwest industrialist Jerome Cade (J. T. Walsh), who is contesting the seat in the wake of the surprise resignation of Sam Hastings (E. G. Marshall). Buckley, who now finds a little too much solace in the contents of a liquor bottle, is assisting the rival candidate, idealistic professor Matt Salinger (Phillip Aarons).

The election campaigns raise a number of murky issues. Ellen wants to know why Hastings has relinquished his seat, whilst St John is worried that someone has been bugging his office and trying to kill him. The shady dealings eventually point to the work of Cade's advisor Arnold Billings

(Denzel Washington), who is linked both to an Arab oil sheikh who is opposed to Hastings and to a populist South American presidential candidate whom St John also represents. St John now has a chance to rekindle his old enthusiasms and rediscover his old integrity by helping Buckley to work for Salinger's victory over his own client Cade.

Sidney Lumet is an extremely fast and efficient worker who always insists on a period of rehearsals on every film that he makes. That time is used to work on camera angles and to give his actors time to make their mistakes, explore their options and decide upon their characterizations. Thus, once filming begins the major decisions have been made and any points of dispute already resolved. He is renowned for shooting within schedule and under budget.

Hackman was impressed by Lumet's skilful professionalism and precision organization. 'Sidney Lumet is such an energetic guy that he really overwhelms you with his kind of energy and his kind of positive attitude about what he's doing and what he wants from his movies and his people,' he told *Films and Filming*. 'He shoots like nobody I've ever seen. For instance, in *Power* we were moving locations in New York City sometimes two, three times a day. They would move the entire crew to another location. Now, some films that I've worked on, you couldn't move once. I mean you'd just lose the rest of the day.'

Lumet's technique was one that Hackman found enormously invigorating and reminiscent of his days as a stage actor. 'It feels a bit like a play,' he admitted, 'especially for the first five days when the creative process is taking place. He allows ideas and he allows one the freedom and the looseness in the area that the actor enjoys most. And then starting the following week you must really know all your lines and it starts to get serious. Because it's all in cement then and you must polish it that next week. It's an interesting process. It's like by the second Friday you're ready to open on Broadway if you could. It's a very involved and calculated process.'

Again, with a view towards his future directorial aspirations, Hackman took the time to follow *Power* through to its final stage as a finished film ready for unveiling to the press in January of 1986. He saw the film and appreciated

[195]

the pitch of performance and commitment that Lumet had secured from his cast.

'I'm very pleased with it,' he told *American Premiere*, 'especially Richard's character and role. I thought he was wonderful. Everybody was good, right down the line. A lot of very theatrical performances – which is refreshing – as opposed to a lot of naturalness that you see in a lot of films with people throwing stuff away. There was nothing to throw away. Everybody was very much intent and knew exactly what they were doing. I thought Denzel Washington was wonderful. A very strong actor.'

Unfortunately, Hackman seems to have been amongst the minority in his critical assessment of *Power*. Leonard Maltin's *TV Guide* review found it 'slick' and 'sanctimonious', adding that '[the] subject isn't headline news anymore, but this movie treats it that way – and then asks us to go along with some pretty silly story points. Downright embarrassing at times.' David Denby in *New York* dubbed it 'American Gigolo Goes to Washington' but did find a word or two of praise for Hackman, observing that 'Hackman, whose mastery of film acting is one of the few remaining glories of American movies, has never been more adept at suggesting the social routines – the little greetings, jokes, delusions – that get a man through the working day.' *Variety* correspondent Rich described the film as 'trite' and 'facile', dismissing Hackman's work with the choice description of his acting efforts as 'a phoned-in turn by Hackman'.

Rich also offered a lamentably accurate forecast of the film's commercial potential, predicting that '[the] box-office outlook is mediocre for a pic with little appeal to teens and questionable prospects among adults at a time when polls show overwhelming popular satisfaction with the most tube-savvy President ever.' *Power* earned a miserable $3 million in America and there are no plans for it to be screened in British cinemas.

Chapter Fifteen

Indiana is known as the basketball capital of America. Although the sport is believed to have originated in Massachusetts in 1891, the first game to be played in Indiana was at the Crawfordsville Tavern in the Spring of 1893. Over the ensuing 94 years, basketball hysteria has become synonymous with the state and its inhabitants, who are affectionately nicknamed 'Hoosiers'. It seems only logical that, at some point, 'Hoosiers' working within the cinema industry would band together and make a film about their shared passion. That time arrived in the mid–1980s.

Angelo Pizzo was born in Bloomington, Indiana and had accumulated ten years of experience within the entertainment industry before taking a sabbatical to write an original screenplay entitled, unsurprisingly, *Hoosiers*.

In 1954 a team from the tiny Milan High School defeated the more favoured Muncie Central to win the State High School Basketball Tournament Championship. Pizzo used that incident to fashion the story of a down-and-out coach who is hired to take charge of a small-town high school basketball team. His controversial presence and methods inspire his players and he is to lead them to the finals of the State Championship. Along the way, the coach has a chance to put his own life in order and to affect the lives of some of the citizens in the small town. Pizzo wrote the role of the coach for Hackman and set his story in the 1951–52 season, 'A time before the intrusion of television, the last era of true regionalism in America.'

Amongst the first people to read Pizzo's script was veteran producer Carter De Haven, who was impressed enough to want to make it his next project. 'What attracted me most to the script of *Hoosiers* was that it rang of truth about a certain time, place and event in America,' he said. 'There's a lot of passion, a lot of caring and a tremendous amount of hard work that's gone into it.'

Pizzo knew that he had found the most sympathetic person to bring his writing to the screen when De Haven asked him to join him as the film's co-producer. 'As a writer, having control was important to me. I would never have let the film be made unless I had control. There were at least three cases where I was offered sums of money to sell the screenplay outright. From the start, I wanted to produce the script and I wanted David Anspaugh to direct. The other condition was that it be shot in Indiana. I wrote the film with Gene Hackman in mind as the coach. One of the most exciting things about the movie was getting him.'

David Anspaugh, a native of Decatur, Indiana, had never previously directed a feature film, although his extensive television credits included *Miami Vice*, *St Elsewhere* and an episode of *Hill Street Blues* for which he had won an Emmy Award and a Director's Guild Award. Hackman expressed few qualms about working for a first-time director, and besides, he liked Pizzo's script.

'What appealed to me about this is that it tells an interesting story and as an actor it stretches you, because the character goes through a lot of changes in the course of events and [through] the people he meets,' he told Barbara Paskin. 'I guess overall it's a sports film, but I wish it were more of a relationship film. Whenever I can put in my two cents in terms of a scene I try to make it with as much human behaviour as possible, as opposed to what one might think of as a sports-orientated film. I think if we can do both then it becomes more attractive for the audience. But this really is a sports film first and a relationship film second.'

The filming of *Hoosiers* began on 21 October 1985 in New Richmond, Indiana. The fictional town of Hickory was a combination of various small towns surrounding Indianapolis, including Knightstown, Ninevah and Lebanon. 'Not one foot was shot inside a soundstage,' was De Haven's proud boast. The rigorous and demanding filming schedule required numerous location moves and intensive preparation of sets. The original intent was to find one town to serve as the primary set. The town, the high school, the gym, everything. But we couldn't find one. If the town looked right, then they'd torn down the gym. If the gym was right, then the town was too modern or too big. So, we made up a composite town of different locations.'

Making *Hoosiers* was a strangely disorienting experience for Hackman, and he must have felt like a refugee from *Back to the Future* as he turned up on a film set to walk into a vivid re-creation of his past. Danville, Illinois, where he had grown up in the 1930s and 1940s, was situated a mere sixty miles from the New Richmond location and the setting of rural small-town life in the rural America of the 1950s was very close to recollections of his own youth. Watching a street full of extras, dressed in the fashions of 1951, he told the film unit's publicist Luis Reyes, 'They seem the same to me, especially since everybody is wearing the same clothes they were when I left Danville, which was about 1948. The styles haven't changed much in those three years from the time our picture is based. So it's really kind of peculiar. It doesn't feel like a period film at all to me.'

In New Richmond he encountered 85–year-old Mrs Fanny Stephens, who had been his mother's best friend when they were children. She brought him photographs of the two of them together as teenagers and told him of how they used to go to the silent movies and act out all the parts when they came home. He was deeply moved by meeting Mrs Stephens and paused to reflect that he might have caught the acting bug from his mother's love of the movies.

Hackman wasn't the only person to be affected by nostalgia during the making of *Hoosiers*. To the small communities of Indiana it became a once-in-a-lifetime experience as whole town populations were galvanized to raid wardrobes, uncover old cars and offer their services as extras. Cars from the period 1940 to 1951 were unearthed from local collectors and enthusiasts. The Hickory team bus, a 1939 Chevy, is the only existing one of that model still in operation outside of the Smithsonian Institute in Washington. Costume designer Jane Anderson, another Indiana native, researched the period and managed to discover cheerleaders' sweaters and senior corduroy skirts that had long been in storage, all to help re-create a 'rural post-World War II and pre-Elvis' look. The recently formed Indiana Film Commission came to the assistance of production designer David Nichols in his quest for a high school gymnasium of the period.

[199]

The combined efforts of all those involved lavished *Hoosiers* with the tender loving care necessary to make it come alive on the big screen.

Hackman plays Norman Dale, a former college coach, who arrives in Hickory in 1951. Early in his career he had been suspended from major-league college coaching when he had struck one of his players. The intervening ten years have been aimlessly spent and his arrival in Hickory is very much a second chance to start afresh. It is his old friend Cletus Summers (Sheb Wooley), the high school principal, who had extended the invitation to coach the modest basketball team of this farming community. The tiny school of less than 80 students fields a team of five players and presents Dale with a formidable challenge.

Dale's status as an outsider and his unconventional methods do not endear him to the locals. During his first game he benches a star player for disobeying his instructions, and his philosophy of building team spirit is slow to catch on. However, he becomes friends with a local schoolteacher, Myra Fleener (Barbara Hershey), and is instrumental in the rehabilitation of the town drunk Shooter (Dennis Hopper), a former basketball star who can still offer expert advice on strategy and gamesmanship.

When Dale's coaching does not produce immediate results his future looks bleak. Then a former star player returns, the other players begin to adapt to Dale's way and the team start winning. Their successful streak takes the Hickory Huskers to the qualifying rounds of the State Championships and, finally, to a shot at the title in Indianapolis.

Hoosiers, it seems, is a film caught in a dilemma of how to reconcile its competing plot threads: one man's redemption through starting over in small-town America, versus a classic *Rocky*-style scenario of sporting underdogs turning into giant-killers.

It drew an admiring review from *Variety*. '[The] first half offers Hackman many special moments,' their critic wrote, 'as he superbly delineates the determination of a man to teach and, in the process, build character in his own way regardless of the negative consequences this might have for himself.' Viewing the film as a whole, Cart said, 'During the opening reels, first-time feature director David Anspaugh paints a richly textured portrait of rural American life, both visually and through glimpses of the guarded reticence of the people.' Overall, *Hoosiers* was hailed as a 'powerful character study in the world of Middle American athletics'. Even the formulaic conclusion was made more palatable by the care and concern that had gone into the characterizations.

In America, *Hoosiers* became Hackman's most successful film in years, accumulating $25 million at the box-office and earning Oscar nominations for Jarry Goldsmith's music and Dennis Hopper's supporting performance. In Britain, the film was retitled and received a premiere at the Brighton Film Festival.

Since his divorce, Hackman has yet to settle himself in any one place and is ever more the vagabond, living life out of a suitcase in one anonymous hotel suite after another. With his profession likely to whisk him off to some unknown location at a moment's notice, it was almost a surprise to find him making a film out of Hollywood in the spring of 1986.

Deceit, now titled *No Way Out*, is a suspense thriller directed by New Zealander Roger Donaldson, whose international career has included the 1984 version of *The Bounty* with Mel Gibson and *Marie* (1985) with Sissy Spacek. In *No Way Out*, Kevin Costner stars as Lieutenant Commander Tom Farrell. Arriving for his first assignment at the Pentagon, he is given 48 hours to find and neutralize the sole witness to a brutal crime that is being covered up. The one complicating factor is that Farrell happens to be that witness. Hackman plays David Brice and further cast members include Sean Young and Howard Duff as Senator Duvall.

No Way Out began filming on 7 April 1986 in Los Angeles and included location shooting in Washington DC and New Zealand. The film was scheduled to be released in 1987.

After *No Way Out*, the suitcase was packed again and Hackman was on his way to England for the production of *Superman IV* and a reprise of his thus far unsatisfactory interpretation of comic villain Lex Luthor. 'I'd hate to be around doing *Superman IX*,' he told *The List*, 'but I enjoyed myself and I stopped worrying about what people think about my doing it a long time ago. It's the kind of role that

[201]

lends itself to a lot of action and scope, and when you get to an age when you're cast in older-man type roles there's a lot of energy inside you that you feel you want to get out. I like playing the Lex Luthor character because I can use up some of this energy.'

The *Superman* rights have now passed from the Salkind family to the Cannon Group, a move that at least pleased Margot Kidder, who had fallen foul of the Salkinds after her outspoken comments on the replacement of Richard Donner as the series director. Number Four is directed by Sidney J. Furie and is budgeted between $30 and $40 million. Christopher Reeve returns as Superman and Clark Kent and has had a hand in the screenplay, feeling that his character should confront some real contemporary issues and even break his mandate not to interfere in the affairs of planet Earth. The plot involves Superman and his struggle with Luthor's latest ally, the superhuman Nuclear Man (Mark Pillow).

In an interview with *Films and Filming* on the last day of production, Christopher Reeve revealed that Hackman had appeared to relish his work on their latest venture. On the first *Superman* film, almost ten years previously, 'he was morose' (said Reeve) 'and when I asked him, "Gee Mr Hackman" – this was me aged 24 – "why did you play Lex Luthor?" he looked at me and said, "You mean besides the $2 million?" This time he really enjoyed himself.'

After extensive post-production and special-effects work, *Superman IV* was scheduled to be released as a major holiday attraction for the summer of 1987.

Chapter Sixteen

Hackman's major project for 1987 is a film version of Ernest Hemingway's *Across the River and Into the Trees*. Over the years it has acquired something of a legendary reputation as one of the cinema's 'unfilmable' novels. It has been announced as a vehicle for William Holden and then Burt Lancaster, and as a directorial venture for John Huston, Robert Altman and others. At the time of writing John Frankenheimer has been chosen to direct the Hackman assault on this unyielding classic. Once again, the actor will be exploring fresh territory in a work that was once described as 'the story of a veteran of two World Wars, staving off death in Venice with one last fling at sport and love with a young, a too-young, child-woman of nineteen.'

The future for Hackman will probably be as unpredictable and checkered as the swings-and-roundabouts pattern of his past. Recent interviewers have noted a certain sadness and wistfulness in his manner, an indication perhaps that the pressures of stardom and growing old have begun to make him careworn and regretful of some of his mistakes along the way. He is a workaholic and a perfectionist whose paramount regard for his professional life has exacted a price from his personal relations. A Broadway actor can go home to his wife and family after every performance. A prolific movie actor retires to the loneliness of his trailer or the four-walled nondescript world of room service and deluxe hotels.

Over the past twenty years Hackman has talked often of returning to the theatre, and one suspects that time is running out if the move is to become anything more than a pipe dream. He gave his most detailed and honest assessment of the prospect in a 1972 interview:

'I keep telling myself that I will return to the theatre; I suppose realistically I probably won't. The kind of energy and the amount of reward involved, not only monetary but in terms of satisfaction, it seems to make no sense, plus, I find it very difficult to live in New York anymore. It seems to have got too big for me, or I have outgrown it. I would like to have played some of the classic contemporary theatre roles, the Eugene O'Neill or the Tennessee Williams roles that some of our better actors have performed. I was always involved in new plays. I never got to do the classics.'

He continues to express a desire to perform in *The Iceman Cometh* or *Long Day's Journey Into Night*, but it now seems unlikely that he will. Doubt continues to cloud over his directorial aspirations as time passes and he seems no nearer achieving that goal either. Scores of actors have managed, with varying degrees of success, to insist on the possibility of directing a film. The list stretches endlessly from Hackman's professional associates Warren Beatty and Robert Redford, to his close friend Robert Duvall, to Richard Attenborough, Richard Benjamin, Ron Howard, Anthony Perkins, James Caan, Clint Eastwood, *et al*.

When Hackman was at the peak of his box-office popularity he felt it unwise to expend valuable time and energy on setting up a directorial assignment when there were so many attractive acting offers competing for his attention. Later, he seems to have lacked the willpower or proper timing to embark upon his cherished plan.

In 1982 he said, 'I want to direct. I have this property *Open and Shut* about a rape case. But I would never allow myself to be in the position of going on the set that first morning without having some experience. What I would do, what I fully intend to do, is to do some second-unit work before principal photography starts – and I'm talking about a lot of it – even if I had to be *very* prepared. Also, I'd prefer not to play in the film as well. But it's very tough for an actor not to direct a film, unless it's a tremendous script. Here you have somebody untried, and I think the reality is that it would be very tough for me *not* to have to perform in it.'

The reality, thus far, has been that Hackman has found it impossible to direct a film of any kind. He claims a dearth of finance and a lack of time as the main obstacles to his plans, plus the fact that he still finds challenges in the art of acting to divert his attention. Another property he now owns is the right to remake a compelling French thriller called *Garde à Vue* (1981) that was known in English as *The Inquisitor*. It is set in a French provincial town on New Year's Eve and is a very contained and claustrophobic piece about a wealthy lawyer who is arrested on suspicion of the rape and murder of two children. Most of the film centres on his interrogation, offering insights into the characters of the lawyer and the inspector investigating the case as well as painting a shadowy picture of the uneasy relations between the lawyer and his mysterious wife. It is an eminently sensible choice for a first-time director as it requires only a modest budget and can allow the debutant to concentrate on the quality of the performances. Hackman's sensibilities and working experience should ensure that he is finely attuned to the needs of his performers.

'I'd like to be sensitive,' he has said. 'I'd like to be able to understand the actor's problems, which I do to some degree, and also to be able to put the story on film. It's very hard for actors sometimes to be objective. Actors tend to want to do moments, which is fine. But directors want to do scenes and large chunks – ideas. So, the problem, as I see it, is trying to make the transition from what the actor wants to what the film needs.'

It is comforting, in a way, that an actor of Hackman's stature and years still holds unfulfilled ambitions and dreams for the future. At 57, his career is still in full flow and it would be as unwise to offer pat conclusions on the story so far as it would be to idly speculate that the best is yet to come. His career does not embrace some meteoric rise to fame, or an intense fashionability balanced by an equally intense indifference on the part of the public. He was a late starter as an actor and a slow developer as a star. His working life has been one of steady progression and growth; he has been durable and dependable as opposed to short-lived and hysterical. He has moved at his own pace and when his career became too much to handle he walked away, re-charging his batteries for another day. By and large, his actions betoken the character of a man who is sensible, thoughtful and hard-working. His 'potato face' may not have destined him for stardom, but his integrity and craftsmanship have placed him in the rare category of stars who are accepted as such because of their acting prowess and not on the basis of an irresistible personality.

Since he returned from his 'retirement', Hackman has expressed few doubts about continuing as an actor. He had simply stepped off the treadmill of money-spinning clinkers, rediscovering his passion and self-respect in the process. The prospect of a genuine and permanent retirement now seems laughable and mercifully distant, although he has forecast, 'I don't think I'll ever do anything else but act. I don't think I could be so successful in anything else. But when I retire, I see myself painting on a small farm in Connecticut. I started painting in 1952 at the Art Student League in New York, but I didn't hang in there. Now I paint a lot. I've been studying with a Russian painter the last couple of years, and would like to be good at it.'

His mention of retirement is, one suspects, merely a passing notion. A healthy dissatisfaction with his work means that there is always more to be achieved – new horizons, new challenges, further opportunities to practise his craft with more refinement and *élan* than ever before.

The perennial prospect of better things in store staves off staleness and boredom. After thirty years Gene Hackman can still surprise and delight with his attention to detail, naturalism and powerful conviction. A few years back he was asked to name what he considered his consummate performance. He paused to contemplate the question and replied, with characteristic modesty, that he didn't consider there to be any.

'There are a few moments in *Scarecrow*, and in *Conversation*, and the withdrawal scene in *French Connection II*, but I've never come away from seeing one of my pictures without thinking I could have given more. I've yet to give it all.'

His answer begged the question of why he had never given his all, and his response to that offers optimism over what the future may hold for both lovers of fine acting and fans of Hackman's unfussy charisma:

'It would mean committing myself to it too much,' he said. 'It's fear, I think. I'm afraid to commit myself that much. It's something I'm working on. Something I've got to look forward to. Maybe in the end that's one of the things which keeps me in the game.'

Filmography

MAD DOG COLL (1961)

A Thalia Films Production. Running Time: 87 minutes. Director: Burt Balaban. Producer: Edward Schreiber. Production Manager: Harrison Starr. Assistant Directors: Arthur Steckler and Ulu Grosbard. Screenplay: Edward Schreiber, based on material by Leo Lieberman. Photography: Gayne Reschner. Editor: Ralph Rosenblum. Art Direction: Richard Sylbert. Set Decoration: Gene Callahan. Music: Stu Phillips. Title Song by Stu Phillips and Eddie D. Trush. Sung by Hal Waters. Sound: Maurice Rosenblum.

Cast: John Davis Chandler (Vincent Coll), Neil Nephew (Rocco), Brooke Hayward (Elizabeth), Jerry Orbach (Joe), Telly Savalas (Lt Darro), Vincent Gardenia (Dutch Schultz), Kay Doubleday (Cleo), Glenn Cannon (Harry), Tom Castronova (Ralphie), Joy Harmon (Caroline), Gene Hackman (Cop).

LILITH (1964)

Centaur Productions for Columbia. Running Time: 114 minutes. Director/Producer: Robert Rossen. Production Manager: Jim Di Gangi. Assistant Directors: Larry Sturhahn and Bob Vietro. Screenplay: Robert Rossen and Robert Alan Aurthur, based on the novel by J. R. Salamanca. Photography: Eugen Shuftan. Assistant Photographers: Bert Siegal and Tibor Sands. Camera Operator: Joe Coffey. Editor: Aram Avakian. Art Director: Richard Sylbert. Set Decoration: Gene Callahan. Music: Kenyon Hopkins. Costume Design: Ruth Morley. Titles: Elinor Bunin. Sound Recording: James Shields and Richard Vorisek. Horse Trainer: Curly Baker.

Cast: Warren Beatty (Vincent Bruce), Jean Seberg (Lilith Arthur), Peter Fonda (Stephen Evshevsky), Kim Hunter (Bea Brice), Anne Meacham (Mrs Yvonne Meaghan), James Patterson (Dr Lavrier),

Jessica Walter (Laura), Gene Hackman (Norman), Robert Reilly (Bob Clayfield), Rene Auberjonois (Howie), Lucy Smith (Vincent's Grandmother), Maurice Brenner (Mr Gordon), Jeanne Barr (Miss Glassman), Richard Higgs (Mr Palakis), Elizabeth Bader (Girl at the Bar), Alice Spivak (Lonely Girl), Walter Arnold (Lonely Girl's Father), Kathleen Phelan (Lonely Girl's Mother), Cecilia Ray (Lilith's Mother in Dream), Gunnar Peters (The Chauffeur in Dream), L. Jerome Offutt (Tournament Judge), W. Jerome Offutt (Tournament Announcer), Robert Jolivette (Older Watermelon Boy), Jason Jolivette (Younger Watermelon Boy), Jeno Mate (Assistant to Dr Lavrier), Ben Carruthers (Benito, the Dancer), Dina Paisner (Psychodrama Moderator), Pawnee Sills (Receptionist).

HAWAII (1966)

A Mirisch Company Production. Running Time: 186 minutes. Director: George Roy Hill. Producer: Walter Mirisch. Associate Producer: Lewis J. Rachmil. Screenplay: Dalton Trumbo and Daniel Taradash, based on the novel by James A. Michener. Photography: Russell Harlan. Editor: Stuart Gilmore. Production Design: Cary Odell. Music: Elmer Bernstein. Song: 'My Wishing Doll' (Lyrics: Mack David; Music: Elmer Bernstein). Costume Design: Dorothy Jeakins. Prologue Sequence supervised by: James Blue. Art Direction: James Sullivan. Set Decoration: Edward G. Boyle and Ray Boltz Jnr. Production Managers: Robert Anderson and Emmett Emerson. Sound: Robert Martin. Second Unit Director: Richard Talmadge. Assistant Director: Ray Gosnell. Music Editor: Richard Carruth. Sound Editor: Wayne B. Fury. Second Unit Cameraman: Harold Wellman. Prologue Sequence Cameraman: Chuck Wheeler. Special Effects: Paul Byrd.

Cast: Julie Andrews (Jerusha Bromley), Max Von Sydow (Abner Hale), Richard Harris (Rafet Hoxworth), Carroll O'Connor (Charles Bromley), Elizabeth Cole (Abigail Bromley), Diane Sherry (Charity Bromley), Heather Menzies (Mercy Bromley), Torin That-cher (Reverend Thorn), Gene Hackman (John Whipple), John Cullum (Immanuel Quigley), Lou Antonio (Abraham Hewlett), Jocelyn La Garde (Queen Malama), Manu Tupou (Keoki), Ted Nobriga (Kelolo), Elizabeth Logue (Noelani), Lokelani S. Chicarell (Iliki), Malcolm Atterbury (Gideon Hale), Dorothy Jeakins (Hepzibah Hale), George Rose (Captain Janders), Michael Constantine (Mason), John Harding (Collins), Robert Crawford (Cridland), Robert Oakley (Micah Hale, 4 years), Henrik Von

Sydow (Micah Hale, 7 years), Clas S. Von Sydow (Micah Hale, 12 years), Bertil Werjefelt (Micah Hale, 18 years).

FIRST TO FIGHT (1966)

A Warner Brothers Production. Running Time: 97 minutes (UK: 71 minutes). Director: Christian Nyby. Executive Producer: William Conrad. Screenplay: Gene L. Coon. Photography: Harold Wellman. Art Direction: Art Loel. Editor: George Rohrs. Sound: Robert B. Lee. Set Decoration: Hal Overell. Dialogue Supervisor: Stacy Harris. Music: Fred Steiner. Production Manager: J. R. Llewellyn. Technical Advisor: Major Fred A. Kraus (USMC, Ret.). Make-Up Supervisor: Gordon Bau. Hair Stylist: Jean Burt Reilly. Assistant Director: Victor Vallejo.

Cast: Chad Everett (Jack Connell), Marilyn Devlin (Peggy Sanford), Dean Jagger (Lt Col Baseman), Bobby Troup (Lt Overman), Claude Akins (Capt Mason), Gene Hackman (Sgt Tweed), James Best (Sgt Carnavan), Norman Alden (Sgt Schmidtmer), Bobs Watson (Sgt Maypole), Ken Swofford (O'Brien), Ray Reese (Hawkins), Garry Goodgion (Karl), Robert Austin (Adams), Clint Ritchie (Sgt Slater), Stephen Roberts (President Franklin D. Roosevelt).

COVENANT WITH DEATH (1966)

A Warner Brothers-Seven Arts Production. Running Time: 96 minutes (UK: 72 minutes). Director: Lamont Johnson. Executive Producer: William Conrad. Screenplay: Larry Marcus and Saul Levitt, based on the novel by Stephen Becker. Photography: Robert Burks. Art Direction: Howard Hollander. Editor: William Ziegler. Set Decoration: Ralph S. Hurst. Music: Leonard Rosenman. Production Manager: J. Russell Llewellyn. Sound: Stanley Jones. Dialogue Supervisor: Stacy Harris. Make-Up Supervisor: Gordon Bau. Hair Stylist: Jean Burt Reilly. Assistant Director: Gil Kissel.

Cast: George Maharis (Benjamin Morrealis Lewis), Laura Devon (Rosemary), Katy Jurado (Eulalia), Earl Holliman (Bryan Talbot), Sidney Blackmer (Colonel Oates), Gene Hackman (Harmsworth), John Anderson (Dietrich), Wende Wagner (Rafaela), Emilio Fernandez (Ignacio), Kent Smith (Parmalee), Lonny Chapman (Musgrave), Arthur O'Connell (Judge Hochstadter), Jose De Vega

(Digby), Larry D. Mann (Chillingworth), Whit Bissell (Bruce Donnelly), Russell Thorson (Dr Schilling), Paul Birch (Governor), Erwin Neal (Willie Wayne).

BANNING (1967)

A Universal Production. Running Time: 100 minutes (originally 102). Director: Ron Winston. Producer: Dick Berg. Assistant Producer: David Hammond. Production Manager: Wallace Worsley. Assistant Director: Edward K. Dodds. Screenplay: James Lee, based on a story by Hamilton Maule. Photography: Loyal Griggs. Art Direction: Alexander Golitzen and Henry Bumstead. Set Decoration: John McCarthy and George Milo. Sound: Waldon O. Watson and William Russell. Editor: J. Terry Williams. Music: Quincy Jones. Costumes: Jean Louis. Make-Up: Bud Westmore. Hair Stylist: Larry Germain.

Cast: Robert Wagner (Mike Banning), Anjanette Comer (Carol Lindquist), Jill St John (Angela Barr), Guy Stockwell (Jonathan Linus), James Farentino (Chris Patton), Susan Clark (Cynthia Linus), Howard St John (J. Pallister Young), Mike Kellin (Harry Kalielle), Gene Hackman (Tommy Del Gaddo), Sean Garrison (Richard Tyson), Logan Ramsey (Doc Brewer), Edmond Ryan (Stuart Warren), Oliver McGowan (Senator Brady), Lucille Meredith (Maggi Andrews), Bill Cort (Tony).

BONNIE AND CLYDE (1967)

A Tatira-Hiller-Warner Brothers Production. Running Time: 111 minutes. Director: Arthur Penn. Producer: Warren Beatty. Production Manager: Russ Saunders. Screenplay: David Newman and Robert Benton. Photography: Burnett Guffey. Editor: Dede Allen. Art Direction: Dean Tavoularis. Set Design: Raymond Paul. Music: Charles Strouse. Costumes: Theadora Van Runkel. Sound: Francis E. Stahl.

Cast: Warren Beatty (Clyde Barrow), Faye Dunaway (Bonnie Parker), Michael J. Pollard (C. W. Moss), Gene Hackman (Buck Barrow), Estelle Parsons (Blanche), Denver Pyle (Frank Hamer), Dub Taylor (Ivan Moss), Evan Evans (Velma Davis), Gene Wilder (Eugene Grizzard).

THE SPLIT (1968)

A Spectrum Production for Metro-Goldwyn-Mayer. Running
Time: 89 minutes. Director: Gordon Flemyng. Producers: Robert
Chartoff and Irwin Winkler. Production Manager: Jim Henderling.
Assistant Director: Al Jennings. Screenplay: Robert Sabaroff, based
on the novel *The Seventh* by Richard Stark. Photography: Burnett
Guffey. Editor: Rita Roland. Art Direction: Urie McCleary and
George W. Davis. Set Decoration: Henry Grace and Keogh
Gleason. Music: Quincy Jones. Songs: 'The Split' by Quincy Jones
and Ernie Shelby, sung by Billy Preston; 'A Good Woman's Love'
by Quincy Jones and Sheb Wooley, sung by Sheb Wooley; 'It's
Just a Game, Love' by Quincy Jones and Ernie Shelby, sung by
Clydie King and Billy Preston. Sound: Franklin Milton and Larry
Jost.

Cast: Jim Brown (McClain), Diahann Carroll (Ellie), Ernest Borg-
nine (Bert Clinger), Julie Harris (Gladys), Gene Hackman (Lt
Walter Brill), Jack Klugman (Harry Kifka), Warren Oates (Marty
Gough), James Whitmore (Herb Sutro), Donald Sutherland (Dave
Negli), Joyce Jameson (Jenifer), Harry Hickoz (1st Detective), Jackie
Joseph (Jackie), Warren Vanders (Mason).

RIOT (1968)

William Castle Productions. Running Time: 96 minutes (UK: 94
minutes). Director: Buzz Kulik. Producer: William Castle.
Associate Producer: Dona Holloway. Production Manager: Bill
Gray. Assistant Director: Danny McCauley. Screenplay: James
Poe, based on the novel by Frank Elli. Photography: Robert B.
Hauser. Editor: Edwin H. Bryant. Art Direction: Paul Sylbert.
Music: Christopher Komeda. Songs: '100 Years' by Christopher
Komeda and Robert Wells, sung by Bill Medley; 'Rag Mop' by
Johnnie Lee Willis and Deacon Anderson. Sound: John H.
Wilkinson and Clem Portman. Sound Recording: Vic Carpenter
and Walter Goss.

Cast: Jim Brown (Cully Briston), Gene Hackman (Red Fletcher),
Ben Carruthers (Surefoot), Mike Kellin (Bugsy), Gerald O'Loughlin
(Grossman), Clifford David ('Big Mary' Sheldon), Bill Walker
(Jake), Ricky Summers ('Gertie'), Michael Byron (Murray), Jerry
Thompson (Fisk), M. Gerri and John Neiderhauser (Homosexuals),
Warden Frank A. Eyman (Warden).

THE GYPSY MOTHS (1969)

A John Frankenheimer-Edward Lewis Production for Metro-Goldwyn-Mayer. Running Time: 106 minutes. Director: John Frankenheimer. Producers: Hal Landers and Bobby Roberts. Production Manager: Jim Henderling. Assistant Director: Al Jennings. Screenplay: William Hanley, based on the novel by James Drought. Photography: Philip Lathrop. Special Photographic Effects: J. McMillan Johnson and Carroll L. Shepphird. Aerial Photography: Carl Boenisch. Editor: Henry Berman. Art Direction: George W. Davis and Cary Odell. Set Decoration: Henry Grace and Jack Mills. Music: Elmer Bernstein. Sound: Franklin Milton and Tommy Overton. Costumes: Bill Thomas.

Cast: Burt Lancaster (Mike Rettig), Deborah Kerr (Elizabeth Brandon), Gene Hackman (Joe Browdy), Scott Wilson (Malcolm Webson), William Windom (V. John Brandon), Bonnie Bedelia (Annie Burke), Sheree North (Waitress), Carl Reindel (Pilot), Ford Rainey (Stand Owner), John Napier (Dick Donford).

MAROONED (1969)

A Frankovich-Sturgess Production. Running Time: 133 minutes. Director: John Sturges. Producer: Mike J. Frankovich. Associate Producer: Frank Capra Jnr. Production Manager: William O'Sullivan. Second Unit Director: Ralph Black. Assistant Director: Daniel J. McCauley. Screenplay: Mayo Simon, from the novel by Martin Caidin. Photography: Daniel Fapp. Photography Consultant: William Widmayer. Second Unit Photography: W. Wallace Kelley. Special Visual Effects: Lawrence W. Butler, Donald C. Glouner and Robie Robinson. Aerial Photography: Nelson Tyler. Editor: Walter Thompson. Production Designer: Lyle R. Wheeler. Set Decoration: Frank Tuttle. Costumes: Seth Banks. Sound: Les Fresholtz and Arthur Piantadosi. Technical Advisers: Martin Caidin and George Smith.

Cast: Gregory Peck (Charles Keith), Richard Crenna (Jim Pruett), David Janssen (Ted Dougherty), James Franciscus (Clayton Stone), Gene Hackman (Buzz Lloyd), Lee Grant (Celia Pruett), Nancy Kovack (Teresa Stone), Mariette Hartley (Betty Lloyd), Scott Brady (Public Affairs Officer), Craig Huebing (Flight Director), John Carter (Flight Surgeon), George Gaynes (Mission Director), Tom Stewart (Houston Cap-Com), Frank March (Space Systems Director), Duke Hobbie (Titan Systems Specialist), Dennis

Robertson (Launch Director), George Smith (Cape Weather Officer), Vincent Van Lynn (Cannon), Walter Brooke (Radin), Mauritz Hugo (Hardy), Bill Couch (Russian Cosmonaut), Mary-Linda Rapelye (Priscilla Keith).

DOWNHILL RACER (1969)

A Wildwood International-Paramount Production. Running Time: 101 minutes. Director: Michael Ritchie. Producer: Richard Gregson. Production Manager: Walter Coblenz. Assistant Directors: Kip Gowans and Walter Coblenz. Screenplay: James Salter, based on the novel 'The Downhill Racers' by Oakley Hall. Photography: Brian Probyn. Editor: Nick Archer. Art Direction: Ian Whittaker. Music: Kenyon Hopkins. Sound Recording: Kevin Sutton and Elden Ruberg.

Cast: Robert Redford (David Chappellet), Gene Hackman (Eugene Claire), Camilla Sparv (Carole Stahl), Joe Jay Jalbert (Tommy Erb), Timothy Kirk (D. K. Bryan), Dabney Coleman (Mayo), Jim McMullan (Johnny Creech), Oren Stevens (Tony Kipsmith), Karl Michael Volger (Machet), Rip McManus (Bruce Devore), Jerry Dexter (Ron Engel), Tom J. Kirk (Stiles), Robert Hutton-Potts, Heini Schuler, Peter Rohr, Arnold Alpiger, Eddie Waldburger, Marco Walli.

I NEVER SANG FOR MY FATHER (1970)

A Jamel Production for Columbia Pictures. Running Time: 92 minutes. Director/Producer: Gilbert Cates. Production Manager: George Goodman. Assistant Directors: Stanley Panesoff and Allan Wertheim. Screenplay: Robert Anderson, based on his own play. Photography: Morris Hartzband and George Stoetzel. Editor: Angelo Ross. Art Direction: Hank Aldrich. Music: Al Gorgoni and Barry Mann. Song: 'Strangers' by Barry Mann and Cynthia Weil, sung by Roy Clark. Costumes: Theoni V. Aldredge. Titles: Bert Gold. Sound: Charles Federmack. Sound Recording: Stanley Mittledorf and James Sabat. Sound Re-Recording: Richard Vorisek.

Cast: Melvyn Douglas (Tom Garrison), Gene Hackman (Gene Garrison), Dorothy Stickney (Margaret Garrison), Estelle Parsons (Alice), Elizabeth Hubbard (Peggy), Lovelady Powell (Norma), Daniel Keyes (Dr Mayberry), Conrad Bain (Rev Pell), Jon Richards (Marvin Scott), Nikki Counselman (Waitress), Carol Peterson (1st

Nurse), Sloane Shelton (2nd Nurse), James Karen (Old Age Home Director), Gene Williams (State Hospital Director).

DOCTORS' WIVES (1970)

Frankovich Productions Incorporated for Columbia Pictures. Running Time: 102 minutes. Director: George Schaefer. Producer: Mike J. Frankovich. Production Manager: William O'Sullivan. Assistant Director: Philip L. Parslow. Screenplay: Daniel Taradash, based on the novel by Frank G. Slaughter. Photography: Charles B. Lang. Special Photographic Effects: Butler-Glouner. Editor: Carl Kress. Production Design: Lyle R. Wheeler. Set Decoration: Marvin March. Music: Elmer Bernstein. Song: 'The Costume Ball' by Elmer Bernstein and Alan and Marilyn Bergman, sung by Mama Cass Elliot. Costumes: Moss Mabry. Titles: Richard Kuhn, National Screen Services. Sound: Les Fresholtz and Arthur Piantadosi. Technical Adviser: Pete Morrow.

Cast: Richard Crenna (Peter Brennan), Janice Rule (Amy Brennan), John Colicos (Mort Dellman), Diana Sands (Helen Straughn), Gene Hackman (Dave Randolph), Rachel Roberts (Della Randolph), Dyan Cannon (Lorrie Dellman), Carroll O'Connor (Joe Gray), Cara Williams (Maggie Gray), George Gaynes (Paul McGill), Marian McCargo (Elaine McGill), Richard Anderson (District Attorney Douglas), Ralph Bellamy (Jake Porter), Anthony Costello (Mike Traynor), Kristina Holland (Sybil Carter), Scott Brady (Sgt Malloy), Mark Jenkins (Lew Saunders), Vincent Van Lynn (Barney Harris), Ernie Barnes (Dr Penfield), Paul Martin (Dr Deemster), William Bramley (Dr Hagstrom), Jon Lormer (Elderly Doctor).

THE HUNTING PARTY (1971)

A Brighton Pictures/Levy-Gardner-Laven Production. Running Time: 108 minutes (UK: 102 minutes). Director: Don Medford. Producer: Lou Morheim. Executive Producers: Jules Levy and Arthur Gardner. Production Supervisor: Geoffrey Haine. Production Manager: Julio Vallejo. Assistant Director: José Maria Ochoa. Screenplay: William Norton, Gilbert Alexander and Lou Morheim, from a story by Gilbert Alexander and Lou Morheim. Photography: Cecilio Pania Gua. Editor: Tom Rolf. Art Direction: Enrique Alarcon. Special effects: Manuel Baquero. Music/Music Direction: Riz Ortolani. Sound Recording: Les Hammond.

Cast: Oliver Reed (Frank Calder), Candice Bergen (Melissa Ruger), Gene Hackman (Brandt Ruger), Simon Oakland (Matthew Gunn), Mitchel Ryan (Doc Harrison), L. Q. Jones (Hog Warren), G. D. Spradlin (Sam Bayard), William Watson (Loring), Ronald Howard (Watt Nelson), Rayford Barnes (Crimp), Bernard Kay (Buford King), Eugenio Escudero Garcia (Mario), Dean Selmier (Collins), Ritchie Adams (Owney Clark), Claro Bravo and Bud Strait (Cowboys), Ralph Brown (Sheriff Johnson), Marian Collier (Schoolteacher), Max Slaten (Telegraph Man), Rafael Escudero Garcia (Mexican), Emilio Raodriques Guiar (Priest), Sara Atkinson (Redhaired Girl), Lilibeth Solison (Blonde Girl), Francisca Tu (Chinese Girl), Marisa Tovar (Mexican Girl), Christine Larroude and Stephanie Pieritz (Prostitutes).

CISCO PIKE (1971)

An Acrobat Production. Running Time: 94 minutes.
  Director: Bill L. Norton. Producer: Gerald Ayres. Associate Producer/Production Manager: Herbert Wallerstein. Assistant Director: Sheldon Schrager. Screenplay: Bill L. Norton. Photography: Vilis Lapenieks. Editor: Robert C. Jones. Art Direction: Alfred Sweeney. Set Decoration: Ray Malyneaux. Music Supervision: Bob Johnston. Songs: 'Lovin' Her Was Easier', 'I'd Rather Be Sorry', 'Pilgrim: Chapter 33' and 'Breakdown' written and sung by Kris Kristofferson; 'Wailin' and Whoopin'' written and sung by Sonny Terry; 'Michoacan' written by A. Allen and K. Fowley, performed by Sir Douglas Quintet; 'Funky Lady' written and sung by Les Montgomery. Sound: Jack Solomon and Arthur Piantadosi. Technical Adviser: John Hartman.

Cast: Kris Kristofferson (Cisco Pike), Karen Black (Sue), Gene Hackman (Officer Leo Holland), Harry Dean stanton (Jesse Dupre), Viva (Merna), Joy Bang (Lynn), Roscoe Lee Browne (Music Store Owner), Chuy Franco (Mexican Man), Severn Darden (Lawyer), Herb Weil (Suspicious Customer), Antonio Fargas (Buffalo), Douglas Sahm (Rex), Don Sturdy (Recording Engineer), Alan Arbus (Sim Valensi), Frank Hotchkiss (Motorcycle Officer), Hugh Romney (Reed), James Oliver (Narc), Nawana Davis (Mouse), Timothy Near (Waitress), Lorna Thayer (Swimming Lady), William Traylor (Jack).

THE FRENCH CONNECTION (1971)

D'Antoni Productions in association with Schine-Moore Productions for Twentieth Century Fox. Running Time: 104 minutes.

Director: William Friedkin. Producer: Philip D'Antoni. Executive Producer: G. David Schine. Associate Producer: Kenneth Utt. Production Manager: Paul Ganapoler. Assistant Directors: William C. Gerritty and Jerry Donnelly. Screenplay: Ernest Tidyman, based on the book by Robin Moore. Photography: Owen Roizman. Editor: Jerry Greenberg. Art Direction: Ben Kazaskow. Set Decoration: Ed Garzero. Special Effects: Sass Bedig. Music/Music Direction: Don Ellis. Sound: Chris Newman and Theodore Soderberg. Technical Consultants: Eddie Egan and Sonny Grosso. Stunt Coordinator: Bill Hickman.

Cast: Gene Hackman (Jimmy 'Popeye' Doyle), Fernando Rey (Alain Charnier), Roy Scheider (Buddy Russo), Tony LoBianco (Sal Boca), Marcel Bozzuffi (Pierre Nicoli), Frédéric de Pasquale (Devereaux), Bill Hickman (Mulderig), Ann Rebbot (Marie Charnier), Harold Gary (Weinstock), Arlene Farber (Angie Boca), Eddie Egan (Simonson), André Ernotte (La Valle), Sonny Grosso (Klein), Pat McDermott (Chemist), Alan Weeks (Drug Pusher), Al Fann (Informant), Irving Abrahams (Police Mechanic), Randy Jurgenson (Police Sergeant), William Coke (Motorman), the Three Degrees (Themselves).

PRIME CUT (1972)

A Cinema Center Films Production. Running Time: 86 minutes. Director: Michael Ritchie. Producer: Joe Wizan. Executive Producer: Kenneth Evans. Associate Producer: Mickey Borofsky. Production Manager: David Salven. Assistant Director: Michael Daves. Screenplay: Robert Dillon. Photography: Gene Polito. Editor: Carl Pingatore. Art Direction: Bill Malley. Set Decoration: James Payne. Special Effects: Logan Frazee. Music: Lalo Schifrin. Titles: Don Record. Sound: Barry Thomas.

Cast: Lee Marvin (Nick Devlin), Gene Hackman ('Mary Ann'), Angel Tompkins (Clarabelle), Gregory Walcott (Weenie), Sissy Spacek (Poppy), Janit Bladwin (Violet), William Morey (Shay), Clint Ellison (Delancy), Howard Platt (Shaugnessy), Les Lannom (O'Brien), Eddie Egan (Jake), Therese Reinsch (Jake's Girl), Bob Wilson (Reaper Driver), Gordon Signer (Brockman), Gladys

Watson (Milk Lady), Hugh Gillin Jnr (Desk Clerk), P. Lunda (Mrs O'Brien), David Savage (Ox-Eye), Craig Chapman (Farmer Bob), Jim Taksas (Big Jim), Wayne Savagne (Freckle Face).

THE POSEIDON ADVENTURE (1972)

Kent Productions for Twentieth century Fox. Running Time: 117 minutes. Director: Ronald Neame. Producer: Irwin Allen. Associate Producer: Sidney Marshall. Production Manager: Hal Herman. Assistant Directors: Norman Cook and Les Warner. Screenplay: Stirling Silliphant and Wendell Mayes, based on the novel by Paul Gallico. Photography: Harold Stine. Special Photographic Effects: L. B. Abbot. Editor: Harold F. Kress. Production Design: William Creber. Set Decoration: Raphael Bretton. Mechanical Effects: A. D. Flowers. Music: John Williams. Song: 'The Morning After' by Al Kasha and Joel Hirschhorn. Orchestration: Alexander Courage. Sound: Herman Lewis. Stunt Co-ordinator: Paul Stader.

Cast: Gene Hackman (Rev Frank Scott), Ernest Borgnine (Mike Rogo), Red Buttons (James Martin), Carol Lynley (Nonnie Parry), Roddy McDowall (Acres), Stella Stevens (Linda Rogo), Shelly Winters (Belle Rosen), Jack Albertson (Manny Rosen), Pamela Sue Martin (Susan Shelby), Arthur O'Connell (Ship's Chaplain), Eric Shea (Robin Shelby), Fred Sadoff (Linarcos), Sheila Mathews (Ship's Nurse), Jan Arvan (Dr Caravello), Byron Webster (Purser), John Crawford (Chief Engineer), Bob Hastings (Master of Ceremonies), Leslie Nielsen (Ship's Captain).

SCARECROW (1973)

A Warner Brothers Production. Running Time: 112 minutes. Director: Jerry Schatzberg. Producer: Robert M. Sherman. Assistant Directors: Tom Shaw and Charles Bonniwell. Screenplay/Story: Garey Michael White. Photography: Vilmos Zsigmond. Editor: Evan Lottman. Production Design: Al Brenner. Special Effects: Candy Flanagin. Music: Fred Myrow. Titles: Anthony Goldschmidt. Sound Editors: Edward Beyer and Robert M. Reitano. Sound Recording: Barry Thomas and Victor Goode. Sound Re-Recording: Arthur Piantadosi.

Cast: Gene Hackman (Max), Al Pacino (Lion), Dorothy Tristan (Coley), Ann Wedgeworth (Frenchy), Richard Lynch (Jack Riley),

Eileen Brennan (Darlene), Penny Allen (Annie), Richard Mackman (Mickey), Al Cingolani (Skipper), Rutanya Alda (Woman in Camper).

THE CONVERSATION (1974)

A Coppola Company-Directors Company Production for Paramount. Running Time: 113 minutes. Director: Francis Ford Coppola. Producers: Francis Ford Coppola and Fred Roos. Associate Producer: Mona Skager. Screenplay: Francis Ford Coppola. Photography: Bill Butler. Production Design: Dean Tavoularis. Sound: Walter Murch. Set Decoration: Doug von Koss. Production Manager: Clark Paylow. Music: David Shire. Editor: Richard Chew. Costumes: Aggie Guerard Rogers. Technical Advisers: Hal Lipset and Leo Jones.

Cast: Gene Hackman (Harry Caul), John Cazale (Stan), Allen Garfield (Bernie Moran), Frederic Forrest (Mark), Cindy Williams (Ann), Michael Higgins (Paul), Elizabeth MacRae (Meredith), Teri Garr (Amy), Harrison Ford (Martin Stett), Mark Wheeler (Receptionist), Robert Shields (The Mime), Phoebe Alexander (Lurleen), Robert Duvall (uncredited).

ZANDY'S BRIDE (1974)

A Harvey Matogsky Production for Warner Brothers. Running Time: 116 minutes. Director: Jan Troell. Producer: Harvey Matofsky. Assistant Directors: Miles Middough and Barry Stern. Screenplay: Marc Norman, based on the novel *The Stranger* by Lillian Bos Ross. Photography: Jordan Cronenweth. Production Design: Al Brenner. Set Decoration: George Gaines. Production Manager: Phillip Parslow. Editor: Gordon Scott. Music: Fred Karlin. Sound: Charles Knight. Costumes: Pat Norris.

Cast: Gene Hackman (Zandy Allan), Liv Ullmann (Hannah Lund), Eileen Heckart (Ma Allan), Harry Dean Stanton (Songer), Joe Santos (Frank Gallo), Frank Cady (Pa Allan), Sam Bottoms (Mel Allan), Susan Tyrrell (Maria Cordova), Bob Simpson (Bill Pincus), Fabian Gregory Cordova (Paco), Don Wilbanks (Farraday), Vivian Gordon (Street Girl).

YOUNG FRANKENSTEIN (1974)

A Gruskoff-Venture Films-Crossbow Production-Jouer Production
Presentation. Running Time: 108 minutes (UK: 106 minutes).
Director: Mel Brooks. Producer: Michael Gruskoff. Production
Manager: Frank Baur. Assistant Directors: Marvin Miller and Barry
Stern. Screenplay: Gene Wilder and Mel Brooks, based on charac-
ters from the novel *Frankenstein* by Mary Shelley. Photography:
Gerald Hirschfeld. Editor: John Howard. Art Direction: Dale
Hennesy. Set Design: Robert De Vestel. Special Effects: Hal Millar
and Henry Miller Jnr. Music/Music Direction: John Morris. Orches-
trations: Jonathan Tunick and John Morris. Violin solo: Gerald
Vinci. Costumes: Dorothy Jeakins. Make-Up: William Tuttle.
Titles: Anthony Goldschmidt. Sound Editor: Don Hall. Sound
Recording: Gene Cantamesa. Sound Re-Recording: Richard
Portman. Frankenstein Laboratory Equipment: Kenneth
Strickfaden.

Cast: Gene Wilder (Dr Frederick Frankenstein), Peter Boyle
(Monster), Marty Feldman (Igor), Madeline Kahn (Elizabeth),
Cloris Leachman (Frau Blücher), Teri Garr (Inga), Kenneth Mars
(Inspector Kemp), Gene Hackman (Blind Hermit), Richard Haydn
(Herr Falkstein), Liam Dunn (Mr Hilltop), Danny Goldman
(Medical Student), Leon Askin (Herr Waldman), Oscar Beregi
(Sadistic Jailer), Lou Cutell (Frightened Villager), Arthur Malet
(Village Elder), Richard Roth (Kemp's Aide), Monte Landis and
Rusty Blitz (Gravediggers), Anne Beesley (Little Girl), Terrence
Pushman (1st Villager), Ian Abercrombie (2nd Villager), Randolph
Dobbs (3rd Villager), John Dennis, Lidia Kristen, Michael Fox,
Patrick O'Hara, John Madison, Rick Norman, Rolfe Seden, Norbert
Schiller.

NIGHT MOVES (1975)

A Hiller Productions-Layton Production. Running Time: 99
minutes. Director: Arthur Penn. Producer: Robert M. Sherman.
Associate Producer: Gene Lasko. Production Manager: Thomas
J. Schmidt. Assistant Directors: Jack Roe and Patrick H. Kehoe.
Screenplay: Alan Sharp. Photography: Bruce Surtees. Underwater
Photography: Jordan Klein. Editors: Dede Allen and Stephen A.
Rotter. Production Design: George Jenkins. Set Decoration: Ned
Parsons. Special Effects: Marcel Vercouters and Joe Day. Music:
Michael Small. Titles: Wayne Fitzgerald. Sound Editors: Craig
McKay, Robert Reitano and Richard Cirincione. Sound Recording:

Jack Solomon. Sound Re-Recording: Richard Vorisek. Aerial Co-ordinator: Dean Engel Hardt.

Cast: Gene Hackman (Harry Moseby), Jennifer Warren (Paula), Edward Binns (Joey Ziegler), Harris Yulin (Marty Heller), Kenneth Mars (Nick), Janet Ward (Arlene Iverson), James Woods (Quentin), Anthony Costello (Marv Ellman), John Crawford (Tom Iverson), Melanie Griffith (Delly Grastner), Susan Clarke (Ellen Moseby), Ben Archibeck (Charles), Dennis Dugan (Boy), C. K. Hincks (Girl), Maxwell Gail Jnr (Stud), Susan Barrister and Larry Mitchell (Ticket Clerks).

BITE THE BULLET (1975)

A Persky-Bright-Vista Production. Running Time: 131 minutes.
Director/Producer: Richard Brooks. Production Supervisor: Gene Levy. Assistant Directors: Tom Shaw and Charles Bonniwell. Screenplay: Richard Brooks. Photography: Harry Stradling Jnr. Editor: George Granville. Art Direction: Robert Boyle. Set Decoration: Robert Signorelli. Special Effects: Chuck Gaspar. Music: Alex North. Orchestration: Hershy Kay. Sound Editor: Kay Rose. Sound Recording: Al Overton Jnr. Sound Re-Recording: Arthur Piantadosi, Les Fresholtz and Richard Tyler. Horses: Rudy Ugland Jnr.

Cast: Gene Hackman (Sam Clayton), Candice Bergen (Miss Jones), James Coburn (Luke Matthews), Ben Johnson ('Mister'), Ian Bannen (Norfolk), Jan Michael Vincent (Carbo), Mario Arteaga (Mexican), Robert Donner (Reporter), Robert Hoy (Lee Christie), Paul Stewart (J. B. Parker), Jean Willes (Rosie), John McLiam (Gebhardt), Dabney Coleman (Jack Parker), Jerry Gatlin (Wood Chopper), Sally Kirkland (Honey), Walter Scott Jnr (Steve), Bill Burton (Billy), Buddy Van Horn (Slim), Hoe Brooks (Barber), Lucia Canales, Darwin Lamb.

FRENCH CONNECTION II (1975)

A Twentieth Century Fox Production. Running Time: 119 minutes.
Director: John Frankenheimer. Producer: Robert L. Rosen. Production Supervisor: Pierre Saint-Blancat. Production Manager: Robert Fugier. Second Unit Director: Marc Monnet. Assistant Directors: Bernard Stora and Thierry Chabert. Screenplay: Robert Dillon, Laurie Dillon and Alexander Jacobs. Photography: Claude

Renoir. Editor: Tom Rolf. Production Design: Jacques Saulnier. Art Direction: Gérard Viard and George Glon. Special Effects: Logan Frazee. Music: Don Ellis. Sound: Bernard Bats and Theodore Soderberg. Sound Effects Editor: Don Hall, William Hardman and Edward Rossi. Stunt Co-ordinator: Hal Needham.

Cast: Gene Hackman (Jimmy 'Popeye' Doyle), Fernando Rey (Alain Charnier), Bernard Fresson (Barthelemy), Jean-Pierre Castaldi (Raoul Diron), Charles Millot (Miletto), Cathleen Nesbitt (Mère Charnier), Pierre Collet (Old Pro), Alexandre Fabre (Young Tail), Philippe Leotard (Jacques), Jacques Dynam (Inspector Genevoix), Raoul Delfasse (Dutch Captain), Patrick Floersheim (Manfredi), Ed Lauter (US Colonel), Daniel Vérité.

LUCKY LADY (1975)

A Gruskoff-Venture Production for Twentieth Century Fox. Running Time: 118 minutes. Director: Stanley Donen. Producer: Michael Gruskoff. Production Executive: Arthur Carroll. Production Managers: Al Burgess, Ted Swanson and Claude Hudson. Assistant Directors: Nigel Wooll, Terry Clegg, Jesus Marin and Vincent Winter. Screenplay and Story: Willard Huyck and Gloria Katz. Photography: Geoffrey Unsworth. Second Unit Photography: Ernest Day and Austin Dempster. Second Unit Battle Shots: Ricou Browning. Editors: Peter Boita and George Hively. Battle Sequence Editor: Tom Rolf. Production Design: John Barry. Art Direction: Norman Reynolds and Jorge Fernandez. Special Effects: John Richardson. Music: Ralph Burns. Songs: 'Get While the Gettin' Is Good' and 'Lucky Lady' by Fred Ebb and John Kander, sung by Liza Minnelli; 'If I Had a Talking Picture of You' by Ray Henderson, Lew Brown and B. G. De Sylva and 'All I Do is Dream of You' by Nancio Herb Brown and Arthur Freed, sung by Pamela Barlow; 'Empty Bed Blues' written and sung by Bessie Smith; 'Ain't Misbehavin'' by Fats Waller, sung by Burt Reynolds. Costumes: Lilly Fenichel. Titles: Dan Perri. Sound Editors: Peter Best and Edward D. Rossi. Sound Recording: Jesus Gonzalez. Sound Re-Recording: Theodore Soderberg. Stunt Co-Ordinator: Paul Stader. Stunt Double: Steve Shaw.

Cast: Gene Hackman (Kibby), Liza Minnelli (Claire), Burt Reynolds (Walker), Geoffrey Lewis (Capt Aaron Mosely), John Hillerman (Christy McTeague), Robby Benson (Billy Weber), Michael Hordern (Capt Rockwell), Anthony Holland (Mr Tully), John McLiam (Ross Huggins), Val Avery (Dolph), Louis Guss (Bernie),

William H. Bassett (Charley), Emilio Fernandez ('Ybarra'), Raymond Guth (Brother Bob), Duncan McLeod (Auctioneer), Richard Caine (Young Bootlegger), Milt (Lewis) Kogan (Supercargo), Suzanne Zenor (Brunette), Stuart Nisbett (Second Independent), Richard Armbruster (Hanson), Doyle Baker (Gene), Michael Greene (Turley), Laura Hippe (Lady Legger), John Furlong (Third Independent), Janit Baldwin (Dopey Girlfriend), Joseph Estevez (Young Boy), Marjorie Battles (Redhead), Tris Coffin (Skipper), Richard Stahl (Capt Lithgoe), Basil Hoffman (Auctioneer's Assistant), Pamela Barlow (Singer), James E. Brodhead (Telegraph Operator), Sue Casey (Lady), Ancel Cook (First Independent), Olive Dunbar (Wife), Walker Edmiston (Pilot), Nicholas Frasca (Claire's Son), Willard Huyck (Boatbuilder), Jacquelyn Hude (American Lady), Sam Jarvis (Husband), Ray Middleton (Stingray Jake), Thomas Merceum Runyon (Fourth Independent), Paul Stader (McTeague Heavy), Mills Watson (Giff), Eleanor Zee (American Woman).

THE DOMINO PRINCIPLE (1976) (UK: THE DOMINO KILLINGS)

An Associated General Films-Domino Principle Associates Production. Running Time: 100 minutes (later 93 minutes). Director/Producer: Stanley Kramer. Executive Producer: Martin Starger. Associate Producer: Terry Morse Jnr. Screenplay: Adam Kennedy, based on his own novel. Photography: Fred Koenekamp and Ernest Laszlo. Aerial Photography: Don Morgan. Editor: John F. Burnett. Production Design: William J. Greber. Art Direction: Ron Hobbs. Set Decoration: Rafael Bretton. Music: Billy Goldenberg. Songs: 'Some Day Soon' by Billy Goldenberg and Harry Shannon, sung by Shirley Eikhard; 'No Puedo Olvidar' by Billy Goldenberg and Orlando Perez. Costumes: Rita Riggs. Sound: David Ronne. Narrator: Patrick Allen.

Cast: Gene Hackman (Roy Tucker), Candice Bergen (Ellie), Richard Widmark (Tagge), Mickey Rooney (Spiventa), Edward Albert (Ross Pine), Eli Wallach (General Tom Reser), Ken Swofford (Warden Ditcher), Neva Patterson (Gaddis), Jay Novello (Captain Ruiz), Robert Karnes (Lefty), Calire Brennan (Ruby), Ted Gehrig (Schnaible), Joseph Perry (Bowcamp), George Memmoli (Cab Driver), Majel Barrett (Mrs Schnaible), George Fisher (Henemyer), Bob Herron (Brookshire), Denver Mattson (Murdock), Jim Gavin (Lenny), Arnesio De Bernal (Bank Official), Patricia Luke (Travel Woman), Charles Hovarth (Harley).

MARCH OR DIE (1977)

A Dick Richards Films Production for Associated General Films/ITC Entertainment. Running Time: 107 minutes. Director: Dick Richards. Producers: Dick Richards and Jerry Bruckheimer. Associate Producer (Morocco): Georges-Patrick Salvy-Guide. Production Supervisors: Ted Lloyd, Mike Moder, Luis Roberts and Mohamed Tazi. Production Managers (Spain): Diego Sempere and Miguel Angel Recuero. Assistant Directors: José Lopez Rodero, André Delacroix, Larry Franco and Mustapha Laghaz. Screenplay: David Zelag Goodman, from a story by David Zelag Goodman and Dick Richards. Photography: John Alcott. Editors: John C. Howard, Stanford C. Allen and O. Nicholas Brown. Production Design: Gil Parrondo. Art Direction: José Maria Tapiador. Set Decoration: Julian Mateos and Dennis Parrish. Special Effects: Robert MacDonald. Music: Maurice Jarre, performed by the National Philarmonic Orchestra; Band of the Garde Républicaine. Songs: 'La Marseillaise' by Claude Joseph Rouget de Lisle; 'Plaisir D'Amour' performed by André Penvern. Make-Up: José Antonio Sauchez. Titles: Wayne Fitzgerald. Sound Effects Supervisor: William Stevenson. Sound Editors: Jim Bullock and Bill Phillips. Sound Recording: Ivan Sharrock. Sound Re-Recording: Richard Portman. Production Assistants: Christina Anderson and Michael Dempsey. Stunt Co-ordinators: Glenn Wilder, Chuck Hayward and Juan Majan.

Cast: Gene Hackman (Maj William Sherman Foster), Terence Hill – AKA Mario Giotti (Marco Segrain), Catherine Deneuve (Simone Picard), Max Von Sydow (François Marneau), Ian Holm (El Krim), Rufus (Sgt Triand), Jack O'Halloran (Ivan), Marcel Bozzuffi (Lt Fontaine), André Penvern (François Gilbert – 'Top Hat'), Paul Sherman (Fred Hastings), Vernon Dobtcheff (Mean Corporal), Marne Maitland (Lēon), Gigi Bonos (André), Wolf Kahler (First German), Mathias Hell (Second German), Jean Champion (Minister), Walter Gotell (Col Lamont), Paul Antrim (Mollard), Catherine Willmer (Petite Lady), Arnold Diamond (Husband), Maurice Arden (Pterre Lahoud), Albert Woods (Henri Delacorte), Liliane Rovere (Lola), Elisabeth Mortensen (French Street Girl), Leila Shenna (Arab Street Girl), François Valorbe (Detective), Villena (Gendarme), Ernest Misko (Aide in Minister's Office), Guy Deghy (Ship's Captain), Jean Rougerie (First Legionnaire at Station), Guy Mairesse (Second Legionnaire at Station), Eve Brenner (Singing Girl), Guy Marley (Singing Legionnaire), Margaret Moldin (Lady in Black).

A BRIDGE TOO FAR (1977)

A Joseph E. Levine Production. Running Time: 175 minutes. Director: Richard Attenborough. Producers: Joseph E. Levine and Richard P. Levine. Assistant Directors: David Tomblin, Steve Lanning, Roy Button, Peter Waller and Geoffrey Ryan. Screenplay: William Goldman, based on the book by Cornelius Ryan. Photography: Geoffrey Unsworth. Editor: Antony Gibbs. Production Design: Terence Marsh. Art Direction: Roy Stannard, Stuart Craig and Alan Tomkins. Set Decoration: Peter Howitt. Special Effects: John Richardson. Music: John Addison. Costumes: Antony Mendleson. Sound: Simon Kaye. Technical Advisor: Kathryn Morgan Ryan.

Cast: Dirk Bogarde (Lt-Gen Frederick Browning), James Caan (Staff Sgt Eddie Dohun), Michael Caine (Lt-Col J. O. E. Vandeleur), Sean Connery (Maj-Gen Robert Urquhart), Edward Fox (Lt-Gen Brian Horrocks), Elliott Gould (Col Bobby Stout), Gene Hackman (Maj-Gen Stanislaw Sosabowski), Anthony Hopkins (Lt-Col John Frost), Hardy Kruger (Maj-Gen Ludwig), Laurence Olivier (Dr Spaander), Ryan O'Neal (Brig-Gen James M. Gavin), Robert Redford (Maj Julian Cook), Maximilian Schell (Lt-Gen Wilhelm Bittrich), Liv Ullmann (Kate ter Horst).

SUPERMAN (1978)

A Dovemead-International Film Production. Running Time: 143 minutes. Director: Richard Donner. Producer: Pierre Spengler. Executive Producer: Ilya Salkind. Associate Producer: Charles F. Greenlaw. Screenplay: Mario Puzo, David Newman, Leslie Newman and Robert Benton, based on the characters created by Jerry Siegel and Joe Shuster. (Story: Mario Puzo. Creative Consultant: Tom Mankiewicz. Additional Material: Norman Enfield). Flying Co-ordinator: Dominic Fulford. Photography: Geoffrey Unsworth. Additional Photography: Alex Thomson, Jack Atcheler, Robert E. Collins, Reginald Morris and Sol Negrin. Production Designer: John Barry. Art Direction: Norman Dorne, Norman Reynolds, Ernest Archer, Tony Reading, Les Dilley, Stuart Craig, Gene Rudolf, Philip Bennet and Stan Jolley. Set Decoration: Peter Howitt and Fred Weiler. Supervising Editor: Stuart Baid. Editor: Michael Ellis. Music: John Williams. Song: 'Can You Read My Mind' by John Williams and Leslie Bricusse, performed by Margot Kidder. Costumes: Yvonne Blake. Sound: Gordon K. McCallum, Roy Charman, Norman Bolland, Ronnie

Fox Rogers, Ginger Gemmell, Roy Ford, Jack Lowen, George Pink, Charles Schmitz, Dick Ragusa and Chris Large.

Cast: Christopher Reeve (Clark Kent, Superman), Margot Kidder (Lois Lane), Gene Hackman (Lex Luthor), Valerie Perrine (Eve Teschmacher), Ned Beatty (Otis), Jackie Cooper (Perry White), Marc McClure (Jimmy Olsen). Krypton: Marlon Brando (Jor-El), Susannah York (Lara), Trevor Howard (1st Elder), Harry Andrews (2nd Elder), Vass Anderson (3rd Elder), John Hollis (4th Elder), James Garbutt (5th Elder), Michael Gover (6th Elder), David Neal (7th Elder), William Russell (8th Elder), Penelope Lee (9th Elder), John Stuart (10th Elder), Alan Cullen (11th Elder), Lee Quigley (Baby Kal-El), Aaron Sholinski (Baby Clark Kent), Jack O'Halloran (Non), Maria Schell (Vond-Ah), Terence Stamp (General Zod), Sarah Douglas (Ursa). Smallville: Glenn Ford (Pa Kent), Phyllis Thaxter (Ma Kent), Jeff East (Young Clark Kent), Diane Sherry (Lana Lang), Jeff Atcheson (Coach), Brad Flock (Football Player), David Petrou (Team Manager). Daily Planet: Billy J. Mitchell (First Editor), Robert Henderson (2nd Editor), Larry Lamb (1st Reporter), James Brockington (2nd Reporter), John Cassady (3rd Reporter), John F. Parker (4th Reporter), Antony Scott (5th Reporter), Ray Evans (6th Reporter), Su Shifrin (7th Reporter), Miquel Brown (8th Reporter), Vincent Marzello (1st Copy Boy), Benjamin Feitelson (2nd Copy Boy), Lise Hilboldt (1st Secretary), Leueen Willoughby (2nd Secretary), Jill Ingham (Perry's Secretary), Pieter Stuyck (Window Cleaner). Metropolis: Rex Reed (Himself), Weston Gavin (Mugger), Stephen Kahan (1st Officer), Ray Hassett (2nd Officer), Randy Jurgenson (3rd Officer), Matt Russo (News Vendor).

SUPERMAN II (1980)

A Dovemead-International Film Production. Running Time: 127 minutes. Director: Richard Lester. Producer: Pierre Spengler. Executive Producer: Ilya Salkind. Screenplay: Mario Puzo, David Newman and Leslie Newman. (Story: Mario Puzo. Creative Consultant: Tom Mankiewicz.) Based on the characters created by Jerry Siegel and Joe Shuster. Photography: Geoffrey Unsworth and Bob Paynter. Production Managers: John Barry and Peter Murton. Art Direction: Charles Bishop, Terry Ackland-Snow, Norman Reynolds and Ernest Archer. Set Decoration: Peter Young and Peter Howitt. Flying Effects: Bob Harman. Editor: John Victor-Smith. Music: Ken Thorne, based on original material composed by John Williams. Costumes: Yvonne Blake and Susan Yelland. Sound: Roy Charman.

Cast: Gene Hackman (Lex Luthor), Christopher Reeve (Clark Kent, Superman), Ned Beatty (Otis), Jackie Cooper (Perry White), Sarah Douglas (Ursa), Margot Kidder (Lois Lane), Jack O'Halloran (Non), Valerie Perrine (Eve Teschmacher), Susannah York (Lara), Clifton James (Sheriff), E. G. Marshall (US President), Marc McClure (Jimmy Olsen), Terence Stamp (General Zod), Leueen Willoughby (Leueen), Robin Pappas (Alice), Roger Kemp (Spokesman), Roger Brierley, Anthony Milner and Richard Griffiths (Terrorists), Melissa Wiltsie (Nun), Alain Dehay (Gendarme), Marc Boyle (CRS Man), Alan Stuart (Cab Driver), John Ratzenberger and Shane Rimmer (Controllers), John Morton (Nate), Jim Dowdell (Boris), Angus McInnes (Prison Warden), Anthony Sher (Bell Boy), Elva May Hoover (Mother), Hadley Kay (Jason), Todd Woodcroft (Father), John Hollis (Krypton Elder), Gordon Rollings (Fisherman), Peter Whitman (Deputy), Bill Bailey (J. J.), Dinny Powell (Boog), Hal Galili (Man at Bar), Marcus D'Amico (Willie), Jackie Cooper (Dino), Richard Parmentier (Reporter), Don Fellows (General), Michael J. Shannon (President's Aide), Tony Sibbald (Presidental Imposter), Tommy Duggan (Diner Owner).

ALL NIGHT LONG (1981)

A Universal Production. Running Time: 87 minutes. Director: Jean-Claude Tramont. Producers: Leonard Goldberg and Jerry Weintraub. Associate Producers: Terence A. Donnelly and Fran Roy. Screenplay: W. D. Richter. Photography: Philip Lathrop. Editor: Marion Rothman. Production Design: Peter Jamison. Set Decoration: Linda Spheeris. Music: Ira Newborn and Richard Hazard. Costumes: Albert Wolsky. Sound: John S. Kean and Albert Morrone.

Cast: Gene Hackman (George Dupler), Barbra Streisand (Cheryl Gibbons), Diane Ladd (Helen Dupler), Dennis Quaid (Freddie Dupler), Kevin Dobson (Bobby Gibbons), William Daniels (Richard H. Copleston), Ann Doran (Grandmother Gibbons), Jim Nolan (Grandfather Gibbons), Judy Kerr (Joan Gibbons), Marlyn Gates (Jennifer Gibbons), Raleigh Bond (Ultra-Sav Doctor), Mitzi Hoag (Nurse), Charles Siebert (Nevins), James Ingersoll (Hutchinson), Tandy Cronyn (Shuster's Secretary), Len Lawson (Barney), Terry Kiser (Ultra-Sav Day Manager), Annie Girardot (French Teacher).

REDS (1981)

A Paramount Production. Running Time: 196 minutes.
Director/Producer: Warren Beatty. Executive Producers: Simon
Relph and Dede Allen. Associate Producer: David L. MacLeod.
Screenplay: Warren Beatty and Trevor Griffiths. Photography:
Vittorio Storaro. Editors: Dede Allen, Craig McKay, Katherine
Wenning, Sam Fine, David Reibman. Production Design: Richard
Sylbert. Art Direction: Simon Holland, Fernando Gonzalez and
Vesa Tapola. Set Decoration: Thomas Roysden and Paul
Heffernan. Original Music: Stephen Sondheim. Additional Music:
Dave Grusin. Costumes: Shirley Russell. Sound: Simon Kaye,
Bruce Bisenz, Al Mian and Frank Kulaga.

Cast: Warren Beatty (John Reed), Diane Keaton (Louise Bryant),
Edward Herrmann (Max Eastman), Jerzy Kosinski (Grigory Zino-
viev), Jack Nicholson (Eugene O'Neill), Paul Sorvino (Louis
Fraina), Maureen Stapleton (Emma Goldman), Nicolas Coster
(Paul Trullinger), M. Emmet Walsh (Speaker, Liberal Club), Ian
Wolfe (Mr Partlow), Bessie Love (Mrs Partlow), MacIntyre Dixon
(Carl Walters), Pat Starr (Helen Walters), Eleanor D. Wilson (Mrs
Reed), Max Wright (Floyd Dell), George Plimpton (Horace
Whigman), Harry Ditson (Maurice Becker), Leigh Curran (Ida
Rauh), Kathryn Grody (Crystal Eastman), Brenda Currin (Marjorie
Jones), Nancy Duiguid (Jane Heap), Norman Chancer (Barney),
Dolph Sweet (Big Bill Haywood), Ramon Bieri (Police Chief), Jack
O'Leary (Pinkerton Guard), Gene Hackman (Peter Van Wherry).

EUREKA (1982)

A Recorded Picture Company (London)-JF Productions (Los Ange-
les)-Sunley Feature for MGM/UA. Running Time: 129 minutes.
Director: Nicolas Roeg. Producer: Jeremy Thomas. Associate
Producer: Tim Van Rellim. Screenplay: Paul Mayersberg, based
on the book *Who Killed Sir Harry Oakes?* by Marshall Houts.
Photography: Alex Thomson. Editor: Tony Lawson. Production
Design: Michael Seymour. Art Direction: John Beard. Music:
Stanley Myers. Costumes: Marit Allen. Sound: Paul Le Mare and
John Richards.

Cast: Gene Hackman (Jack McCann), Theresa Russell (Tracy),
Rutger Hauer (Claude Maillot/Van Horn), Jane Lapotaire (Helen
McCann), Mickey Rourke (Aurelio D'Amato), Ed Lauter (Charles
Perkins), Joe Pesci (Mayakofsky), Helena Kallianiotes (Frieda),

[227]

Cavan Kendall (Pierre de Valois), Corin Redgrave (Worsley), Joe Spinell (Pete), Frank Pesce (Stefano), Michael Scott Addis (Joe), Norman Beaton (Byron Judson), Emrys James (Judge), James Faulkner (Roger), Ann Thornton (Jane), Emma Relph (Mary), John Vine (Julian), Tim Van Rellim (Police Chief), Ellis Dale (Jury Foreman), Mico Blanco Group, accompanied by The Aklowa Master Drummers (Tonnelle Dancers), Lloyd Berry (Olaf), Tom Heaton (Man Blowing Off Head), Timothy Scott (Jim Webb), Geri Dewson (Whore), Annie Kidder (Rita), Ian Tracey (Joey), Brad Sakiyama (Phil), Sandra Friesen (Mother), Raimund Stamm (Patron), Suzette Collins (Esther), Tommy Lane (Miami Chauffeur).

MISUNDERSTOOD (1983)

An Accent Films-Keith Barish Production in association with Tarak Ben Ammar. Running Time: 91 minutes. Director: Jerry Schatzberg. Producer: Tarak Ben Ammar. Executive Producers: Keith Barish and Craig Baumgarten. Associate Producer: Mark Lombardo. Screenplay: Barra Grant, based on the novel by Florence Montgomery. Photography: Pasqualino de Santis. Production Design: Joel Schiller. Editor: Marc Laub. Set Decoration: Franco Fumagalli. Music: Michael Hoppe. Sound: Arthur Rochester. Costumes: Jo Ynocencio.

Cast: Gene Hackman (Ned), Henry Thomas (Andrew), Rip Torn (Will), Huckleberry Fox (Miles), Maureen Kerwin (Kate), Susan Anspach (Lily), June Brown (Mrs Paley), Helen Ryan (Lucy), Nadim Sawalhs (Ahmed), Nidal Ashkar (Mrs Jallouli), Khaled Akrout (Electronic Salesman), Rajah Gafsi (Cafe Owner), Moheddine Mrad (Kassir), James R. Cope (Mr Grace), Halima Daoud (Aisha), Raad Rawi (Doctor), Habiba (Girl), Fathia Boudabous (Woman in Red Light District), Nabil Massad (Jallouli), Anick Allieres (Marie), Mohamed Ben Othman (Chocolate Merchant), Abdellatif Hamrouni (Holy Man), Salah Rahmouni (Rachid), Mohamed Dous (Judo Instructor), Tarak Sancho (Ned's Driver), Hattab Dhib (Kassir's Driver), Andre Valiquette (Bob), Dirk Holzapfel (Luicen).

UNDER FIRE (1983)

An Under Fire Associates (Greenberg Brother Partnership)-Lion's Gate Film for Orion. Running Time: 127 minutes. Director Roger

Spottiswoode. Producer: Jonathan Taplin. Executive Producer: Edward Teets. Associate Producer: Anna Roth. Screenplay: Ron Shelton and Clayton Frohman, based on a story by Frohman. Photography: John Alcott. Supervising Editor: John Bloom. Editor: Mark Conte. Art Direction: Augustin Ytuarte and Toby Rafelson. Set Decoration: Enrique Estevez. Music: Jerry Goldsmith. Songs: 'Dear John' and '1979' written and performed by Pat Metheny; 'Our Love May Never See tomorrow' by Peggy Turner. Costumes: Cynthia Bales. Sound: Kirk Francis and John Richards.

Cast: Nick Nolte (Russell Price), Gene Hackman (Alex Grazier), Joanna Cassidy (Claire Stryder), Jean-Louis Trintignant (Marcel Jazy), Ed Harris (Oates), Richard Masur (Hub Kittle), Hamilton Camp (Regis Seydor), Alma Martinez (Isela), Holly Palance (Journalist), Ella Laboriel (Night-club singer), Samuel Zarzosa (Jazz combo: Drums), Jonathan Zarzosa (Pianist), Raul Picasso (Bass Player), Oswaldo Doria (Boy Photographer), Fernando Elizondo (Businessman), Jorge Santoyo (Guerrilla Leader), Lucina Rojas (Guerrilla Woman), Raul Garcia (Waiter), Victor Alcocer (Captured Businessman), Eric Valdez (*Time* stringer), Andaluz Russel (Young Journalist), E. Villavicencio (Arresting Officer), Enrique Lucero (Prison Priest), Enrique Beraza (Interrogation Officer), Jenny Gago (Miss Panama), Elpidia Carrillo, Martin Palmares and Gerardo Moreno (Sandinistas at Leon).

UNCOMMON VALOR (1983)

A Paramount Production. Running Time: 105 minutes. Director/Executive Producer: Ted Kotcheff. Producers: John Milius and Buzz Feitshans. Associate Producers: Burton Elias and Wings Hauser. Production Manager: Mel Dellar. Assistant Directors: Craig Huston, Richard Prince and Pamela Eilerson. Screenplay: Joe Gayton. Photography: Stephen H. Burum and Ric Waite. Editor: Mark Melnick. Production Design: James L. Schoppe. Art Direction: Jack G. Taylor Jnr. Set Decoration: John Anderson and George Gaines. Music: James Horner. Songs: 'Badman' by Ray Kennedy and 'Brothers in the Night' by Ray Kennedy, Kevin Dukes and David Ritz, performed by Ray Kennedy; 'Sunshine of Your Love' by Jack Bruce, Peter Brown and Eric Clapton. Wardrobe: Steve Shubin. Make-Up: Michael Westmore and Monty Westmore. Sound Recording: Joe Kenworthy and Eric Tomlinson. Technical Adviser: Larry N. Neber. Stunt Co-ordinator: Conrad E. Palmisano.

Cast: Gene Hackman (Colonel Jason Rhodes), Robert Stack (Hugh

MacGregor), Fred Ward (Wilkes), Reb Brown (Blaster), Randall 'Tex' Cobb (Sailor), Patrick Swayze (Scott), Harold Sylvester (Johnson), Tim Thomerson (Charts), Lau Nga Lai (Lai Fun), Kwan Hi Lim (Jiang), Kelly Yunkerman (Paul MacGregor), Todd Allen (Frank Rhodes), Gail Strickland (Helen Rhodes), Jane Kaczmarek (Mrs Wilkes), Gloria Stroock (Mrs MacGregor), Constance Forslund (Mrs Charts), Charles Aidman (Senator Hastings), Debi Parker (Mai Ling), Jan Triska (Gericault), Jeremy Kemp (Ferryman), Emmett Dennis III (First Medic), Charles Faust (First GI), David Austin (Second GI), Le Tuan (First Guard), James Edgcomb (CIA Agent), Ken Farmer (Jail Guard), Tad Horino (Mr Ky), Michael Dudikoff (Blaster's Assistant), Bruce Paul Barbour (Helicopter Pilot), Steven Solberg (First POW), Laurence Neber (Second POW), Don Mantooth (Third POW), Jerry Supiran (Frank, age 9), Brett Johnson (First Kid), Barret Oliver (Second Kid), Marcello Krakoff (Third Kid), Justin Bayly (Fourth Kid), Kevin Brando (Fifth Kid), Angela Lee (Sixth Kid), Juan Fernandez (Orderly), Darwyn Carson (Secretary), Nancy Linari and David Dangler (Reporters), Joseph Dypwick, William S. Hamilton, Napoleon Hendrix, Chip Lally, Michael P. May, Tom Randa and Larry Charles White (American Soldiers),

TWICE IN A LIFETIME (1985)

A Yorkin Company Production. Running Time: 117 minutes (UK version 111 minutes). Director/Producer: Bud Yorkin. Executive Producer: David Salven. Associate Producer: David Yorkin. Screenplay: Colin Welland. Photography: Nick McLean. Editor: Robert Jones. Production Design: William Creber. Set Design: Kenneth Creber. Set Decoration: Antony Mondello. Music: Pat Metheny. Costumes: Erica Phillips. Sound: Darin Knight and Josh Abbey.

Cast: Gene Hackman (Harry Mackenzie), Ann-Margret (Audrey Minnelli), Ellen Burstyn (Kate Mackenzie), Amy Madigan (Sunny), Ally Sheedy (Helen Mackenzie), Stephen Lang (Keith), Darrell Larson (Jerry Mackenzie), Brian Dennehy (Nick), Chris Parker (Tim), Rachel Street (Joanne), Kevin Bleyer (Chris), Micole Mercurio (Betty), Doris Hugo Drewien (Millie), Lee Corrigan (Milos), Ralph Steadman (Mike), Rod Pilloud (Mick), Art Cahn (Nikos), Anne Ludlum (Susie), Evelyn Purdue (Lucy), Gayle Bellows (Jean), Kit Harris (Dolores), George Catalano (Shoe Repairman), Tawnya Pettiford (Harry's Neighbour), Mary Ewald (Saleswoman), Daniel Mahar (Foreman), Sharon Collar (Maya),

Gary Kowalski (Minister), Keith Nicholai (Photographer), Ken Clark (Flower Man), Audrey Flod (Bingo Caller), Loretta Adair (Bingo Assistant), Eileen Cornwell (Bingo Checker), Mary Thielen (Checkout Clerk), Denise Aiumu (Sales Clerk), Junior Barber (Young Child).

TARGET (1985)

A CBS Production. Running Time: 118 minutes. Director: Arthur Penn. Producers: Richard D. Zanuck and David Brown. Production Co-ordinators: Judith Atwell, (US) Susan Gallegly. Production Managers: Bernard Farrel, William Watkins, (West Germany) Uwe Petersen, and (US) Tom Joyner. Second Unit Director: Gene Lasko. Screenplay: Howard Berk and Don Petersen, based on a story by Leonard Stern. Photography: Jean Tournier, (US) Robert Jessup. Editor: Steve Rotter. Production design: Willy Holt. Art Direction: (US) Richard James. Set Decoration: Gabriel Bechit, (West Germany) Barbara Kloth. Special Effects: René Albouze. Music: Michael Small. Additional Music: Intersound, performed by Robbie Kondor and Cliff Carter. Songs: 'That Old Black Magic' by Johnny Mercer and Harold Arlen, performed by Billy Daniels; 'Lost in Love' by Graham Russell. Costume Design: Marie-Françoise Perochon. Titles: Wayne Fitzgerald. Sound: Bernard Bats, (West Germany) Rainer Jankowski and (US) Bob Wald. Stunt co-ordinators; Rémy Julienne, Michel Julienne, Claude Carliez.

Cast: Gene Hackman (Walter Lloyd), Matt Dillon (Chris Lloyd), Gayle Hunnicutt (Donna Lloyd), Victoria Fyodorova (Lise), Ilona Grubel (Carla), Herbert Berghof (Schroeder), Josef Sommer (Barney Taber), Guy Boyd (Clay), Richard Munch (Colonel), Ray Fry (Mason), Jean-Pol Dubois (Glasses), Werner Pochath (Young Agent), Ulrich Haupt (Older Agent), James Selby (Ross), Ric Krause (Howard), Robert Leinsol (Café Vendor), Jany Holt (Proprietress, Marie-Louise Pension), Catherine Rethi (Nurse), Tomas Hnevsa (Squat Man, Henke), Charlette Bailey (Receptionist, US Consulate), Veronique Guillaud (Secretary, US Consulate), Jacques Mignot (Madison Hotel Clerk), Brad Williams (Forklift Operator), Randy Moore (Tour Director), Jean-Pierre Stewart (Ballard), Robert Ground (Marine Sergeant),

POWER (1985)

A Lorimar/Polar Film. Running Time: 111 minutes. Director:

Sidney Lumet. Producers: Reene Schisgal and Mark Tarlov. Associate Producers: Wolfgang Glattes and Kenneth Utt. Assistant Director: Wolfgang Glattes. Screenplay: David Himmelstein. Photography: Andrzej Bartkowiak. Editor: Andrew Mondshein. Production Design: Peter Larkin. Art Direction: William Barclay. Music: Cy Coleman. Costume Design: Anna Hill Johnstone. Sound: Chris Newman.

Cast: Richard Gere (Pete St John), Julie Christie (Ellen Freeman), Gene Hackman (Wilfred Buckley), Kate Capshaw (Sydney Betterman), Denzel Washington (Arnold Billings), E. G. Marshall (Senator Sam Hastings), Beatrice Straight (Claire Hastings), Fritz Weaver (Wallace Furman), Michael Learned (Gov Andrea Sandard), J. T. Walsh (Jeorme Cade). E. Katherine Kerr (Irene Furman), Polly Rowles (Lucille De Witt), Matt Salinger (Phillip Aarons), Tom Mardirosian (Sheikh), Omar Torres (Roberto Cepeda).

HOOSIERS (1986) (UK: BEST SHOT)

A Carter De Haven Production for Hemdale Presentation and Orion Pictures Release. Running Time: 114 minutes. Director: David Anspaugh. Producers: Carter De Haven and Angelo Pizzo. Associate Producer: Graham Henderson. Executive Producers: John Daly and Derek Gibson. Assistant Director: Herb Adelman. Second Unit Director: Angelo Pizzo. Screenplay: Angelo Pizzo. Photography: Fred Murphy. Editor: C. Timothy O'Meara. Production Design: David Nichols. Art Director: David Lubin. Set Decoration: Janis Lubin and Brendan Smith. Music: Jerry Goldsmith. Costume Design: Jane Anderson. Sound: David Brownlow.

Cast: Gene Hackman (Coach Norman Dale), Barbara Hershey (Myra Fleener), Dennis Hopper (Shooter), Sheb Wooley (Cletus), Fern Parsons (Opal Fleener), Brad Boyle (Whit), Steve Hollar (Rade), Brad Long (Buddy), David Neidorf (Everett), Kent Poole (Merle), Wade Schenck (Ollie), Scott Summers (Strap), Maris Valainis (Jimmy).

NO WAY OUT (1987)

An Orion Production. Director: Roger Donaldson. Producers: Laura Ziskin and Robert Garland. Executive Producer: Mace Neufeld. Screenplay: Robert Garland. Photography: John Alcott.

Editor: Neil Travis. Production Manager: Mel Dellar. Production Design: J. Dennis Washington. Art Direction: Anthony Brocklis.

Cast: Kevin Costner (Lt Commander Tom Farrell), Gene Hackman (David Brice), Sean Young (Susan), Will Patton (Scott Pritchard), Howard Duff (Senator Duvall), George Dzundza.

SUPERMAN IV (1987)

A London Cannon Films Limited Production. Director: Sidney J. Furie. Producers: Menahem Golan and Yoram Globus. Associate Producers: Michael J. Kagan and Graham Easton. Screenplay: Mark Rosenthal and Lawrence Konner, from a story by Christopher Reeve, Mark Rosenthal and Lawrence Konner. Photography: Ernest Day. Editor: John Shirley. Production Design: John Graysmark. Set Decoration: Peter Young. Art Direction: Leslie Tomkins. Costumes: John Bloomfield. Sound: Danny Daniel. Visual Effects Supervisor: Harrison Ellenshaw.

Cast: Christopher Reeve (Superman/Clark Kent), Gene Hackman (Lex Luthor), Margot Kidder (Lois Lane), Jackie Cooper (Perry White), Marc McClure (Jimmy Olsen), Jon Cryer, Mariel Hemingway (Lacy Warfield), Sam Wanamaker and Mark Pillow.

ACROSS THE RIVER AND INTO THE TREES (1987) (Project)

Director: John Frankenheimer. Producer: Robert Haggiag.
A projected film version of the Hemingway novel scheduled to go into production during 1987 in Venice.

Other Work:
Hackman can also be seen in the short film *Confrontation* (1970), directed by Arthur Hiller, in which, according to one source, 'Three men, one of them a religious minister, publicly burn papers relating to US Army conscripts destined for Vietnam. The film deals with their trial and the reasons for their refusal to obey the laws of the land.'

He also appears in three documentaries: Richard Kaplan's *A Look at Liv Ullmann's Norway* (1977); the Italian *Speed Fever* (1978), directed by Oscar Orefici and Mario Morra, which looks at the fascination of Formula 1 motor-racing; and Iain Johnstone's *The Making of Superman – The Movie* (1979).

Television Appearances

(A Selected Chronology adapted from *Actors' Television Credits* by James Robert Parish)

US Steel Hour	'Little Tin God' (22 April 1959)
US Steel Hour	'Big Doc's Girl' (4 November 1959)
US Steel Hour	'Bride of the Fox' (24 August 1960)
The Defenders	'Quality of Mercy' (16 September 1961)
US Steel Hour	'Brandenburg Gate' (4 October 1961)
US Steel Hour	'Far From the Shade Tree' (10 January 1962)
The Defenders	'Judgment Eve' (20 April 1963)
Dupont Show of the Month	'Ride with Terror' (1 December 1963)
The Trials of O'Brien	Episode (18 March 1966)
Hawk	'Do Not Mutilate or Spindle' (8 September 1966)
FBI	'The Courier' (15 January 1967)
The Invaders	'The Spores' (17 October 1967)
Iron Horse	'Leopards Try' (28 October 1967)
CBS Playhouse	'My Father and My Mother' (13 February 1968)
I Spy	Episode (26 February 1968)
Shadow on the Land	TV Movie (4 December 1968)

Hackman has also appeared as himself on television chat shows and profiles including *Insight* (1971), *The South Bank Show* (1983) and *Wogan* (1986).

Bibliography

Books:

Downing, David	*Robert Redford* (UK: W. H. Allen, 1982)
Lenburg, Jeff	*Dustin Hoffman: Hollywood's Anti-Hero* (US: St. Martin's Press, 1983)
McNeil, Alex	*Total Television* (UK: Penguin Books, 1980)
Marrill, Alvin H.	*Movies Made for Television* (UK: LSP, 1980)
Munshower, Suzanne	*Warren Beatty* (UK: W. H. Allen, 1983)
Parish, James Robert	*Actor's Television Credits* (US: Scarecrow Press, 1973)
Peary, Danny	*Close-Ups*, Workman Publishing, NY, 1978
Steinberg, Cobbett	*Reel Facts* (US: Vintage Books, 1978)
Wake, Sandra & Hayden, Nicola	*The Bonnie and Clyde Book* (UK: Lorrimer, 1972)
Wiley, Mason & Bona, Damien	*Inside Oscar* (UK: Columbus, 1986)

Periodical Articles:

Anderson, Beth	'Uncommon Valor' (*On Location*, December 1983)
Austin, John	'Lucky Lady' (*Photoplay*, November 1975)
Bergson, Phillip	'Just Visiting' (*What's On*, 29/3/1984)
Bygrave, Mike	'Hackman at 51, Still Looking

	for a Direction' (*Mail on Sunday Magazine*, 31/10/1982)
Castell, David	'Will the real Gene Hackman, Stand Up Please?' (*Films Illustrated*, September 1978)
Cates, Gilbert	'Life with Father' (*Action*, August-September 1970)
Colvin, Clare	'The Madness and the Ecstasy' (*The Times*, 2/5/1983)
Combs, Richard	'Winter Tales' (*Monthly Film Bulletin*, August 1986)
Cort, Gavin	'Gene Hackman: The Aftermath of the Oscars' (*Show*, July 1972)
Dangaard, Colin	'Move Over Barbra . . . This is Gene's Make or Break Movie' (*Daily Express*, 6/10/1980)
Davis, Victor	'Popeye Doyle is Back on Spinach' (*Daily Express*, 11/1/1985)
Edwards, Sydney	'No More Mr Nice Guy' (*Evening Standard*, 24/9/1976)
Friedkin, William	'Anatomy of a Car Chase' (*Action*, March-April 1972)
Gallagher, Tad	'Night Moves' (*Sight and Sound*, Spring 1975)
Hamill, Pete	'Hackman' (*Film Comment*, September-October 1974)
Hamill, Pete	'Recognizing Roy Scheider' (*New York*, 23/5/1983)
Hinxman, Margaret	'Actor By Accident' (*Woman*, 1972)
Hutchinson, Curtis	'Flying Tonight' (*LM*, January 1987)
Lewin, David	'Hard Man Gene, Back as Mr Nice Guy' (*Sunday Mirror*, 1/3/1981)
Lewis, Brent	'The War Goes On' (*Nine to Five*, 2/4/1984)
Luft, Herbert G.	'Gene Hackman – An American of Strength and Doubts' (*Films in Review*, January 1975)
McAsh, Ian F.	'March or Die' (*Photoplay*, February 1977)

Malcolm, Derek — 'Cops and Robbers' (*The Guardian*, 24/1/1972)

Mann, Roderick — 'What Gene Discovered When He Quit' (*Sunday Express*, 14/1/1979)

Mills, Bart — 'Blue Gene' (*The Guardian*, 21/10/1974)

Mills, Nancy — 'Uncommon Actor' (*Stills*, April 1986)

Milne, Tom — 'Eureka' (*Sight and Sound*, Autumn 1982)

Mitchell, Ann — 'Gene Hackman – How his Wife's Love Helped Him Sneer at Defeat' (*Photoplay*, June 1973)

Munn, Mike — 'March or Die' (*Photoplay*, February 1977)

Neame, Ronald — *Dialogue on Film* (Vol 2 No 7 May 1973)

Paskin, Barbara — 'Gene Hackman – A Busy Fella, but a bit of a Yeller' (*Film Review*, November 1977)

Paskin, Barbara — 'Gene Hackman – The Common Man' (*Films and Filming*, May 1986)

Perry, George — 'Penn Connection, Part 3' (*Sunday Times*, 2/12/1984)

Pickard, Roy — 'Attenborough's Battles' (*Photoplay*, July 1977)

Pirie, David — 'Making the Sonofabitch Fly' (*Time Out*, 22/12/1978 and 5/1/1979)

Ritchie, Michael — 'Snow Job' (*Action*, August-September 1970)

Rivers, Tim — 'Hackman's Choice' (*The List*, 9–22/1/1987)

Royal, Susan — 'Gene Hackman – An Interview' (*American Premiere*, Spring 1986)

Russell, Mike — 'What in Means to be Gene Hackman' (*Photoplay*, October 1982)

Sibley, Adrian — 'Superman and Beyond' (*Films and Filming*, March 1987)

Simon, John	'Jan Troell' (*Film Heritage*, Summer 1974)
Sragow, Michael	'Jan Troell: Hypnotist on a Grand Scale' (*Rolling Stone*, 9/6/1983)
Taylor, Paul	'Out of the Cutting Room – Into the Fire' (*Monthly Film Bulletin*, January 1984)
Thompson, Douglas	'Money and Me by Old Potato Face' (*TV Times*, 6–12/7/1985)
Ward, Robert	'I'm Not a Movie Star; I'm An Actor' (*American Film*, March 1983)
Weller, Sheila	'Bull's Eye!' (*Movie Digest*, May 1972)

The following uncredited articles were also useful:
'Third Time Lucky' (*Films Illustrated*, July 1973)
'Liza, Burt, Gene and Lucky Lady' (*Photoplay*, February 1976)
'Hackman' (*Photoplay*, May 1976)
'Alan Sharp Interview' (*Literature/Film Quarterly*, Summer 1983)
'Hackman – Hard Guy, Soft Centre' (*Film Review*, June 1986)

Index